THE OLYMPIC OATH

We swear that we will take part in the Olympic Games in fair competition, respecting the regulations which govern them and with the desire to participate in the true spirit of sportsmanship for the honour of our country and for the glory of sport.

Administered to competitors
at the Opening Ceremonies.

THE OLYMPIC GAMES HANDBOOK

Distributed in Canada by Burns & MacEachern Limited, 62 Railside Road, Toronto C

the Olympic Games handbook

An authentic history of both the Ancient and Modern Olympic Games. Complete results and records. Fully illustrated.

By
David Chester

CHARLES SCRIBNER'S SONS

NEW YORK

A-7.71 (I)

Printed and Bound in Canada

Library of Congress Catalog Card Number 74-162947

SBN 684 12602-8 (cl)
SBN 684 12607-9 (pa)

36,668

CONTENTS

CHAPTER   PAGE

1   THE ANCIENT OLYMPIC GAMES 9

       THE MODERN OLYMPIC GAMES

2   I Olympiad. Athens. 1896 13
3   II Olympiad. Paris. 1900 17
4   III Olympiad. St. Louis. 1904 22
5   IV Olympiad. London. 1908 30
6   V Olympiad. Stockholm. 1912 37
       VI Olympiad. *Cancelled*
7   VII Olympiad. Antwerp. 1920 45
8   VIII Olympiad. Paris. 1924 53
9   IX Olympiad. Amsterdam. 1928 62
10   X Olympiad. Los Angeles. 1932 71
11   XI Olympiad. Berlin. 1936 82
       XII and XIII Olympiads. *Cancelled*
12   XIV Olympiad. London. 1948 92
13   XV Olympiad. Helsinki. 1952 104
14   XVI Olympiad. Melbourne. 1956 119
15   XVII Olympiad. Rome. 1960 134
16   XVIII Olympiad. Tokyo. 1964 149
17   XIX Olympiad. Mexico. 1968 163

       THE WINTER OLYMPIC GAMES
18   I Winter Olympiad. Chamonix. 1924 183
19   II Winter Olympiad. St. Moritz. 1928 185
20   III Winter Olympiad. Lake Placid. 1932 187
21   IV Winter Olympiad. Garmisch-Partenkirchen. 1936 190
22   V Winter Olympiad. St. Maritz. 1948 192
23   VI Winter Olympiad. Oslo. 1952 195
24   VII Winter Olympiad. Cortina d'Ampezzo. 1956 .. 199
25   VIII Winter Olympiad. Squaw Valley. 1960 203
26   IX Winter Olympiad. Innsbruck. 1964 208
27   X Winter Olympiad. Grenoble. 1968 213

       OLYMPIC RECORDS 219

Chapter 1
THE ANCIENT OLYMPIC GAMES

"REJOICE! We conquer!"

Those were the last words of Pheidippides who dropped dead from exhaustion after running twenty-five miles from the plains of Marathon to Athens to spread the news of the Greeks' victory over the Persians in 490 B.C.

The marathon cross-country race, the glamour event of the modern Olympic games, commemorates the heroism of Pheidippides.

However, there was no marathon race in the Ancient Olympics which began in the 13th century B.C. and ended in 394 A.D. Their origin is obscure. The ancient Greeks believed it all began with a feud between Zeus and Kronos, two Greek gods who battled on Mount Olympus for possession of the earth. Zeus won.

The poet Pindar, however, thought that the Games celebrated Heracles' victory over King Augeas of Elis. Heracles had been offered one tenth of the king's horses if he could clean out his vast stables within 24 hours. Heracles is supposed to have dammed up two nearby rivers and diverted the waters through the stables. Augeas refused to give him his award. So Heracles assassinated the king and his family and took the entire stables.

Another version is that Pelops instituted the Games in celebration of his marriage to Hippodamia after defeating her father, King Oenamaus, who had decreed that suitors must abduct her in a chariot and elude the pursuing chariots of the king. Until Pelops fell in love with Hippodamia, the king's men had caught 13 abductors and killed them. But Pelops bribed the royal charioteer into loosening the wheels of the king's chariot. The king broke his neck when a wheel fell off during the chase.

The early Games became part of the religious rites of the early Greeks and the athletes were treated as demi-gods. Kings and commoners competed. The winners were awarded sprigs of olive.

The first record of the Ancient Olympics was Coroebus' victory in a 200-yard foot race in 776 B.C. when the Greeks began reckoning time by Olympiads, the four year intervals between the Games. The foot race was the only event until the 14th Olympiad when a second foot race of two lengths of the stadium, about 400 yards, was added.

Later, discus and spear throwing, long jumping, boxing and wrestling were included. And there was a vicious event called the pancratium in which no holds were barred except for biting and gouging. Strangling was a necessary skill. There were several fatalities.

At first, all athletes competed in the nude. Women were barred at least until the 128th Olympiad when a girl won a chariot race.

All competitors had to undergo ten months of intensive training. During the three months before the Games, all fighting between Greek villages and states was suspended.

The entire religious significance of the Games was lost with the rise of the Roman empire. They became a pagan carnival. After athletes began demanding money and corruption set in, Roman Emperor Theodosius banned the Games in 394 A.D. Earthquakes and floods destroyed what was left of the Olympic temples after Barbarians had pillaged them.

THE
MODERN
OLYMPIC
GAMES

Chapter 2

THE I OLYMPIAD

Athens, 1896

THE French government commissioned Baron Pierre de Coubertin to study physical culture in 1889, and three years later Coubertin proposed a revival of the Olympic Games, convinced that athletics combined with education could improve international understanding.

In 1894, 34 nations supported the idea during a conference held at the Sorbonne. Coubertin wanted Paris to hold the first Olympic revival in 1900 during an international exposition. But the other delegates did not want to wait that long and unanimously voted to hold the first modern Olympiad in Athens in 1896. French delegate Michel Breal offered a trophy for a marathon race and this became the prime attraction of the modern Olympic Games.

Greek Prime Minister Trikoupes did not like the idea of holding the Olympics in Athens, but Coubertin, convinced that the idea had the support of the Athenians, persuaded the Greek Crown Prince to head the organizing committee.

Competitors came from England, France, Germany, Denmark, Switzerland, Hungary, Austria, Greece and the United States.

The United States won nine of the twelve track and field events. Tom Burke won the 100 and 400 metre runs. Tom Curtis took the 110 metre hurdles, W. H. Hoyt the pole vault and Ellery Clark the high jump and broad jump. They all belonged to the Boston Athletic Club.

Shot putter Bob Garrett, captain of the Princeton track and field team, paid his own way to Athens. He beat Miltiades Gouscos of Greece by three quarters of an inch.

The discus throw was not practised in the United States at the time, but Garrett had been practising on a home made one on the Princeton campus. When he arrived in Athens, he discovered that the regulation discus was much lighter than the one he had been used to, so he entered the event and beat Greek champion Panagiotis Paraskevopoulos by more than seven inches for a second gold medal.

Harvard University refused to give James B. Connolly permission to go to the Olympics so he left school and became the first of the modern Olympic champions, winning the triple jump on opening day. Connolly became a well known writer and many years later returned to Harvard to lecture on literature.

Until the final day, the only non-American winner was Edwin Flack, an Australian running for Great Britain who won the 800 and 1,500 metres.

The Greeks had by far the most athletes in competition, but the best they had been able to do was finish second in the discus, shot put and triple jump. But they almost scored a sweep in the marathon, the last event on the program. Spiridon Louis, a shepherd and post office messenger, fasted and prayed the day before the race. He took the lead with about seven miles to go on the 25 mile course from Marathon to Athens. The crowd of 60,000 roared with delight when he was first into the stadium and the Crown Prince and his brother left their seats to greet him at the finish line. Two other Greek runners followed him but Gyula Kellner of Hungary was awarded the bronze medal after one of them was disqualified.

In all, the Greek athletes picked up nine gold medals in other events, including three for shooting, to tie with the United States for number of gold medals won. Each country had collected ten.

France won four of six cycling events, Greece two of the three fencing competitions, Germany four of the seven gymnastics medals, Hungary two of the four swimming events and Great Britain won both tennis medals.

14

OFFICIAL I OLYMPIAD RESULTS

Athens, 1896

TRACK AND FIELD

100 Metres
1. T. Burke, U.S.—12.0
2. F. Hoffmann, Germany
3. A. Szokolyi, Hungary

400 Metres
1. T. Burke, U.S.—54.2
2. H. Jamieson, U.S.
3. F. Hoffmann, Germany

800 Metres
1. E. Flack, Australia—2:11.0
2. N. Dani, Hungary
3. D. Golemis, Greece

1500 Metres
1. E. Flack, Australia—4:33.2
2. A. Blake, U.S.
3. A. Lermusiaux, France

Marathon
1. S. Louis, Greece—2:58:50
2. C. Vasilakos, Greece—3:06:03
3. G. Kellner, Hungary—3:06:35

110 Metres Hurdles
1. T. Curtis, U.S.—17.6
2. G. Goulding, Great Britain—18.0

High Jump
1. E. Clark, U.S.—5′ 11¼″
2. J. Connolly, U.S.—5′ 9¼″
3. R. Garrett, U.S.—5′ 9¼″

Broad Jump
1. E. Clark, U.S.—20′ 10″
2. R. Garrett, U.S.—20′ 3¾″
3. J. Connolly, U.S.—20′ 0½″

Triple Jump
1. J. Connolly, U.S.—44′ 11¾″
2. A. Tuffere, France—41′ 8″
3. J. Persakis, Greece—41′ ⅞″

Pole Vault
1. W. Hoyt, U.S.—10′9⅞″
2. A. Tyler, U.S.—10′7 $\frac{11}{16}$″
3. J. Theodoropoulos, Greece—9′6 $\frac{9}{16}$″

Shot Put
1. R. Garrett, U.S.—36′9¾″
2. M. Gouscos, U.S.—36′9″
3. G. Papasideris, Greece—33′11⅞″

Discus Throw
1. R. Garrett, U.S.—95′7⅝″
2. P. Parakevopoulos, Greece—94′11 $\frac{11}{16}$″
3. S. Versis, Greece—91′1 $\frac{11}{16}$″

SWIMMING

100 Metres Free-Style
1. A. Hajos, Hungary—1:22.2
2. G. Williams, U.S.
3. O. Herschmann, Austria

500 Metres Free-Style
1. Newmann, Austria—8:12.6
2. Pepanos, Greece

1,200 Metres Free-Style
1. A. Hajos, Hungary—18:22.2
2. Andreou, Greece

100 Metres Free-Style between Sailors
1. Melokinis, Greece
2. Hazapis, Greece

WRESTLING
1. K. Schumann, Germany
2. G. Tsitis, Greece
3. S. Christopulos, Greece

WEIGHTLIFTING

Two Hands
1. V. Jensen, Denmark—245¾ lb.
2. E. Elliott, Great Britain
3. S. Versis, Greece

One Hand
1. L. Elliott, Great Britain
2. V. Jensen, Denmark

CYCLING

Road Race—54 Miles
1. A. Konstantinidis, Greece— 3:22.31.0
2. A. Goedrich, Germany
3. F. Battel, Great Britain

Track Race—10 kilometers
1. Masson, France—17:54.2
2. Flamen, France

Track Race—2 kilometers
1. Masson, France—4:56.0
2. Nicolopoulos, Greece

Track Race—100 kilometers
1. Flameng, France—3:08.19.2
2. Colettis, Greece

Turn around the Track—333⅓ metres
1. Masson, France—23.0
2. Nicolopoulos, Greece

Twelve-Hour Race
1. Schmal, Austria
2. Keeping, Great Britain

FENCING

Foil Between Masters
1. Pirghos, Greece
2. Perronet, France

Foil
1. E. Graveloote, France
2. H. Callott, France
3. P. Pierrakos, Greece

Sabre
1. J. Georgiadis, Greece
2. T. Karakalos, Greece
3. H. Nielsen, Denmark

GYMNASTICS

Horizontal Bar
1. H. Weingartner, Germany
2. A. Flatow, Germany
3. Petmesas, Greece

Horizontal Bar, Team
1. Germany

Parallel Bars
1. A. Flatow, Germany
2. H. Weingartner, Germany
3. L. Zutter, Switzerland

Parallel Bars, Team
1. Germany
2. Greece
3. Greece

Pommelled Horse
1. L. Zutter, Switzerland
2. H. Weingartner, Germany
3. G. Kokas, Hungary

Long Horse Vault
1. K. Schumann, Germany
2. L. Zutter, Switzerland

Flying Rings
1. J. Mitropoulos, Greece
2. H. Weingartner, Germany
3. Persakis, Greece

Rope Climbing
1. Andiakopoulos, Greece
2. Zenakis, Greece

SHOOTING

Automatic Pistol
1. J. Phrangudis, Greece
2. G. Orphanidis, Greece

Military Rifle—200 metres
1. Carassevdas, Greece—2,320 pts.
2. Pavlides, Greece—1,978 pts.

Military Rifle—300 metres
1. G. Orphanidis, Greece
2. J. Frangudis, Greece

Military Revolver—25 metres
1. J. Paine, U.S.—442 pts.
2. S. Paine, U.S.—380 pts.

TENNIS

Singles
1. Boland, Great Britain
2. Casdaglis, Greece

Doubles
1. Boland-Thraun, Great Britain
2. Casdaglis-Petrokokkinos, Greece

Chapter 3
THE II OLYMPIAD
Paris, 1900

ALTHOUGH the Greeks had been somewhat reluctant to hold the first Olympics, they wanted to hang on to them once the inaugural Games proved a success.

Greek newspapers urged Parliament to make Athens a permanent site and even the American athletes in Athens circulated a petition favoring this idea. The King told the closing dinner that Athens would be a "stable and permanent site" for all future Olympiads.

Coubertin, however, wanted the Olympics to be held in different countries. He attempted to placate the Greeks by proposing Pan-Hellenic Games be held in Athens every four years.

He finally succeeded in bringing the II Olympiad to Paris, but the Games turned into a mismanaged side show to the 1900 Paris Exposition. The events were spread over the five month duration of the exposition. Director Charles H. Sherrill of the New York Athletic Club claimed that the American athletes thought they were competing in an exposition international track meet. The winners did not realize they were Olympic champions until they had received their medals, and the Paris newspapers did not mention the word "Olympic" in their accounts. Even the official program identified the Olympic Games as "Championnats Internationaux". Coubertin was so disgusted that he resigned from the organizing committee. Two years later some of the Olympic champions complained that they still had not received their medals.

Americans once again dominated the track and field events, winning 17 of the 22 gold medals. Alvin Kraenzlein won four of them—the 60 metre dash, both hurdling races and the running broad jump. He beat John McLean of the U.S. by a foot and a half in the 110 metre hurdles and Myer Prinstein of the U.S. by less than half an inch in the broad jump. He won

17

the 200 metre hurdles in a close finish, with Norman Pritchard of India second, and Walter Tewkesbury of the U.S. third. The 60 metre dash was held on a Sunday and some of the more religious competitors withdrew, leaving Kraenzlein to defeat Tewkesbury.

Tewkesbury finished second to Frank Jarvis of the U.S. in the 100 metres but beat Pritchard by five yards in the 200 metres.

Ray Ewry of the New York Athletic Club, one of the most remarkable athletes in Olympic history, won all three standing jumps to begin a still unbroken record of ten Olympic championships. Ewry was an invalid doomed to an early death when a doctor told him to try some simple exercises. Later on at Purdue University he took up jumping and became the intercollegiate champion. He was 27 years old when he entered his first Olympic Games.

Myer Prinstein defeated defending champion James B. Connolly and Richard Sheldon in the running triple jump, one of several U.S. sweeps. Sheldon also won a gold medal in the shot put and a bronze medal in the standing high jump.

Irving Baxter of the U.S. won the high jump and pole vault and also three silver medals for the standing jumps. In the pole vault, the favored Bascom Johnson of the New York Athletic Club had left the grounds after being misinformed by a French official that the competition had been postponed. Baxter just happened to be hanging around when he noticed a small crowd gathering around the pole vault pit and he joined in the competition.

Paris bread delivery boy, Michel Theato, defeated Emile Champion by five minutes in the marathon. Some of the losers complained that the two Frenchmen knew the course so well that they took a few shortcuts through the back alleys of Paris.

J. T. Rimmer of Great Britain won the 4,000 metre steeplechase. The favorite, George Orton of the U.S., had spent a sleepless night with indigestion and finished last.

In other sports, Great Britain dominated the swimming; France the fencing, cycling and gymnastics; and Switzerland the shooting.

The United States won a total of 18 gold medals, France won 16, and Great Britain 12.

OFFICIAL II OLYMPIAD RESULTS

Paris, 1900

TRACK AND FIELD

60 Metres
1. A. C. Kraenzlein, U.S.—.7.0
2. J. W. Tewkesbury, U.S.

100 Metres
1. F. Jarvis, U.S.—10.8
2. J. W. Tewkesbury, U.S.
3. S. Rowley, Australia

200 Metres
1. J. W. Tewkesbury, U.S.—22.2
2. N. Pritchard, India
3. S. Rowley, Australia

400 Metres
1. M. Long, U.S.—49.4
2. W. Holland, U.S.
3. E. Schultz, Denmark

800 Metres
1. A. Tysoe, Great Britain—2:01.4
2. J. Cregan, U.S.
3. D. Hall, U.S.

1,500 Metres
1. C. Bennett, Great Britain—4:06.0
2. H. Deloge, France
3. J. Bray, U.S.

Marathon
1. M. Theato, France—2:59:45.0
2. E. Champion, France—3:04:25.0
3. E. Fast, Sweden—3:37:00.0

5,000 Metres Team Race
1. Great Britain—15:20.0
2. France

110 Metres Hurdles
1. A. Kraenzlein, U.S.—15.4
2. J. McLean, U.S.
3. F. Moloney

200 Metres Hurdles
1. A. Kraenzlein, U.S.—25.4
2. G. N. Pritchard, India

400 Metres Hurdles
1. J. W. Tewkesbury, U.S.—57.6
2. H. Tauzin, France
3. G. Orton, U.S.

2,500 Metres Steeplechase
1. G. W. Orton, U.S.—7:34.0
2. S. Robinson, Great Britain

4,000 Metres Steeplechase
1. J. T. Rimmer, Great Britain—12:58.4
2. C. Bennet, Great Britain

Standing High Jump
1. R. Ewry, U.S.—5'5"
2. I. Baxter, U.S.
3. R. Sheldon, U.S.

Running High Jump
1. I. Baxter, U.S.—6'2¾"
2. P. Leahy, Great Britain—5'10¹¹⁄₁₆"
3. L. Gonczy, Hungary—5'8⅛"

Standing Broad Jump
1. R. Ewry, U.S.—10'6¼"
2. I. Baxter, U.S.

Running Broad Jump
1. A. Kraenzlein, U.S.—23'6⅞"
2. M. Prinstein, U.S.—23'6½"
3. C. Leahy, Great Britain—22'9⅝".

Standing Triple Jump
1. R. Ewry, U.S.—34'8½"
2. I. Baxter, U.S.

Running Triple Jump
1. M. Prinstein, U.S.—47'4⅛"
2. J. Connolly, U.S.—45'10"
3. R. Sheldon, U.S.—44'9"

Pole Vault
1. I. Baxter, U.S.—10'9⅞"
2. M. B. Kolkett, U.S.—10'7¹⅜"
3. C. A. Andersen, Norway—10'5⁵⁄₁₆"

Shot Put
1. R. Sheldon, U.S.—46'3⅛"
2. M. McCracken, U.S.—42'1¾".
3. R. Garrett, U.S.—40'7"

Discus Throw
1. R. Bauer, Hungary—118'2⅞"
2. F. Janda, Bohemia—115'3⁷⁄₁₆"
3. R. Sheldon, U.S.—113'2¼"

Hammer Throw
1. J. Flanagan, U.S.—167'4"
2. T. Hare, U.S.—161'2"
3. M. McCracken, U.S.—139'1".

SWIMMING

100 Metres—Free-Style
1. Jarvis, Great Britain—1:16.4
2. Wahle, Austria
3. Halmay, Hungary

400 Metres
1. Jarvis, Great Britain
2. Hulmann, Great Britain
3. Martin, France

200 Metres—Free-Style
1. Lane, Australia—2:25.2
2. Halmay, Hungary
3. Rubert, Austria

200 Metres Back-Stroke
1. E. Hoppenberg, Germany—2:47.0
2. K. Rubert, Austria
3. F. Dooxt, Netherlands

CYCLING

1,000 Metres Sprint
1. G. Taillandier, France
2. Vasserot, France
3. Lanz, France

FENCING

Foil
1. C. Coste, France
2. H. Masson, France
3. J. Boulanger, France

Epée
1. E. Fonst, Cuba
2. L. Peree, France
3. Leon See, France

Sabre
1. G. de la Falaise, France
2. L. Thiebaut, France
3. S. Flesch, Austria

GYMNASTICS

1. S. Sandras, France
2. J. Bass, France
3. G. Demanet, France

ROWING

Single Sculls
1. H. Barrelet, France—7:35.6
2. Gaudin, France—7:41.6
3. G. St. Ashe, Great Britain—8:15.6

Coxwainless Fours
1. France I—7:34.2
   Roubaix
2. France II—7:34.4
   Lyon
3. Germany—7:57.2
   Fav. Hammonia Hamburg

Coxswainless Pairs
1. Van Crombage/De Sonville,
   Belgium I
2. Delattre/Delattre, Belgium II

Coxed Fours
1. Germany—5:59.0
   Germania, Hamburg
2. Netherlands—6:33.0
   Minerva, Amsterdam
3. Germany—6:35.0
   Ruderverein, Ludwigshafen

Coxed Pairs
1. Netherlands
   Minerva, Amsterdam
2. France I
   Soc. de la Marne
3. France II
   Rowing Club de Castillon

Eights
1. U.S.—6:07.8
   Vesper B.C.
   Philadelphia
2. Belgium—6:13.8
   Club Nautique de Ghent
3. Netherlands—6:23.0
   Minerva, Amsterdam

YACHTING

6 Metres
1. Lerina, Switzerland

8 Metres
1. Olle, Great Britain

Boats to 10 Tons
1. Aschembrodel, Germany
2. Scotia, Great Britain
3. Crabe II, France

Boats above 10 Tons
1. Esterel, France
2. Rozenn, France
3. Quand-meme, France

SHOOTING

Free Pistol
1. K. Roderer, Switzerland
2. K. Staeheli, Switzerland
3. L. Ricnardet, Switzerland

Small-Bore Rifles—Prone
1. A. Carnell, Great Britain

Clay Pigeon
1. W. Ewing, Canada

Rifle, 300 Metres
1. M. Kellenberger, Switzerland
   Miniature Rifle, 12 Metres
1. C. Grosset, France

Rifle Teams
1. Switzerland

Revolver Teams
1. Switzerland
2. France
3. The Netnerlands

Game Shooting
1. Mackintosh, Australia
2. Marquis de Villaviciosa, Spain
3. Murphy, U.S.

Running Deer
1. L. de Bray, France

ARCHERY

Au Cordon Doré—50 metres
1. Herouin, France
2. Van Innins, Belgium
3. Fisseux, France

Au Cordon Doré—33 metres
1. Van Innins, Belgium
2. Thibaud, France
3. J. Petit, France

Au Chapelet—50 metres
1. Mougin, France
2. Helle, France
3. Mercier, France

A La Perche
1. Foulon, France
2. Serrurier, France
3. Druart, France

Au Chapelet—33 metres
1. Van Innins, Belgium
2. Thibaud, France
3. J. Petit, France

LAWN TENNIS

Men's Singles
1. L. Doherty, Great Britain
2. H. S. Mahony, Great Britain

Women's Singles
1. Miss Cooper, Great Britain
2. Miss Prevost, Great Britain

Men's Doubles
1. Doherty/Doherty, Great Britain
2. Garmenda/Max Decugis, France

Mixed Doubles
1. F. Doherty/Miss Cooper, Gt. Brit.
2. H. S. Mahony/Miss Prevost, Great Britain

TUG OF WAR
1. Sweden
2. France

WATER POLO
1. Great Britain
2. Belgium
3. France

Chapter 4

THE III OLYMPIAD

St. Louis, 1904

THE III Olympiad at St. Louis, Missouri, was once again lost in the trappings of a world fair.

The biggest crowd to see an Olympic event numbered only 2,000. And only eight foreign countries sent athletes to the United States. France was among the absentees.

Several American cities put in bids for the Olympic Games when Coubertin, impressed with U.S. performance at Athens and Paris, persuaded the International Olympic Committee to award the III Olympiad to the United States. Buffalo wanted the Games to be held there in 1905 during the Pan-American Exposition, but the Europeans blocked that proposal because it did not adhere to the four year interval between Olympics.

The committee initially awarded the Games to Chicago because St. Louis had neglected to send a representative to an International Olympic Committee meeting in Paris in 1901. The promoters of the 1904 Louisiana Purchase Exposition in St. Louis then threatened to hold a rival international track meet while the Olympics would have been taking place in Chicago. Finally, President Theodore Roosevelt, honorary president of the 1904 Olympic Games, asked the IOC to change its mind and the committee voted 14-2 to switch the Olympics from Chicago to St. Louis.

The program once again was stretched out to cover the duration of the exposition from May through November, but this time Americans made sure that everyone knew it was an Olympic Games by giving just about every event at the exposition an Olympic connotation. There was even a quasi-athletic freak show billed as "Olympic Anthropology Days".

However, about 1,300 *bona fide* Olympic athletes did compete. Most of them, of course, were Americans who won 21 of the 22 track and field events and finished one-two-three in 18 of them. Montreal policeman,

Etienne Desmarteau, was the only gold medallist from outside of the U.S., winning the 56-pound weight with a toss of 34' 4". He beat another policeman, John J. Flanagan of New York who won the hammer throw.

Suspicious officials uncovered one of the biggest scandals in Olympic history when Fred Lorz of the United States finished first in the marathon so fresh that he was hardly out of breath. After Alice Roosevelt, the daughter of the president, had decorated him with a laurel wreath and presented him with a gold medal, the officials turned up a truck driver who confessed that he had given Lorz a lift over ten miles of the course. Lorz had been stopped by cramps after running about nine miles. The truck driver picked him up but when the truck broke down Lorz had recovered and said he ran back to the stadium just to keep warm and pick up his clothes. But the spectators started cheering him on, thinking he was the winner, and when he was being congratulated at the finish line he was too ashamed to admit that he had hitched a ride. After his hoax was discovered, the gold medal was given to another American, Thomas Hicks, with Albert Corey and Arthur Newton, also of the U.S., getting the silver and bronze.

The popular hero of the marathon, both among the athletes and the spectators, was Havana postman Felix Carvajal who had boasted that he could win it. He was not chosen on the Cuban national team, so he paid for his trip by daily jaunts around the Havana civic square collecting coins from the crowd. But he lost what was left of his expense money in a dice game at New Orleans and had to hitch-hike to St. Louis. The little Cuban was exhausted and almost starved when he staggered into the Olympic village. Other athletes invited him to their training tables to build up his strength. Felix showed up at the starting line in heavy boots, a long-sleeved shirt and trousers. Someone snipped off his sleeves and trouser legs with a pair of scissors and loaned him a pair of sneakers. During the race, friendly Felix stopped every once in a while to chat with spectators. When he was hungry, he took detours into apple orchards. Somehow or other he still managed to finish fourth and probably could have won if he had had some coaching and a more serious attitude.

A couple of Kaffirs employed at an exposition concession stand also decided to run the marathon and finished ninth and twelfth. One of them said he might have won if he had not been chased nearly a mile off course by a vicious dog.

Ten patriotic Greeks who were not on the national team paid their own way to St. Louis to run in the marathon. However, they all finished far back.

Ray Ewry picked up four more gold medals for the standing jumps; and triple winners were Harry Hillman in the 200 and 400 metre hurdles and the 400 metre run, Archie Hahn in the 60, 100 and 200 metre sprints, and Jim Lightbody in the 800 and 1,500 metres and 2,500 metre steeplechase. Lightbody rested for a couple of hours after winning the 800 metres and then entered the four mile team race. He finished last.

Defending champion Myer Prinstein won the running triple jump and also took the running broad jump; and New York policeman Martin Sheridan added 10 feet to his Olympic discus record.

The seven-man German swimming team won five of the ten events. Emil Rausch won the 880 yard and one mile races as well as a bronze in the 220 yard freestyle. Backstroker Walter Brock won a gold medal in the 100 yard and a silver in the 440 yard races. George Zahanas won the breast stroke as well as a bronze in the backstroke.

Zoltan de Halmay of Hungary won the 50 and 100 yards free-style; and Charles Daniels of the United States, who was second in the 100 yards and third in the 50 yards, beat teammate Francis Gailey in the 220 and 440 yards. Gailey also finished second in the 880 yard and one mile races.

Cuban fencers won all six events with Ramon Fonst getting three individual gold medals.

The Americans won all the rowing events and made sweeps in cycling, rowing, archery, wrestling and boxing. It all added up to 76 gold medals for the United States, six for Cuba, six for Germany, two for Canada, two for Hungary and one for Greece.

The dominance of the United States at St. Louis resulted in the International Olympic Committee sanctioning an extra curricular Olympiad at Athens in 1906 to celebrate the tenth anniversary of the Olympic revival. But here too, the United States again dominated the track and field events winning 11 of the 19 gold medals. Archie Hahn repeated his 100 metre victory at St. Louis; and Paul Pilgrim upset the favored Harry Hillman in the 400 metres and Jim Lightbody in the 800 metres. Lightbody did, however, win the 1,500 metres.

George Bonhag had expected to win the five mile race in Athens but was so disappointed by his fourth place finish to Harry Hawtree of Great Britain that he entered an event he had never tried before, the 1,500 metre walk. A Canadian competitor gave him a few last minute pointers about the tricky heel-and-toe technique. When he won, Bonhag could not help bursting into a fit of hysterical laughter. Ray Ewry won both standing jumps and Martin Sheridan won the shot put and discus.

The results of these international games at Athens are not included in the official Olympic records.

OFFICIAL III OLYMPIAD RESULTS

St. Louis, 1904

TRACK AND FIELD

60 Metres
1. A. Hahn, U.S.—7.0
2. W. Hogenson, U.S.
3. F. R. Moulton, U.S.

100 Metres
1. A. Hahn, U.S.—11.0
2. N. Cartmell, U.S.
3. W. Hogenson, U.S.

200 Metres
1. A. Hahn, U.S.—21.6
2. N. Cartmell, U.S.
3. W. Hogenson, U.S.

400 Metres
1. H. Hillman, U.S.—49.2
2. F. Waller, U.S.
3. H. C. Groman, U.S.

800 Metres
1. J. Lightbody, U.S.—1:56.0
2. H. Valentine, U.S.
3. E. Breitkreutz, U.S.

1,500 Metres
1. J. Lightbody, U.S.—4:05.4
2. Frank Verner, U.S.
3. L. Hearn, U.S.

Marathon
1. T. Hicks, U.S.—3:28:53.0
2. A. Corey, U.S.
3. A. Newton, U.S.

110 Metres Hurdles
1. F. Schule, U.S.—16.0
2. T. Shideler, U.S.
3. L. Ashburner, U.S.

200 Metres Hurdles
1. H. Hillman, U.S.—24.6
2. F. Castleman, U.S.
3. G. C. Poage, U.S.

400 Metres Hurdles
1. H. Hillman, U.S.—53.0
2. F. Waller, U.S.
3. G. Poage, U.S.

2,500 Metres Steeplechase
1. J. Lightbody, U.S.—7:39.6
2. J. Daly, Great Britain
3. A. Newton, U.S.

Standing High Jump
1. R. Ewry, U.S.—4'11"
2. J. F. Stadler, U.S.
3. L. Robertson, U.S.

Running High Jump
1. S. Jones, U.S.—5'10 $\frac{11}{16}$"
2. G. P. Serviss, U.S.—5'10"
3. P. Weinstein, Germany—5'10"

Three Standing Jumps
1. R. Ewry, U.S.—34'7¼"
2. C. M. King, U.S.
3. J. F. Stadler, U.S.

Standing Broad Jump
1. R. Ewry, U.S.—11'4⅞"
2. C. M. King, U.S.
3. J. A. Miller, U.S.

Running Broad Jump
1. M. Prinstein, U.S.—24'1"
2. D. Frank, U.S.—22'7¼"
3. R. Strangland, U.S.—22'7"

Standing Triple Jump
1. R. Ewry, U.S.—34'7¼"
2. C. M. King, U.S.
3. J. F. Stadler, U.S.

Running Triple Jump
1. M. Prinstein, U.S.—47'0"
2. F. Englenardt, U.S.—45'7.2"
3. R. Strangland, U.S.—43'10 $\frac{3}{16}$"

Pole Vault
1. C. Dvorak, U.S.—11'6"
2. L. Samse, U.S.—11'3"
3. L. Wilkins, U.S.—11'3"

Shot Put
1. R. Rose, U.S.—48'7"
2. W. Coe, U.S.—47'3"
3. L. B. Feuerbach, U.S.—43'10⅜"

Discus Throw
1. M. Sheridan, U.S.—128'10 $\frac{1}{16}$"
2. R. Rose, U.S.—128'7½"
3. N. Georgantos, Greece—123'7½"

Hammer Throw
1. J. Flanagan, U.S.—168'0 $\frac{11}{16}$"
2. J. DeWitt, U.S.—164'8⅜"
3. R. Rose, U.S.—150'0½"

SWIMMING

50 Yards Free-Style
1. Z. de Halmay, Hungary—28.0
2. J. S. Leary, U.S.
3. C. M. Daniels, U.S.

100 Yards Free-Style
1. Z. de Halmay, Hungary—1:02.8
2. C. Daniels, U.S.
3. S. Leary, U.S.

220 Yards Free-Style
1. C. Daniels, U.S.—2:44.2
2. F. Gailey, U.S.
3. E. Rausch, Germany

440 Yards Free-Style
1. C. Daniels, U.S.—6:16.2
2. F. Gailey, U.S.
3. O. Wahle, Austria

880 Yards Free-Style
1. E. Rausch, Germany—13:11.4
2. F. Gailey, U.S.
3. G. Kiss, Hungary

1,500 Metres Free-Style
1. E. Rausch, Germany—27:18.2
2. G. Kiss, Hungary—28:28.2
3. F. Gailey, U.S.—28:54.0

1 mile Free-Style
1. E. Rausch, Germany—27:18.2
2. F. Gailey, U.S.
3. G. Kiss, Hungary

100 Yards Backstroke
1. W. Brock, Germany—1:16.8
2. G. Hoffman, Germany
3. G. Zahanus, Germany

440 Yards Breast Stroke
1. G. Zahanus, Germany—7:23.6
2. W. Brock, Germany
3. H. J. Handy, U.S.

Plunge for Distance
1. W. E. Dickey, U.S.—62'6"
2. E. H. Adams, U.S.—57'6"
3. L. B. Goodwin, U.S.—54'0"

Fancy Diving
1. G. E. Sheldon, U.S.
2. A. Brauschwerger, Germany
3. F. H. Kehoe, U.S.

BOXING

Flyweight
1. G. Finnegan, U.S.
2. M. Burke, U.S.

Bantamweight
1. O. L. Kirk, U.S.
2. G. Finnegan, U.S.

Featherweight
1. O. L. Kirk, U.S.
2. F. Haller, U.S.

Welterweight
1. A. Young, U.S.
2. H. Spanger, U.S.
3. J. Lydon, U.S.

Lightweight
1. H. J. Spanger, U.S.
2. J. Eagan, U.S.
3. R. Van Horn, U.S.

Middleweight
1. C. Mayer, U.S.
2. B. Spradley, U.S.

Heavyweight
1. S. Berger, U.S.
2. C. Mayer, U.S.

WRESTLING

Free-Style—Flyweight
1. R. Curry, U.S.
2. J. Heim, U.S.
3. G. Thiefenthaler, U.S.

Free-Style—Lightweight
1. O. Roehm, U.S.
2. R. Tesing, U.S.
3. G. Zukel, U.S.

Free-Style—Bantamweight
1. I. Niflot, U.S.
2. A. Wester, U.S.
3. Z. Strebler, U.S.

Free-Style—Welterweight
1. C. Erickson, U.S.
2. W. Beckmann, U.S.
3. J. Winholtz, U.S.

Free-Style—Featherweight
1. B. Bradsnaw, U.S.
2. T. McLeer, U.S.
3. C. Clapper, U.S.

Free-Style—Heavyweight
1. B. Hansen, U.S.
2. F. Kungler, U.S.
3. F. Warmbold, U.S.

WEIGHT-LIFTING

Heavyweight
1. P. Kakousis, Greece—246 lb.
2. Otto Osthoff, U.S.—186 lb.
3. F. Kungler, U.S.—150 lb.

CYCLING

880 Yards
1. M. Hurley, U.S.—1:00.9
2. T. Billington, U.S.
3. B. Downing, U.S.

1/3 Mile
1. M. Jurley, U.S.—43.8
2. B. Downing, U.S.
3. T. Billington, U.S.

Five Miles
1. C. Schlee, U.S.—13:08.2
2. G. Wiley, U.S.
3. A. F. Andrews, U.S.

440 Yards
1. Marcus Hurley, U.S.—31.8
2. B. Downing, U.S.
3. T. Billington, U.S.

One Mile
1. M. Hurley, U.S.—2:41.6
2. B. Downing, U.S.
3. T. Billington, U.S.

Two Miles
1. B. Downing, U.S.—4:57.8
2. O. Goerke, U.S.
3. M. Hurley, U.S.

25 Miles
1. B. Downing, U.S.—1:10:55.4
2. A. F. Andrews, U.S.
3. G. Wiley, U.S.

FENCING

Foil
1. R. Fonst, Cuba
2. A. Post, Cuba
3. C. Tatham, Cuba

Team Foil
1. Cuba
2. U.S.

Singlestick
1. A. Post, Cuba
2. W. Grebe, U.S.
3. S. O'Connor, U.S.

Epée
1. R. Fonst, Cuba
2. C. Tatham, Cuba
3. A. Post, Cuba

Sabre
1. M. Diaz, Cuba
2. W. Grebe, U.S.
3. A. Post, Cuba

Individual Swords
1. R. Fonst, Cuba

GYMNASTICS

Combined Exercises—Individual
1. A. Spinnler, Germany
2. W. Weber, Germany
3. H. Peitsch, Germany

Rope Climbing
1. G. Eyser, U.S.
2. C. Kraus, U.S.
3. E. Voight, U.S.

Horizontal Bar
1. A. Heida, U.S.
2. E. A. Hennig, U.S.
3. G. Eyser, U.S.

Parallel Bars
1. G. Eyser, U.S.
2. A. Heida, U.S.
3. J. Duha, U.S.

Pommelled Horse
1. A. Heida, U.S.
2. G. Eyser, U.S.
3. W. A. Merz, U.S.

Long Horse Vault
1. A. Heida, U.S.
2. G. Eyser, U.S.
3. W. A. Merz, U.S.

Rings
1. H. Glass, U.S.
2. W. A. Merz, U.S.
3. E. Voight, U.S.

Indian Club
1. E. A. Hennig, U.S.
2. E. Voight, U.S.
3. R. Wilson, U.S.

All Around Individual
1. A. Heida, U.S.
2. G. Eyser, U.S.
3. W. A. Merz, U.S.

ROWING

Single Sculls
1. F. Greer, U.S.—10:08.5
2. J. Juvenal, U.S.
3. C. Titus, U.S.

Double Sculls
1. U.S.—10:03.2
   Atalanta B.C.
   New York
2. U.S.
   Ravenswood B.D.
   Long Island
3. U.S.
   Independent R.C.
   New Orleans

Coxswainless Pairs
1. U.S.—10:57.0
   Seawanhaka C.
2. U.S.
   Atalanta B.C.
3. U.S.
   Western R.C.

Coxswainless Fours
1. U.S.—9:53.8
   Century B.C. St. Louis
2. U.S.
   Western R.C.
3. U.S.
   Independent R.C.
   New Orleans

Eights
1. U.S.—7:50.0
   Vesper B.C. Philadelphia
2. Canada
   Argonaut, Toronto

ARCHERY

Double York Round—Men
1. P. Bryant, U.S.
2. Col. R. Williams, U.S.
3. W. H. Thompson, U.S.

Double American Round—Men
1. P. Bryant, U.S.
2. D. McGowan, U.S.
3. T. F. Scott, U.S.

Team Round—Men
1. U.S. (Potomac)
2. U.S. (Cincinnati A.C.)
3. U.S. (Boston A.A.)

Double National Round—Women
1. Mrs. M. C. Howell, U.S.
2. Mrs. H. C. Pollock, U.S.
3. Mrs. E. C. Cooke, U.S.

Double Columbia Round—Women
1. Mrs. M. C. Howell, U.S.
2. Mrs. E. C. Coolen, U.S.
3. Mrs. H. C. Pollock, U.S.

Women's Team Championship
1. U.S. (Cincinnati)

LACROSSE

1. Canada
2. U.S.

ROQUE

1. C. Jacobus, U.S.—5 wins
2. S. O. Streeter, U.S.—4 wins
3. D. C. Brown, U.S.—3 wins

TENNIS

Men's Singles
1. B. C. Wright, U.S.
2. R. LeRoy, U.S.

Men's Doubles
1. B. C. Wright/W. E. Leonard, U.S.
2. R. LeRoy/A. E. Bell, U.S.

TUG-OF-WAR

1. U.S., Milwaukee
2. U.S., South West T.V., St. Louis

WATER POLO

1. New York A.C., U.S.
2. Chicago A.C., U.S.

Chapter 5

THE IV OLYMPIAD

London, 1908

THE enthusiastic participation of Great Britain in the 1906 international games at Athens after boycotting the St. Louis Olympics led to the IV Olympiad being held in London in 1908.

The marathon from Windsor Castle to Shepherds Bush Stadium was one of the most exciting races in Olympic history. The British fans began lining the 26 mile, 385 yard course the previous evening and an overflow crowd of 70,000 packed the stadium long before the race started. Two British runners led for the first four miles with Charles Hefferson, a South African running for the United States, and Dorando Pietri of Italy, third and fourth. After 15 miles, Hefferson and Pietri passed the British runners. Then, with the stadium almost in sight, Pietri sprinted past Hefferson. He was first into the stadium, but was so exhausted that he collapsed on the cycling track atfer running in the wrong direction. A couple of doctors propped him up and pointed him towards the finish line and several officials helped him across when it looked as if he was going to collapse again. He was finally dragged across the line 30 seconds ahead of John Hayes of the United States who had passed Hefferson as they were entering the stadium. The British officials ran up the Italian flag although it was obvious to everyone else that Pietri would have to be disqualified for receiving assistance. Fights broke out among the fans while the officials argued for almost an hour before disqualifying Pietri and giving the gold medal to Hayes, a New York department store clerk who was the youngest member of the U.S. team. During the debate, doctors trying to revive Pietri thought he was going to die. But he recovered in time to be personally presented with a special gold cup donated by Queen Alexandra.

A disqualification in the 400 metres enabled Wyndham Halswelle of Great Britain to become the only athlete in Olympic history to win a gold medal by running a race by himself. British officials ruled that he had been forced to the outside of the track by two Americans—J. C. Carpenter and W. C. Robbins—who beat him. They ordered a re-run of the race, but the angry Americans refused to compete and Halswelle jogged around the track all by himself in 50 seconds flat.

Reggie Walker, a 19-year-old South African who was added to the team as an afterthought, won the 100 metres over Jimmy Rector of the U.S. and Bobby Kerr of Canada. Kerr later won the 200 metres.

Mel Sheppard of the United States beat Emilio Lunghi of Italy by nine yards in the 800 metre race. He also won the 1,500 metres.

Charley Bacon was pressed by teammate Harry Hillman to set a world record of 55 seconds in the 400 metres hurdles. Forrest Smithson gave the United States the other hurdling event, running the 110 metres in 15 seconds to beat teammates John Garrels and Arthur Shaw by five yards.

British runners took most of the honours in the distance races, placing first, second, fourth and fifth in the steeplechase and first, second and fifth in the five mile run. Arthur Russell won the steeplechase and E. R. Voight the five mile race.

J. E. Deakin, A. J. Robertson and W. Coales gave Great Britain the three mile team race. G. E. Larner of Great Britain beat E. J. Webb and four other British contestants in the 10-mile walk. Larner and Webb also finished one-two in the 3,500 metre walk.

Ray Ewry picked up his ninth and tenth Olympic gold medals by winning the two standing jumps but he was almost beaten in both events by Greek champion C. Tsiclitaris who was young enough to be his son.

New York policeman John F. Flanagan won the hammer throw for the third time in a row.

Defending champion Martin Sheridan repeated his 1904 discus victory, defeating M. H. Griffin and Marquis Horr for a U.S. sweep. Sheridan also defeated Werner Jaervinen of Finland, the defending champion, in the Greek style discus event in which the competitors threw from a classic, stationary position.

31

Erik Lemming of Sweden won both javelin throw events; and Timothy Ahearne, an Irishman competing for Britain, was a surprise winner in the triple jump.

In swimming, Henry Taylor of Great Britain was a triple gold medal winner, winning the 400 and 1,500 metre races and then anchoring the victorious 800 metres relay team. And Charles Daniels of the United States got revenge for his loss to Zoltan Hamay of Hungary at St. Louis by beating him this time in the 100 metres freestyle.

Hjalmar Johansson finished ahead of three other Swedes in high diving, and 18-year-old Albert Zurner of Germany took the springboard diving medal.

Britain won another gold medal in water polo, overwhelming Belgium 9-2 in the final.

The British won all five boxing championships with 38-year-old R. K. Gunn taking the featherweight title. Great Britain also took five of the seven cycling events, as well as the gold medals for lawn tennis, rackets, rowing, yachting, and polo.

British athletes won 57 gold medals followed by the Americans with 22, of which 15 had been won out of the 25 track and field events.

OFFICIAL IV OLYMPIAD RESULTS

London, 1908

TRACK AND FIELD

100 Metres
1. R. Walker, South Africa—10.8
2. J. Rector, U.S.
3. R. Kerr, Canada

200 Metres
1. R. Kerr, Canada—22.6
2. R. Cloughen, U.S.
3. Nathan Cartmell, U.S.

400 Metres
1. W. Halswelle, Great Britain—50.0

800 Metres
1. M. Sheppard, U.S.—1:52.8
2. E. Lunghi, Italy
3. H. Braun, Germany

1,500 Metres
1. M. Sheppard, U.S.—4:03.4
2. H. Wilson, Great Britain
3. N. Hallows, Great Britain

5 Mile Run
1. E. R. Voight, Gt. Britain—25:11.
2. E. Owen, Great Britain—25:24.0
3. J. F. Svanberg, Sweden—25:37.2

Marathon
1. J. Hayes, U.S.—2:55:18.4
2. C. Hefferon, U.S.—2:56:06.0
3. J. Forshaw, U.S.—2:57:10.4

110 Metres Hurdles
1. F. Smithson, U.S.—15.0
2. J. Garrels, U.S.
3. A. Shaw, U.S.

400 Metres Hurdles
1. C. Bacon, U.S.—55.0
2. H. Hillman, U.S.
3. L. Tremeer, Great Britain

3,200 Metres Steeplechase
1. A. Russell, Great Britain—10:47.8
2. A. J. Robertson, Gt. Brit.
3. J. L. Eisele, U.S.

3 Mile Team Race
1. Great Britain
2. U.S.
3. France

1,600 Metres Relay
1. U.S.—3:29.4
2. Germany
3. Hungary

3,500 Metres Walk
1. G. E. Larner, Gt. Brit.—14:55
2. E. J. Webb, Great Britain
3. H. E. Kerr, Australia

Standing High Jump
1. R. Ewry, U.S.—5'2"
2. { C. Tsiclitiras, Greece
     { J. A. Biller, U.S.
3. F. L. Homes—U.S.

Running High Jump
1. H. Porter, U.S.—6'2 $\frac{11}{16}$"
2. { C. Leany, Great Britain—6'2"
     { I. Somodi, Hungary—6'2"
     { G. Andre, France—6'2"

Standing Broad Jump
1. R. Ewry, U.S.—10'11¼"
2. C. Tsiclitiras, Greece
3. M. J. Sheridan, U.S.

Running Broad Jump
1. F. Irons, U.S.—24'6½"
2. D. Kelly, U.S.—23'3⅛"
3. C. Bricker, Canada—23'2¾"

Triple Jump
1. T. Ahearne, Gt. Briz.—48'11⅜"
2. G. MacDonald, Canada—48'5 $\frac{1}{16}$"
3. E. Oarsen, Norway—47'2½"

Pole Vault
1. { A. Gilbert, U.S.—12'2 $\frac{1}{16}$"
     { E. Cook, U.S.
3. { E. Archibald, Canada—11'9 $\frac{11}{16}$"
     { C. S. Jacobs, U.S.
     { B. Soderstrom, Sweden

Shot Put
1. R. Rose, U.S.—46'7½"
2. D. Horgan, Gt. Brit.—44'8 $\frac{3}{16}$"
3. J. Garrels, U.S.—43'2⅞"

Discus Throw
1. M. Sheridan, U.S.—134'1 $\frac{11}{16}$"
2. M. H. Griffin, U.S.—133'6⅝"
3. M. Horr, U.S.—129'5⅛"

Discus Throw (Greek Style)
1. M. J. Sheridan, U.S.—124'8"
2. M. F. Horr, U.S.
3. W. Jarvinen, Finland

Discus Throw (Free Style)
1. M. Sheridan, U.S.—134'1 $\frac{11}{16}$"
2. M. H. Giffin, U.S.
3. M. F. Horr, U.S.

Hammer Throw
1. J. Flanagan, U.S.—170'4 $\frac{1}{16}$"
2. M. McGrath, U.S.—167'10 $\frac{11}{16}$"
3. C. Walsh, U.S.—159'1 $\frac{11}{16}$"

Javelin Throw (Greek Style)
1. E. Lemming, Sweden—179'10½"
2. A. Halse, Norway
3. O. Nilsson, Sweden

Javelin Throw (Free Style)
1. E. Lemming, Sweden—178'7¼"
2. M. Dorizas, Greece
3. A. Halse, Norway

SWIMMING AND DIVING

100 Metres Free-Style
1. C. Daniels, U.S.—1:05.6
2. Z. Halmay, Norway—1:06.2
3. H. Julin, Sweden—1:08.8

400 Metres Free-Style
1. H. Taylor, Gt. Brit.—5:36.8
2. F. Beaurepaire, Australia—5:44.2
3. O. Scheff, Austria—5:46.0

1,500 Metres Free-Style
1. H. Taylor, Great Britain—22:48.4
2. T. Battersby, Gt. Brit.—22:51.2
3. F. Beaurepaire, Australia—22:56.2

200 Metres Breast Stroke
1. F. Holman, Great Britain—3:09.2
2. W. W. Robinson, Gt. Brit.—3:12.8
3. P. Hansson, Sweden—3:14.6

100 Metres Backstroke
1. A. Bieberstein, German—1:24.6
2. L. Dam, Denmark—1:26.6
3. H. N. Haresnape, Great Britain—1:27.0

800 Metres Relay
1. Great Britain—10:55.6
2. Hungary—10:59.0
3. U.S.—11:02.8

Platform Diving
1. H. Johansson, Sweden
2. K. Malmstrom, Sweden
3. A. Spangoerg, Sweden

Fancy Diving
1. A. Zurner, Germany
2. R. Behrens, Germany
3. G. W. Geidzik, U.S.

BOXING

Bantamweight
1. A. Thomas, Great Britain
2. J. Condon, Great Britain
3. W. Webb, Great Britain

Light weight
1. F. Grace, Great Britain
2. R. Spiller, Great Britain
3. H. Johnson, Great Britain

Featherweight
1. R. K. Gunn, Great Britain
2. C. Morris, Great Britain
3. H. Roddin, Great Britain

Middleweight
1. J. Douglas, Great Britain
2. R. Baker, Australia
3. W. Philo, Great Britain

Heavyweight
1. A. L. Oldman, Great Britain
2. S. Evans, Great Britain
3. F. Parks, Great Britain

WRESTLING

Free-Style—Bantamweight
1. G. Mehnert, U.S.
2. W. J. Press, Great Britain
3. A. Cote, Canada

Greco-Roman—Lightweight
1. E. Porro, Italy
2. N. Orlov, Russia
3. A. Linden-Linko, Finland

Free-Style—Featherweight
1. G. Dole, U.S.
2. J. Slim, Great Britain
3. W. McKie, Great Britain

Greco-Roman—Middleweight
1. F. Martensson, Sweden
2. M. Andersson, Sweden
3. A. Andersen, Denmark

Free-Style—Lightweight
1. G. de Relwyskow, Great Britain
2. W. Wood, Great Britain
3. A. Gingell, Great Britain

Greco-Roman—Light-Heavyweight
1. V. Weckman, Finland
2. Y. Saarela, Finland
3. K. Jensen, Denmark

Free-Style—Middleweight
1. S. Bacon, Great Britain
2. G. de Relwyskow, Great Britain
3. F. Beck, Great Britain

Free-Style—Heavyweight
1. G. C. O'Kelly, Great Britain
2. J. Gundersen, Norway
3. E. Barrett, Great Britain

Greco-Roman—Heavyweight
1. R. Weisz, Hungary
2. O. Petrov, Russia
3. S. Jensen, Denmark

CYCLING

20 Kilometres
1. C. B. Kingsbury, Gt. Brit.—34:13.6
2. B. Jones, Great Britain
3. G. Werbrouck, Belgium

Pursuit Race—4,000 Metres
1. Great Britain—2:18:6
2. Germany—2:18:6
3. Canada—2:29:6

100 Kilometres
1. C. H. Bartlett, Gt. Brit.—2:41:48.6
2. C. A. Denny, Great Britain
3. O. Lapize, France

660 Yards
1. V. L. Johnson, Gt. Brit.—51.2
2. E. Demangel, France
3. K. Neumer, Germany

2,000 Metres Tandem
1. M. Schilles/A. Auffray, France—3:7.6
2. F. G. Hamlin/H. T. Johnson, Great Britain
3. C. Brooks/W. H. T. Isaacs, Gt. Br.

5,000 Metres
1. B. Jones, Great Britain—8:36.2
2. M. Schilles, France
3. A. Auffray, France

FENCING

Epée—Individual
1. G. Alibert, France
2. A. Lippmann, France
3. E. Olivier, France

Sabre—Individual
1. J. Fuchs, Hungary
2. B. Zulavsky, Hungary
3. V. Goppold, Bohemia

Epée—Team
1. France
2. Great Britain
3. Belgium

Sabre—Team
1. Hungary
2. Italy
3. Bohemia

GYMNASTICS

Combined Exercises—Individual
1. A. Braglia, Italy
2. S. W. Tysal, Great Britain
3. J. Segura, France

Hepthlon Team
1. Sweden
2. Norway
3. Finland

ROWING

Single Sculls
1. H. Blackstaffe, Gt. Brit.—9:26.0
2. A. McCullough, Gt. Brit.
3. B. von Gaza, Germany

Coxswainless Fours
1. Great Britain—8:34.0
   (Magdalene B.C. Oxford)
2. Great Britain—(Leander)

Coxswainless Pairs
1. Fenning/Thomson, Gt. Brit.—
   9:41.0 (Leander I)
2. Fairbairn/Verdon, Gt. Brit.
   (Leander II)
3. Toms/Jackes, Canada

Eights
1. Great Britain—7-52.0
   (Leander)
2. Belgium—
   (Club Nautique de Ghent)
3. Great Britain
   (Cambridge B.C. University)

YACHTING

6 Metres
1. Dormy, Great Britain
2. Zut, Belgium

8 Metres
1. Cobweb, Great Britain
2. Vinga, Sweden
3. Sorais, Great Britain

12 Metres
1. Hera, Great Britain
2. Mouchette, Great Britain

SHOOTING

Free Pistol
1. P. Van Asbroeck, Belgium
2. R. Storms, Belgium
3. J. Gorman, U.S.

Miniature Rifles, Team
1. Great Britain
2. Sweden
3. France

Free Rifle—300 Metres
1. A. Helgerud, Norway
2. H. Simon, U.S.
3. O. Saether, Norway

Miniature Rifles, Moving Target
1. A. F. Fleming, Great Britain
2. M. K. Matthews, Great Britain
3. W. B. Marsden, Great Britain

Miniature Rifles
1. W. E. Styles, Great Britain
2. H. I. Hawkins, Great Britain
3. E. J. Amoore, Great Britain

Revolver and Pistol, Team
1. U.S.
2. Belgium
3. Great Britain

Small-Bore Rifles—Prone
1. A. Carnell, Great Britain
2. H.Humby,GreatBritain
3. G. Barnes, Great Britain

Running Deer, Team
1. Sweden
2. Great Britain

Team Competition, Six Distances
1. U.S.
2. Great Britain
3. Canada

Running Deer, Single Shot
1. O G. Swahn, Sweden
2. Capt. T. Ranken, Great Britain
3. A. E. Rogers, Great Britain

Running Deer, Double Shot
1. W. Winans, U.S.
2. Capt. T. Ranken, Great Britain
3. O. G. Swahn, Sweden

1,000 Yards, Individual
1. Col. J. K. Miller, Great Britain
2. Capt. K. K. V. Casey, U.S.
3. M. Blood, Great Britain

Clay Pigeon
1. W. Ewing, Canada
2. G. Beattie, Canada
3. { A. Maunder, Gt. Brit.
     A. Metaxas, Greece

300 Metres, Team
1. Norway
2. Sweden
3. France

Clay Pigeon—Team
1. Great Britain
2. Canada
3. Great Britain

35

ARCHERY

York Round—Men	*National Round—Women*
1. W. Dodd, Great Britain	1. Miss Q. Newall, Great Britain
2. R. Brooks-King, Great Britain	2. Miss Dodd, Great Britain
3. H. B. Richardson, U.S.	3. Mrs. Hill-lowe, Great Britain

Continental Style

1. M. Grisot, France
2. M. Vernet, France
3. M. Cabaret, France

FIELD HOCKEY

1. England
2. Ireland
3. ⎰Scotland
   ⎱Wales

LACROSSE

1. Canada
2. Great Britain

RACOUETS

Men's Singles	*Men's Doubles*
1. E. B. Noel, Great Britain	1. W. H. Pennell/J. J. Astor, Gt. Brit.

RUGBY FOOTBALL

1. Australia
2. Great Britain

SOCCER

1. Great Britain
2. Denmark
3. Netherlands

TENNIS—LAWN

Men's Singles	*Men's Doubles*
1. M. J. G. Ritchie, Great Britain	1. G. W. Hillyard/F. R. Doherty, Great Britain
2. O. Froitzheim, Germany	2. M. J. G. Ritchie/J. C. Parke, Great Britain
3. W. V. Eaves, Great Britain	3. C. H. L. Cazalet/C. P. Dixon Great Britain

Women's Singles

1. Mrs. L. Chambers, Great Britain
2. Miss Boothby, Great Britain
3. Mrs. Winch, Great Britain

TENNIS—COVERED COURTS

Men's Singles	*Men's Doubles*
1. A. W. Gore, Great Britain	1. A. W. Gore/H. R. Barrett, Great Britain
2. C. A. Caridia, Great Britain	2. C. M. Simond/C A. Caridia, Great Britain

Women's Singles	*Tennis (Jeu de Paume)*
1. Miss Eastlake-Smith, Gt. Britain	1. J. Gould, U.S.
2. Miss A. N. G. Greene, Gt. Britain	2. E. H. Miles, Great Britain
	3. Hon. N. S. Lytton, Great Britain

TUG-OF-WAR

1. Great Britain—City Police
2. Great Britain—Liverpool Police
3. Great Britain—K. Division

POLO

1. Great Britain (Roehampton)
2. Great Britain (Hurlingham)

WATER POLO

1. Great Britain
2. Belgium
3. Sweden

FIGURE SKATING—MEN

1. U. Slachow, Sweden
2. R. Johansson, Sweden
3. P. Thoren, Sweden

FIGURE SKATING—WOMEN

1. M. Syers, Great Britain
2. El. Rendschmidt, Germany
3. D. Greenhough-Smith, Gt. Brit.

PAIR SKATING

1. Anna Hubler/Heinrich Berger, Germany—56.0 pts.
2. P. W. Johnson/J. H. Johnson, Great Britain—51.5 pts.
3. M. Syers/E. Syers, Great Britain —48.0 pts.

Chapter 6

THE V OLYMPIAD

Stockholm, 1912

IN the two summers before the 1912 Olympic Games, American Indian Jim Thorpe had accepted $25 a month for playing semi-pro baseball. The indiscretion cost Thorpe the two gold medals he won at Stockholm. The Amateur Athletic Union, almost a year after the Olympics were over, disqualified him for professionalism and ordered him to turn over the medals to the runners-up in the decathlon and pentathlon. However, Hugo Wieslander of Sweden and F. R. Bie of Norway refused to accept them.

After his double victory, King Gustav V of Sweden hailed Thorpe as "the greatest athlete in the world". He was not exaggerating. The year before, Thorpe won nine out of ten events in a track meet involving his Carlisle Indian School and the much larger University of Syracuse team.

At Stockholm in 1912, he won four out of the five events in the pentathlon and came third in the other, a performance that has never been equalled.

In the decathlon, he won seven of the ten events and scored 8,412 out of a possible 10,000 points compared with only 5,377 for Wieslander. That record, later scratched from the books, was not beaten until 1952 when Bob Mathias scored 8,887.

Thorpe later rewrote the record books in U.S. pro football and compiled an incredible .324 batting average during a six year career in the National Baseball League. He also excelled in archery, swimming, hockey, shooting, canoeing, basketball, lacrosse, squash, handball and horseback riding.

Hannes Kolehmainen of Finland, who won the 5,000 and 10,000 metres and the 8,000 metres cross-country, did not get a medal for his best performance. Kolehmainen set a world record 8:36.9 in a preliminary heat of the 3,000 metres team race, but the rest of the

Finnish runners did so badly that they did not qualify for the final.

In the 10,000 metres, Kolehmainen increased his lead on every lap and beat American Indian Lewis Terwanima by 45 seconds.

His victory margin in the 5,000 metres was a tenth of a second. Kolehmainen trailed Jean Bouin of France for most of the three miles and beat him with a last second lunge to the tape after they had sprinted neck-and-neck for the last quarter mile.

South African mounted policeman, Ken McArthur, beat compatriot Chris Gitsham by a minute in the marathon. It was the fifth straight time that runners from the same country had finished first and second. McArthur's champagne celebration was dampened by the news that a Portuguese runner who was overcome by the heat had died in hospital.

The first five finishers in the 800 metres were only two fifths of a second apart. Eighteen-year-old Ted Meredith beat defending champion Mel Sheppard who had set the pace most of the way, and Ira Davenport was third for an American sweep.

Meredith also took an early lead in the 400 but faded to finish fourth behind Charles Reidpath of the United States, Hans Braun of Germany and Edward Lindberg of the U.S. The race was run in lanes for the first time to prevent the crowding which gave the race to Lieut. Wyndham Halswelle by default at London.

Ralph Craig of the United States won both the sprints. In the 100 metres, Craig and Donald Lippincott of the U.S. ran the distance twice over because they did not hear the starter calling them back after a false start and they sprinted all the way to the finish line. That tired Lippincott, who finished third behind Alvin Meyer of the U.S., but it was just a warmup for Craig. Lippincott came second in the 200 metres.

Oxford University student, Arnold Jackson, came from behind to steal the 1,500 metres from the favored Americans, Abel Kiviat, Norman Taber and John Paul Jones, who had no energy left to beat off Jackson's finishing kick after they had fought amongst themselves for the lead most of the way. Edvin Wide of Sweden who finished fifth, was only four fifths of a second behind the winner.

The United States had five of the six finalists in the 110 metre hurdles and Fred Kelly led an American sweep.

In the modern pentathlon, a new Olympic event, G. M. Lilliehook of Sweden won the gold medal without finishing first in any of the five events. Lieut. George Patton, who became a famous U.S. general in World War II, won the cross country race and was favored to win the medal until he did so badly in target shooting that he wound up fifth behind four Swedes.

Ralph Rose, the shot put champion of 1904 and 1908, missed a third gold medal when he slept in and was still drowsy when the final started. His 50′ ½″ toss was longer than his previous Olympic performances, but New York policeman Babe McDonald beat him by 3½″. By afternoon, Rose was wide awake and won the shot put event in which both hands were used.

With the great Ray Ewry now retired, Greek champion C. Tsiclitiras who had finished second in both standing jumps at London, won the standing broad jump over brothers Platt and Ben Adams of the U.S. who were first and second in the standing high jump with Tsiclitiras third.

The pole vault provided one of the closest contests at Stockholm, with Marc Wright of Dartmouth and Frank Nelson of Yale tied for second behind Harry Babcock of Columbia and Bill Happeny of Canada; D. Murphy of the U.S. and B. Uggla of Sweden tied for third.

Matthew McGrath of the United States, who had finished second to John Flanagan in 1908, won the hammer throw. McGrath's career spanned 16 years, ending in 1924 when he came second to Fred Tootell of the U.S. after missing a medal in 1920.

Duke Kahanamoku, one of the great swimmers of the first half of the century, made his debut in the 1912 Olympics, winning the 100 metres freestyle. He successfully defended his championship eight years later at Antwerp, but he was beaten in 1924 by Johnny Weissmuller who won five gold medals in Olympic competition.

The Duke, like Weissmuller, became a movie actor after his swimming career was over. He then returned to his native Hawaii where he was the official greeter until his death in 1968. He was given the traditional beachboy funeral—burial at sea beyond the Waikiki Reef.

OFFICIAL V OLYMPIAD RESULTS

Stockholm, 1912

TRACK AND FIELD

100 Metres
1. R. Craig, U.S.—10.8
2. A. Meyer, U.S.—10.9
3. D. Lippincott, U.S.—10.9

200 Metres
1. R. Craig, U.S.—21.7
2. D. Lippincott, U.S.—21.8
3. W. Applegarth, Gt. Brit.—22.0

400 Metres
1. C. Reidpath, U.S.—48.2
2. H. Braun, Germany—48.3
3. E. Lindberg, U.S.—48.4

800 Metres
1. T. Meredith, U.S.—1:51.9
2. M. Sheppard, U.S.—1:52.0
3. I. Davenport, U.S.—1:52.0

1,500 Metres
1. A. Jackson, Great Britain—3:56.8
2. A. Kiviat, U.S.—3:56.9
3. N. Taber, U.S.—3:56.9

5,000 Metres
1. H. Kolehmainen, Finland—14:36.6
2. Jean Bouin, France—14:36.7
3. G. Hutson, Great Britain—15:07.6

10,000 Metres
1. H. Kolemainen, Finland—31:20.8
2. L. Tewanima, U.S.—32:06.6
3. A. Stenroos, Finland—32:21.8

3,000 Metres Team
1. U.S.—8:44.6
2. Sweden
3. Great Britain

Marathon
1. K. McArthur, S. Africa—2:36:54.8
2. C. Gitsham, S. Africa—2:37:52.0
3. G. Strobino, U.S.—2:38:42 4

8,000 Mtres Cross-Country
1. H. Kolehmainen, Finland—45:11:6
2. H. Anderson, Sweden
3. J. Eke, Sweden

110 Metres Hurdles
1. F. Kelly, U S —15.1
2. J. Wendell, U S —15.2
3. M. Hawkins, U S —15.3

400 Metres Relay
1. Great Britain—42.4
2. Sweden—42.6

1,600 Metres Relay
1. U S —3:16.6
2. France—3:20.7
3. Great Britain—3:23.2

10,000 Metres Walk
1. G. H. Goulding, Canada—46:28.4
2. E. J. Webb, Great Britain
3. F. Altimani, Italy

Standing High Jump
1. P. Adams—U.S.—5'4⅛"
2. B. Adams, U.S.
3. C. Tsiclitiras, Greece

Running High Jump
1. A. Richards, U.S.—6'3" ¹¹⁄₁₆
2. H. Leische, Germany—6'3 ³⁄₁₆
3. G. Horine, U.S.—6'2⅜"

Standing Broad Jump
1. C. Tsiclitiras, Greece—11'0⅝"
2. Platt Adams, U.S.
3. B. W. Adams, U.S.

Running Boad Jump
1. A. Gutterson, U.S.—24'11 ³⁄₁₆"
2. C. Bricker, Canada—23'7⅞"
3. G. Aberg, Sweden—23'6¹¹⁄₁₆"

Triple Jump
1. G. Lindblom, Sweden—48'5 ¹⁄₁₆"
2. G. Aberg, Sweden—47'7¼"
3. E. Almlof, Sweden—46'5⅞"

Pole Vault
1. H. Babcock, U.S.—12'11½"
2. { F. Nelson, U.S.—12'7½"
   { M. Wrignt, U.S.—12'7½"

Shot Put
1. P McDonald, U.S.—50'4"
2. R Rose, U.S.—50'0⅜"
3. L Whitney, U.S.—45'8 ⁷⁄₁₆"

Discus Throw
1. A Taipole, Finland—145'0 ⁹⁄₁₆"
2. R Byrd, U.S.—142'1½"
3. J Duncan, U.S.—138'8 ⁹⁄₁₆"

Hammer Throw
1. M McGrath, U.S.—179'7⅛"
2. D Gillis, Canada—158'9½"
3. C Childs, U.S.—158'0 ⁷⁄₁₆"

Javelin Throw
1. E. Lemming, Sweden—198′11 ⅜″
2. J. Saaristo, Finland—192′5¹⁄₁₆″
3. M. Kovacs, Hungary—182′1″

Javelin Throw, both hands
1. J. Saaristo, Finland—358′10¾″
2. W. Siikaniemi, Finland
3. U. Peltonen, Finland

Discus Throw, both hands
1. A. Taipole, Finland—274′
2. E. Niklander, Finland
3. E. Magnusson, Sweden

Shot Put, both hands
1. R. Rose, U.S.—90′5½″
2. P. McDonald, U.S.
3. E. Niklander, Finland

Pentathlon
1. F. R. Bie, Norway
2. J. J. Donahue, U.S.
3. F. Lukeman, Canada

Decathlon
1. H. Wieslander, Sweden
2. C. Lomberg, Sweden
3. G. Holmer, Sweden

SWIMMING AND DIVING—MEN

100 Metres Free-Style
1. D. Kahanamoku, U.S.—1;03.4
2. C. Healy, Australia—1:04.6
3. K. Huszagh, U.S.—1:05.6

400 Metres Free-Style
1. G. Hodgson, Canada—5:24.4
2. J. Hatfield, Great Britain—5:25.8
3. H. Hardwick, Australia—5:31.2

1,500 Metres Free-Style
1. G. Hodgson, Canada—22:00.0
2. J. Hatfield, Great Britain—22:39.0
3. H. Hardwick, Australia—23:15.4

200 Metres Breast Stroke
1. W. Bathe, Germany—3:01.8
2. W. Lutzow, Germany—3:05.0
3. P. Malisch, Germany—3:08.0

400 Metres Breast Stroke
1. W. Bathe, Germany—6:29.6
2. T. Henning, Sweden
3. P. Courtman, Great Britain

100 Metres Backstroke
1. H. Hebner, U.S.—1:21.2
2. O. Fahr, Germany—1:22.4
3. P. Kellner, Germany—1:24.0

800 Metres Free-Style Relay
1. Australia—10:11.2
2. U.S.—10:20.2
3. Great Britain—10:28.2

Platform Diving
1. E. Adlerz, Sweden
2. A. Zurner, Germany
3. G. Blomgren, Sweden

Springboard Diving
1. P. Gunther, Germany
2. H. Luber, Germany
3. K. Behrens, Germany

High Diving
1. E. Adlerz, Germany
2. H. Johansson, Sweden
3. J. Jansson, Sweden

SWIMMING AND DIVING—WOMEN

100 Metres Free-Style
1. F. Durack, Australia—1:22.2
2. W. Wylie, Australia—1:25.4
3. J. Fletcher, Great Britain—1:27.0

400 Metres Relay
1. Great Britain—5:52.8
2. Germany—6:04.6
3. Austria—6:17.0

Platform Diving
1. G. Johansson, Sweden
2. L. Regnell, Sweden
3. I. White, Great Britain

WRESTLING

Greco-Roman—Featherweight
1. K. Koskelo, Finland
2. G. Gerstacker, Germany
3. O. Lasanen, Finland

Greco-Roman—Lightweight
1. E. Ware, Finland
2. G. Malmstrom, Sweden
3. E. Matiasson, Sweden

Greco-Roman—Middleweight
1. C. Johansson, Sweden
2. M. Klein, Russia
3. A. Asikainen, Finland

Greco-Roman—Light-Heavyweight
1. A. Ahlgren, Sweden
2. I. Bohling, Finland
3. B. Vargya, Hungary

Greco-Roman—Heavyweight
1. Y. Saarela, Finland
2. J. Olin, Finland
3. S. Jensen, Denmark

CYCLING

Road Race—Individual
1. R. Lewis, South Africa
2. F. Grubb, Great Britain
3. C. Schutte, U.S.

Road Race—Team
1. Sweden
2. Great Britain
3. U.S.

EQUESTRIAN SPORTS

Grand Prix Jumping—Individual
1. J. Cariou, France—186 pts.
2. von Krocher, Germany—186 pts.
3. E. Blommaert de Soye, Belgium—185 pts.

Grand Prix Dressage
1. C. Bonde, Sweden—15 pts.
2. G. Boltenstern, Sweden—21 pts.
3. H. von Blixen Finecke, Sweden—32 pts.

Grand Prix Jumping—Team
1. Sweden—545 pts.
2. France—538 pts.
3. Germany—530 pts.

Three-Day Event—Individual
1. A. Nordlander, Sweden—46.59 pts.
2. von Rochow, Germany—46.42 pts.
3. J. Cariou, France—46.32 pts.

Three-Day Event—Team
1. Sweden—139.06 pts.
2. Germany—138.48 pts.
3. U.S.—137.33 pts.

FENCING

Foil—Individual
1. N. Nadi, Italy
2. P. Speciale, Italy
3. R. Verderber, Austria

Epée—Team
1. Belgium
2. Great Britain
3. Netherlands

Epée—Individual
1. P. Anspach, Belgium
2. I. Osiier, Denmark
3. P. de Beaulieu, Belgium

Sabre—Individual
1. J. Fuchs, Hungary
2. B. Bekessy, Hungary
3. E. Meszaros, Hungary

Sabre Team
1. Hungary
2. Austria
3. Netherlands

GYMNASTICS

Combined Exercises—Individual
1. A. Braglia, Italy
2. L. Segura, France
3. A. Tunesi, Italy

Free System—Team
1. Norway
2. Finland
3. Denmark

Swedish System—Team
1. Sweden
2. Norway
3. Denmark

Special Conditions—Team
1. Italy
2. Hungary
3. Great Britain

ROWING

Single Sculls
1. W. Kinnear, Gt. Brit.—7:47.6
2. P. Veirman, Belgium
3. E. Butler, Canada

Eights
1. Great Britain—6:15.0
   Leander Club
2. Great Britain
   New College, Oxford
3. Germany
   Berliner Ruder Gesellschaft

Coxed Fours
1. Germany—6:59.4
2. Great Britain
3. Norway

Inrigger Fours
1. Denmark—7:47
2. Sweden

YACHTING

6 Metres
1. "MacMiche,", France
2. "Nurdug II," Denmark
3. "Kerstin," Sweden

10 Metres
1. "Kitty," Sweden
2. "Nina," Finland
3. "Gallia II," Russia

8 Metres
1. "Taifun," Norway
2. "Sans Atout," Sweden
3. "Lucky Girl," Finland

12 Metres
1. "Magda IX," Norway
2. "Erna-Signe," Sweden
3. "Heatherbell," Finland

SHOOTING

Four Distances—Team
1. U.S.
2. Great Britain
3. Sweden

Individual—600 Metres
1. P. R. Colas, France
2. C. T. Osburn, U.S.
3. J. E. Jackson, U.S.

Individual—300 Metres
1. A. Prokopp, Hungary
2. C. T. Osburn, U.S.
3. E. E. Skogen, Norway

Team—300 Metres
1. Sweden
2. Norway
3. Denmark

Miniature Rifle, 50 Metres—Team
1. Great Britain
2. Sweden
3. U.S.

Miniature Rifle, 25 Metres—Team
1. Sweden
2. Great Britain
3. U.S.

Miniature Rifle, 25 Metres
1. W. Carlberg, Sweden
2. H. von Holst, Sweden
3. G. Ericsson, Sweden

Revolver and Pistol, 50 Metres—Team
1. U.S.
2. Sweden
3. Great Britain

Revolver and Pistol, 30 Metres—Team
1. Sweden
2. Russia
3. Great Britain

Revolver and Pistol, 30 Metres
1. A. P. Lane, U.S.
2. A. P. Palen, Sweden
3. H. von Holst, Sweden

Clay Pigeon—Team
1. U.S.
2. Great Britain
3. Germany

Running Deer—Team
1. Sweden
2. U.S.
3. Finland

Running Deer—Single Shot
1. A. G. Swahn, Sweden
2. A. Lundeberg, Sweden
3. N. Toivonen, Sweden

Running Deer—Double Shot
1. A. Lundeberg, Sweden
2. E. Benedicks, Sweden
3. O. G. Swahn, Sweden

Free Pistol
1. A. Lane, U.S.
2. P. Dolfen, U.S.
3. G. E. Stewart, Great Britain

Free Rifle
1. P. R. Colas, France
2. L. J. Madsen, Denmark
3. N. Larsen, Denmark

Small-Bore Rifles—Prone
1. F. Hird, U.S.
2. W. Milne, Great Britain
3. H. Burt, Great Britain

Clay Pigeon
1. J. Graham, U.S.—96 pts.
2. A. Goeldel, Germany—94 pts.
3. H. Blau, Russia—91 pts.

Miniature Rifles—50 Metres
1. F. S. Hird, U.S.
2. W. Milne, Great Britain
3. H. Burt, Great Britain

MODERN PENTATHLON

1. G. M. Lilliehook, Sweden   2. K. G. Asbrink, Sweden
3. G. de Laval, Sweden

TENNIS—LAWN

Men's Singles
1. C. L. Winslow, South Africa
2. H. A. Kitson, South Africa
3. O. Kreuzer, Germany

Women's Singles
1. M. Broquedis, France
2. D. Koring, Germany
3. M. Bjurstedt, Norway

Men's Doubles
1. H. A. Kitson/C. L. Winslow, South Africa
2. A. Zborzil/F. Pipes, Austria
3. A. Canet/M. Meny, France

Mixed Doubles
1. D. Koring/H. Scnomburgk, Germ.
2. S. Fick/S. Setterwal, Sweden
3. M. Broquedis/A. Canet, France

TENNIS—COVERED COURTS

Men's Singles

1. A. Gobert, France
2. C. P. Dixon, Great Britain
3. A. F. Wilding, Australia

Women's Singles

1. E. M. Hannam, Great Britain
2. T. G. S. Castenschiold, Denmark
3. M. B. Parton, Great Britain

Men's Doubles

1. A. Gobert/M. Germot, France
2. G. Setterwall/G. Kempe, Sweden
3. C. P. Dixon/A. E. Beamish, Great Britain

Mixed Doubles

1. E. M. Hannam/C. P. Dixon, Great Britain
2. F. H. Aitchison/H. Roper-Barrett, Great Britain
3. S. Fick/G. Setterwall, Sweden

SOCCER

1. Great Britain
2. Denmark
3. Netherlands

TUG-OF-WAR

1. Sweden
2. Great Britain

WATER POLO

1. Great Britain
2. Sweden
3. Belgium

Chapter 7

THE VII OLYMPIAD

Antwerp, 1920

THE VI Olympiad, scheduled for Berlin in 1916, was cancelled because of the war. Eighteen months after Armistice, the VII Olympiad was held in Antwerp.

Germany and Austria were not invited. Their presence might have stirred up animosities with the Allied athletes who had fought against them. A *De Profundis* for athletes killed in the war was sung at an inaugural service at the Antwerp Cathedral.

Paavo Nurmi of Finland, the greatest distance runner of his time, made his Olympic debut at Antwerp, winning the 10,000 metres run and the 10,000 metres cross-country. However, he was beaten in the 5,000 metres by Joseph Guillemot of France who had been gassed during the war and was told he would never be able to run again. He matched Nurmi stride for stride most of the way, usually staying a pace or two behind him until he suddenly sprinted past Nurmi close to the finish.

Nurmi, a keen student of rival runners' styles, reversed his tactics in the 10,000, letting Guillemot set the pace and sprinting past him in the stretch. Guillemot also went to the front in the cross-country, but gashed his foot on a sharp stone, giving Nurmi an easy win. Officials refused to believe that any runner, even Nurmi, could do 10,000 metres in 27 minutes and 15 seconds under such poor conditions. They remeasured the course and discovered it was considerably shorter than 10,000 metres. His time was adjusted to 31:45.8.

Hannes Kolehmainen, the distance champion at Stockholm who helped coach Nurmi, won the marathon in a downpour by sprinting away from Juri Lossman of Estonia and Valerio Arri of Italy.

The most surprising athlete at Antwerp was Albert Hill of Great Britain. Making his Olympic debut at the incredible age of 36, he won both the 800 and 1,500 metre races. In the 800, he beat Earl Eby of the United

States after front-running Bevil Rudd of South Africa wrenched his ankle in a pothole and limped in third. Rudd recovered from his injury just in time to win the 400 metres. The United States had counted on world record holder Joie Ray to win the 1,500 metres, but he developed a sore tendon and finished eighth while Hill got his second gold medal.

The only other double winner in track and field was colorful heel-and-toe stylist Ugo Frigerio of Italy in the 3,000 and 10,000 metre walks. Frigerio, who set a world record in the 3,000 metres, gave the band a selection of tunes he wanted played while he circled the track in time to the music. When he thought the band was not playing loud enough, he stopped and told the conductor to raise the volume. And each time he passed the grandstand, he waved and shouted "Viva!" to the cheering crowd.

World record holder Charley Paddock of the U.S. won the 100 metres over teammate Morris Kirksey and Harry Edwards, a West Indian competing for Britain. But in the 200 metres, Paddock was beaten by Allen Woodring, a last-minute addition to the U.S. team who had not been expected to survive the preliminaries. Woodring had trained so hard in Antwerp that he wore out his only pair of track shoes. For the final, he borrowed a pair with longer spikes than he had been accustomed to and he thought this would slow him down. But the race was run in a heavy rainstorm and the longer spikes gave him better traction.

Earl Thomson, an American-trained athlete running for Canada, and Frank Loomis of the U.S. set world records in winning the 110 and 400 metre hurdles respectively; and Frank Foss set a world record in the pole vault after he had already eliminated the rest of the competition.

Finnish athletes, improving on their impressive performance at Stockholm, took the shot put, discus, javelin and triple jump. Ville Portola beat teammate Erik Niklander in the shot put but Niklander won the discus. In the javelin, Finland's sweep by Jonni Myyra, Urko Peltonen and Pekka Johansson, who all broke the world record, marked the first time that any country other than the United States had finished one-two-

46

three in an Olympic event. For the first time in the modern Olympics, the United States also failed to win the shot put and the long jump.

The U.S. swimming team partially made up for the disappointing performance of its track and field team. Norman Ross won both the 400 and 1,500 metre races and defending champion Duke Kahanamoku won the 100 metres. The Americans also got gold medals in two diving competitions, the backstroke and the 800 metre relay. Hakan Malmroth of Sweden won both breast stroke races.

The U.S. women's swimming team won everything but the platform diving championship, won by Stefani Fryland-Clausen of Denmark. Twelve-year-old Aileen Riggin, the youngest competitor at Antwerp, won the springboard diving for the U.S. Ethelda Belbtrey won three gold medals, for the 100 and 300 metres freestyle and the 400 metre relay.

In rowing, Jack Kelly of the U.S., father of Princess Grace of Monaco, won the single skulls and then partnered Paul Costello for a win in the double skulls.

Although the American athletes were the overall winners at Antwerp, the U.S. for the first time did not run away with the track and field honors. Of the 27 events, the United States and Finland each won eight gold medals.

OFFICIAL VII OLYMPIAD RESULTS

Antwerp, 1920

TRACK AND FIELD

100 Metres
1. C. Paddock, U.S.—10.8
2. M. Kirksey, U.S.
3. H. Edwards, Great Britain

200 Metres
1. A. Woodring, U.S.—22.0
2. C. Paddock, U.S.
3. H. Edwards, Great Britain

400 Metres
1. B. Rudd, South Africa—49.6
2. G. Butler, Great Britain
3. N. Engdahl, Sweden

800 Metres
1. A. Hill, Great Britain—1:53.4
2. E. Eby, U.S.
3. B. Rudd, South Africa

1,500 Metres
1. A. Hill, Great Britain—4:01.8
2. P. Baker, Great Britain
3. L. Shields, U.S.

5,000 Metres
1. J. Guillemot, France—14:55.6
2. P. Nurmi, Finland
3. E. Backman, Sweden

10,000 Metres
1. P. Nurmi, Finland—31:45.8
2. J. Guillemot, France
3. J. Wilson, Great Britain

3,000 Metre Team Race
1. U.S.
2. Great Britain
3. Sweden

47

Marathon

1. H. Kolehmainen, Finland— 2:32:35.8
2. J. Lossman, Estonia—2:32:48.6
3. V. Arri, Italy—2:36:32.8

10,000 Metres Walk

1. U. Frigerio, Italy—48:6.2
2. J. B. Pearman, U.S.
3. C. E. J. Gunn, Great Britain

110 Metres Hurdles

1. E. Thomson, Canada—14.8
2. H. Barron, U.S.
3. F. Murray, U.S.

400 Metres Hurdles

1. F. Loomis, U.S.—54.0
2. J. Norton, U.S.
3. A. Desch, U.S.

3,000 Metres Steeplechase

1. P. Hodge, Great Britain—10:00.4
2. P. Flynn, U.S.
3. E. Ambrosini, Italy

400 Metres Relay

1. U.S.—42.2
2. France
3. Sweden

1,600 Metres Relay

1. Great Britain—3:22.2
2. South Africa
3. France

3,000 Metres Walk

1. U. Frigerio, Italy—13:14.2
2. G. L. Parker, Australia
3. R. F. Remer, U.S.

10,000 Metres Cross-Country

1. P. Nurmi, Finland—27:15.0
2. Eric Backman, Sweden
3. Liimatainen, Finland

High Jump

1. R. Landon, U.S.—6'4 $\frac{3}{16}$"
2. H. Muller, U.S.—6'2 $\frac{13}{16}$"
3. B. Ekelund, Sweden—6'2 $\frac{13}{16}$"

Broad Jump

1. W. Pettersson, Sweden—23'5 $\frac{1}{2}$"
2. C. Johnson, U.S.—23'3 $\frac{5}{16}$"
1. E. Abrahamsson, Sweden—23'2 $\frac{3}{4}$"

Triple Jump

1. V. Tuulos, Finland—47'7 $\frac{1}{16}$"
2. F. Jansson, Sweden—47'6 $\frac{1}{16}$"
3. E. Almlof, Sweden—46'9 $\frac{13}{16}$"

Pole Vault

1. F. Foss, U.S.—12'5 $\frac{5}{8}$"
2. H. Petersen, Denmark—12'3 $\frac{5}{8}$"
3. E. Meyers, U.S.—12'3 $\frac{5}{8}$"

Shot Put

1. V. Porhola, Finland, 48'7 $\frac{1}{16}$"
2. E. Niklander, Finland—46'5 $\frac{1}{4}$"
3. H. Liversedge, U.S.—46'5 $\frac{1}{16}$"

Discus Throw

1. E. Niklander, Finland—146'7 $\frac{1}{12}$"
2. A. Taipale, Finland—144'11 $\frac{3}{4}$"
3. A. Pope, U.S.—138'2 $\frac{11}{12}$"

Hammer Throw

1. P. Ryan, U.S.—173'5 $\frac{11}{12}$"
2. C. J. Lindh, Sweden—158'10 $\frac{11}{16}$"
3. B. Bennet, U.S.—158'3 $\frac{5}{8}$"

Javelin Throw

1. J. Myyra, Finland—215'9 $\frac{3}{4}$"
2. U. Peltonen, Finland—208'4"
3. P. J. Johansson, Finland—207'0 $\frac{1}{16}$'

65-Pound Weight

1. P. J. McDonald, U.S.—36'11 $\frac{3}{4}$"
2. P. Ryan, U.S.
3. C. J. Lind, Sweden

Pentathlon

1. Lehtonen, Finland—14 pts.
2. Bradley, U.S.
3. Lahtinen, Finland

Decathlon

1. H. Lovland, Norway
2. B. Hamilton, U.S.
3. B. Ohlson, Sweden

SWIMMING AND DIVING—MEN

100 Metres Free-Style

1. D. Kahanamoku, U.S.—1:00.4
2. P. Kealona, U.S.—1:02.2
3. W. Harris, U.S.—1:03.2

400 Metres Free-Style

1. N. Ross, U.S.—5:26.8
2. L. Langer, U.S.—5:29.2
3. G. Vernot, Canada—5:29.8

1,500 Metres Free-Style

1. N. Ross, U.S.—22:23.2
2. G. Vernot, Canada—22:36.4
3. F. Beaurepaire, Australia—23:04.0

200 Metres Breast Stroke

1. H. Malmroth, Sweden—3:04.4
2. T. Henning, Sweden—3:09.2
3. A. Aaltonen, Finland—3:12.2

400 Metres Breast Stroke

1. H. Malmroth, Sweden—6:31.8
2. T. Henning, Sweden
3. P. Aaltonen, Finland

100 Metres Backstroke

1. W. Kealoha, U.S.—1:15.2
2. R. K. Kergeris, U.S.—1:16.2
3. G. Blitz, Belgium—1:19.0

800 Metres Free-Style Relay
1. U.S.—10:04.4
2. Australia—10:25.4
3. Great Britain—10:37.2

Platform Diving
1. C. Pinkston, U.S.
2. E. Adlerz, Sweden
3. H. Prieste, U.S.

Springboard Diving
1. L. Kuehn, U.S.
2. C. Pinkston, U.S.
3. L. Balbach, U.S.

Plain Diving
1. A. Vallman, Sweden
2. N. Skoglund, Sweden
3. Y. Jonsson, Sweden

SWIMMING AND DIVING—WOMEN

100 Metres Free-Style
1. E. Bleibtrey, U.S.—1:13.6
2. I. Guest, U.S.—1:17.0
3. F. Schroth, U.S.—1:17.2

400 Metres Free-Style
1. E. Bleibtrey, U.S.—4:34.0
2. M. Woodbridge, U.S.—4:42.4
3. F. Schroth, U.S.—4:52.0

400 Metres Relay
1. U.S.—5:11.6
2. Great Britain—5:40.8
3. Sweden—5:43.6

Platform Diving
1. S. Fryland-Clausen, Denmark
2. E. Armstrong, Great Britain
3. E. Ollivier, Sweden

Springboard Diving
1. A. Riggin, U.S.
2. H. Wainwright, U.S.
3. T. Payne, U.S.

BOXING

Flyweight
1. F. de Genaro, U.S.
2. A. Petersen, Denmark
3. W. Cuthbertson, Great Britain

Bantamweight
1. C. Walker, South Africa
2. C. Graham, Canada
3. J. McKenzie, Great Britain

Featherweight
1. P. Fritsch, France
2. Gauchet, France
3. E. Garzena, Italy

Lightweight
1. S. Mosberg, U.S.
2. G. Johanssen, Denmark
3. Newton, Canada

Welterweight
1. T. Schneider, Canada
2. A. Ireland, Great Britain
3. F. Colberg, U.S.

Middleweight
1. H. Mallin, Great Britain
2. Prudhomme, Canada
3. Herzowitch, Canada

Light-Heavyweight
1. E. Eagan, U.S.
2. S. Sorsdal, Norway
3. H. Frank, Great Britain

Heavyweight
1. R. Rawson, Great Britain
2. Soren Petersen, Denmark
3. Elvere, France

WRESTLING

Free-Style—Featherweight
1. C. Ackerley, U.S.
2. S. Gerson, U.S.
3. P. Bernard, Great Britain

Free-Style—Lightweight
1. K. Antilla, Finland
2. G. Svensson, Sweden
3. P. Wright, Great Britain

Free-Style
1. Eino Leino, Finland
2. V. Penttala, Finland
3. C. Johnson, U.S.

Free-Style—Light-Heavyweight
1. A. Larsson, Sweden
2. C. Courant, Switzerland
3. W. Maurer, U.S.

Free-Style—Heavyweight
1. R. Rothe, Switzerland
2. N. Pendleton, U.S.
3. E. Nilsson, Sweden
   F. Meyer, U.S.

Greco-Roman—Featherweight
1. O. Friman, Finland
2. K. Kahkonen, Finland
3. F. Svensson, Sweden

Greco-Roman—Lightweight
1. E. Ware, Finland
2. T. Tamminen, Finland
3. F. Andersen, Norway

Greco-Roman—Middleweight
1. C. Westergren, Sweden
2. A. Lindfors, Finland
3. M. Perttila, Finland

Greco-Roman—Light-Heavyweight
1. C. Johansson, Sweden
2. E. Rosenquist, Finland
3. J. Eriksen, Denmark

Greco-Roman—Heavyweight
1. A. Lindfors, Finland
2. P. Hansen, Denmark
3. M. Nieminen, Finland

WEIGHT-LIFTING

Featherweight
1. F. de Haes, Belgium—485 lb.
2. A. Schmidt, Estonia—468 ½ lb.
3. E. Ritter, Switzerland—463 lb.

Middleweight
1. B. Gance, France—540lb.
2. U. Bianchi, Italy—523 ½ lb.
3. A. Pettersson, Sweden—523 ½ lb.

Lightweight
1. A. Neyland, Estonia—567 ¾ lb.
2. R. Williquet, Belgium—529 lb.
3. J. Rooms, Belgium—507 lb.

Light-Heavyweight
1. E. Cadine, France—639 lb.
2. F. Hunenberger, Switz.—606 lb.
3. E. Pettersson, Sweden—600 ½ lb.

Heavyweight
1. F. Bottino, Italy—595 lb.
2. J. Alzin, Luxemburg—562 lb.
3. L. Bernot, France—551 lb.

CYCLING

1,000 Metres Sprint
1. M. Peeters, Netherlands
2. H. T. Johnson, Great Britain
3. H. Ryan, Great Britain

50 Kilometres
1. H. George, Belgium—1:16:43.2
2. C. A. Alden, Great Britain
3. P. Ikelaar, Netherlands

2,000 Metres Tandem
1. Harry Ryan/Thomas Lance, Great Britain
2. J. R. Walker/W. R. Smith, South Africa

Road Race—Individual
1. H. Stenquist, Sweden
2. H. Kaltenbrun, South Africa
3. F. Canteloube, France

4,000 Metres Team Pursuit
1. Italy—5:20.0
2. Great Britain
3. South Africa

Road Race—Team
1. France
2. Sweden
3. Belgium

EQUESTRIAN SPORTS

50 Kilometers
1. Lt. Johansen, Norway—3:05.0
2. Capt. Vidart, France—3:06.30
3. Lt. d'Emars, Belgium

Grand Prix—Jumping—Team
1. Sweden—14 faults
2. Belgium—16.25 faults
3. Italy—18.75 faults

20 Kilometers
1. Lt. Misonna, Belgium—55.33
2. Capt. de Sabtigues, France—56.29
3. Lt. Bonvalet, Belgium

Grand Prix—Dressage
1. J. Lundblad, Sweden—27,937 pts.
2. B. Sandstrom, Sweden—26,312pts.
3. H. von Rosen, Sweden—25,125 pts.

Vaulting
1. Bonckaert, Belgium
2. Field, France
3. Finet, Belgium

Three-Day Event—Individual
1. H. Morner, Sweden
2. A. Lundstrom, Sweden
3. E. Caffaratti, Italy

Grand Prix—Jumping—Individual
1. T. Lequio, Italy—0 faults
2. A. Valerio, Italy—3 faults
3. G. Lewenhaupt, Sweden—4 faults

Three-Day Event—Team
1. Sweden
2. Italy
3. Belgium

FENCING

Foil—Individual
1. N. Nadi, Italy
2. P. Cattiau, France
3. R. Ducret, France

Epée—Team
1. Italy   2. Belgium   3. France

Foil—Team
1. Italy   2. France   3. U.S.

Sabre—Individual
1. N. Nadi, Italy
2. A. Nadi, Italy
3. A. E. W. de Jong, Netherlands

Epée—Individual
1. A. Massard, France
2. A. Lippmann, France
3. E. Gevers, Belgium

Sabre—Team
1. Italy
2. France
3. Netherlands

GYMNASTICS

Combined Exercises—Individual
1. G. Zampori, Italy
2. M. Torres, France
3. J. Gounot, France

European Style—Team
1. Italy 2. France 3. Belgium

Swedish System—Team
1. Sweden 2. Denmark 3. Belgium

ROWING

Single Sculls
1. J. Kelly, U.S.—7:35.0
2. J. Beresford, Gt. Brit—7:36.0
3. C. d'Arcy, New Zealand—7:48.0

Double Sculls
1. J. Kelly/P. Costello, U.S.—7:09.0
2. E. Dones/P. Anoni, Italy —7:19.0
3. A. Ple/G. Giran, France—7:21.0

Coxwainless Pairs
1. E. Olgeni/G. Scatturin, Italy—7:56.0
2. Poix/Bouton, France—7:57.0
2. E. Candeveau/A. Felber, Switz.

Coxed Fours
1. Switzerland—6:54.0
2. U.S.—6:58.0
3. Norway—7:01.0

Eights
1. U.S. (Navy)—6:02.6
2. Great Britain (Leander)—6:05.8
3. Norway—6:36.0

YACHTING

12-foot Dinghies
1. Beatriss III, Holland
   Boreas (tie), Holland

6 Metres
1. Jo, Norway
2. Tan-Fe-Pas, Belgium

8 Metres
1. Sildra, Norway
2. Lyn, Norway
3. Antwerpia, Belgium

10 Metres
1. Mosk II, Norway

12 Metres
1. Heira II, Norway

30 Metres
1. Kullan, Sweden

40 Metres
1. Sif, Sweden
2. Elsie, Sweden

SHOOTING

Free Pistol
1. C. Frederick, U.S.
2. A. da Costa, Brazil
3. A. Lane, U.S.

Free Rifle
1. M. Fisher, U.S.
2. N. Larsen, Denmark
3. O. Ostensen, Norway

Small-Bore Rifles—Prone
1. L. Nuesslein, U.S.
2. A. Rothrock, U.S.
3. D. Fenton, U.S.

Army Rifle—Individual
1. Osburn, U.S.
2. Madson, Denmark
3. Nuesslein, U.S.

Army Rifle—Team
1. Denmark
2. U.S.
3. Sweden

Odd Distances
1. U.S.
2. Norway
3. Switzerland

Clay Pigeon
1. M. Aric, U.S.
2. F. Troeh, U.S.
3. F. Wright, U.S.

Clay Pigeon—Team
1. U.S.
2. Belgium
3. Sweden

Pistol and Revolver, 50 Metres—Team
1. U.S.
2. Sweden
3. Brazil

Revolver, 30 Metres—Team
1. U.S.
2. Greece
3. Switzerland

Revolver—Individual
1. Paraines, Brazil
2. Bracken, U.S.

Running Deer—Single Shot
1. Norway 2. Finland 3. Sweden

Running Deer—Double Shots
1. Norway 2. Sweden 3. Finland

Military Rifle, 300 Metres Prone—Team
1. U.S. 2. France 3. Finland

Military Rifle, 300 Metres Prone—Individual
1. Olsen, Norway
2. Johnson, France
3. Kuchen, Switzerland

Military Rifle, 600 Metres Prone—Team
1. U.S. 2. South Africa 3. Sweden

Military Rifle, 600 Metres Prone—Individual
1. Johansson, Sweden
2. Erickson, Sweden
3. Spooner, U.S.

Any Rifle—Team
1. U.S. 2. Norway 3. Finland

Any Rifle—Individual
1. Morris Fisher, U.S.
2. Larsen, Denmark
3. unknown, Sweden

Miniature Rifle—Team
1. U.S. 2. Sweden 3. Norway

Miniature Rifle—Individual
1. Nusslein, U.S.
2. Rothrock, U.S.
3. Fenton, U.S.

MODERN PENTATHLON
1. G. Dryssen, Sweden
2. E. de Laval, Sweden
3. G. Runo, Sweden

FIELD HOCKEY
1. Great Britain
2. Denmark
3. Belgium

RUGBY FOOTBALL
1. U.S.
2. France

SOCCER
1. Belgium
2. Spain
3. Netnerlands

LAWN TENNIS

Men's Singles
1. Raymond, South Africa
2. Kumagae, Japan

Women's Singles
1. Mlle S. Lenglen, France
2. Miss Holman, Great Britain

Men's Doubles
1. Turnbull/Woosnam, Gt. Britain
2. Kumagae/Kashio, Japan

Women's Doubles
1. Mrs. McNair/Miss McKane, Great Britain
2. Mrs. Beamish/Miss Holman, Great Britain

Mixed Doubles
1. Decugis/Mlle. S. Lenglen, France
2. Woosnam/Miss McKane, Gt. Brit.

TUG-OF-WAR
1. Great Britain
2. U.S.

WATER POLO
1. Great Britain
2. Belgium
3. Sweden

ICE HOCKEY
1. Canada 2. U.S. 3. Czechoslovakia

FIGURE SKATING

Men
1. G. Grafstrom, Sweden
2. A. Krogh, Norway
3. M. Stuxrud, Norway

Women
1. M. Julin-Mauroy, Sweden
2. S. Noren, Sweden
3. T Weld, U.S.

Pairs
1. L. Jakobsson/W. Jakobsson, Finland
2. A. Bryn/Y. Bryn, Norway
3. P. W. Johnson/B. Williams, Great Britain

Chapter 8

THE VIII OLYMPIAD

Paris, 1924

PAAVO Nurmi, who won the 10,000 metre and cross-country races at Antwerp, won four gold medals at Paris. The tireless Finn won the 1,500 metre and 5,000 metre races, the 10,000 metre cross-country and led his team to victory in the 3,000 metre team race. He probably would have made it five gold medals if he had entered the 10,000 metres.

With little more than an hour's rest between races, Nurmi set Olympic records for both the 1,500 and 5,000 metres. He won the 1,500 metre race by nearly two seconds from Willy Scherrer of Switzerland. However, he only beat fellow Finn Ville Ritola by a fifth of a second in the 5,000 metres.

The cross-country race was run during a heat wave and only 15 of the 39 starters were able to finish. One of the dropouts collapsed in a pool of blood after running into a concrete wall, but the heat did not bother Nurmi who beat Ritola by two minutes.

Ritola, a U.S. resident who retained his Finnish citizenship, cut more than 12 seconds off the world record in the 10,000 metres despite a rain-soaked track. He also set a world record in the 3,000 metres steeplechase.

Albin Steenroos, a 40-year-old Helsinki sewing machine salesman who had finished third to Hannes Kolehmainen in the 10,000 metres 14 years earlier, gave Finland a clean sweep of the distance races by beating Romeo Bertini of Italy by six minutes in the marathon.

British runners upset the favored Americans in three of the four shorter distances.

Cambridge University student Harold Abrahams, who continued drinking beer and smoking cigars during training, won the 100 metres although broad jumping had been his specialty. He took the lead at the halfway mark from defending champion Charles Paddock of the U.S. who faded to finish fifth.

Paddock was also favored in the 200 metres but he was beaten by half a yard by Jackson Scholz of the U.S. who had finished second in the 100 metres. Scholz passed Paddock near the finish line when Paddock looked over his shoulder to see how much of a lead he had.

Glasgow divinity student Eric Liddell refused to compete in his specialty, the 100 metres, because it was run on a Sunday. So he entered the 200 and came third and then went into the 400 and won in a world record 47.6 seconds, much to his own surprise and to the astonishment of Horatio M. Fitch who came second after setting the world record in a preliminary.

Henry Stallard of Great Britain, who had earned a bronze medal in the 1,500 metres, was considered a certainty to win the 800 metres. He had a big lead until the 600 metre mark where he began to fall back and finished fourth behind Douglas Lowe of Great Britain, Paul Martin of Switzerland and Schuyler Enck of the U.S.

F. Morgan Taylor of the United States set a world record 52.6 seconds in the 400 metres hurdles but it was disallowed because he knocked down a hurdle. Dan Kinsey of the U.S. and Syd Atkinson of South Africa took all the jumps together in the 110 metres hurdles but Kinsey pulled away in the stretch to win by six inches.

De Hart Hubbard of the U.S. won the broad jump at 24'5⅛" but another American, Bob Legendre, set a world record of 25'6" while competing in the pentathlon. Legendre did not do as well in the other events, finishing third behind defending champion E. R. Lehtonen of Finland and E. Somfay of Hungary.

Harold Osborn of the United States won both the decathlon and the high jump. And another American double winner was Bud Houser in the shot put and discus.

Tony Winter of Australia set a world record 50'11¼" in the triple jump, defeating Luis Brunetto of Argentina and defending champion Vilho Tuulos of Finland.

The United States scored a sweep in the pole vault with Californians Lee Barnes, 17, and Glenn Graham

18, tied for first and James Brooker third. Barnes won the gold medal in a jump-off.

Defending champion Jonni Myyra of Finland won the javelin again. And defending champion Ugo Frigerio of Italy lapped all but one of his competitors in the 10,000 metre walk.

The Americans set world records in the 400 and 1,600 metre relays, and U.S. swimmers won 13 of the 17 aquatic events. Johnny Weissmuller set world records for the 100 and 400 metres freestyle. In the 100, he beat two-time Olympic champion Duke Kahanamoku, the only man he was afraid to swim against. Weissmuller had never competed against the Duke before, but in a pre-Olympic race, U.S. swimming coach Bill Bachrach convinced him that he could beat him. Weissmuller was swimming in Kahanamoku's native Hawaii in the U.S. national championships. Bachrach invited the Duke to watch Weissmuller training without telling his nervous protégé. He gave Kahanamoku a stop watch while Weissmuller swam 100 metres. After watching him beat his world record by three seconds, the Duke ducked out of the competition.

At the Olympics, Weissmuller won a third gold medal by swimming the first leg of the world record breaking U.S. 800 metre relay team. Weissmuller, the world's best swimmer for the first half century, did not learn to swim until he was ill when a doctor told him he would grow up to be a weakling if he did not start exercising. When he retired in 1929 to play Tarzan in movies, he held every world freestyle record from 50 yards to half a mile. One record, 51 seconds in the 100 metres, lasted until 1944 when Alan Ford of Yale knocked it down to 49.7.

Andrew Charlton, who was a close third to Weissmuller and Arne Borg of Sweden in the 400 metres at Paris, beat Borg in the 1,500 metres in a world record 20:6.6. Australian veteran Frank Beaurepaire was third to complete a remarkable Olympic career. He had a silver medal in the 400 and a bronze in the 1,500 metres in 1908 and another bronze in the 1,500 in 1920.

In cycling, France won all the events except the 50-kilometer endurance race won by Jacobus Willem of Holland and the 4,000 metre team race won by Italy.

OFFICIAL VIII OLYMPIAD RESULTS

Paris, 1924

TRACK AND FIELD—MEN

100 Metres
1. H. Abrahams, Gt. Brit—10.6
2. J. Scholz, U.S.
3. A. Porritt, New Zealand

200 Metres
1. J. Scholz, U.S.—21.6
2. C. Paddock, U.S.
3. E. Liddell, Great Britain

400 Metres
1. E. Liddell, Great Britain—47.6
2. H. Fitch, U.S.—48.1
3. G. Butler, Great Britain—48.4

800 Metres
1. D. Lowe, Great Britain—1:52.4
2. P. Martin, Switzerland—1:52.6
3. S. Enck, U.S.—1:53.1

1,500 Metres
1. P. Nurmi, Finland—3:53.6
2. W. Scherrer, Switzerland—3:54.8
3. H. Stallard, Great Britain—3:55.0

5,000 Metres
1. P. Nurmi, Finland—14:32.2
2. V. Ritola, Finland—14:31.4
3. E. Wide, Sweden—15:01.3

10,000 Metres
1. V. Ritola, Finland—30:23.2
2. E. Wide, Sweden—30:50.8
3. E. Berg, Finland—31:59.0

10,000 Metres Cross-Country
1. P. Nurmi, Finland—32:54.8
2. V. Ritola, Finland
3. J. Johnson, U.S.

3,000 Metres Team
1. Finland
2. Great Britain
3. U.S.

10,000 Metres Cross-Country Walk
1. U. Frigerio, Italy—47:49.0
2. G. Goodwin, Great Britain
3. C. MacMaster, South Africa

Marathon
1. A. Stenroos, Finland—2:41:22.6
2. R. Bertini, Italy—2:47:19.6
3. C. de Mar, U.S.—2:48:14.0

110 Metres Hurdles
1. D. Kinsey, U.S.—15.0
2. S. Atkinson, South Africa—15.0
3. S. Pettersson, Sweden—15.7

400 Metres Hurdles
1. F. M. Taylor, U.S.—52.6
2. E. Vilen, Finland—53.8
3. I. Riley, U.S.—54.1

3,000 Metres Steeplechase
1. V. Ritola, Finland—9:33.6
2. E. Katz, Finland
3. P. Bontemps, France

400 Metres Relay
1. U.S.—41.0
2. Great Britain—41.2
3. Netherlands—41.8

1,600 Metres Relay
1. U.S.—3:16.0
2. Sweden—3:17.0
3. Great Britain—3:17.4

High Jump
1. H. Osborn, U.S.—6'5 $\frac{5}{16}$"
2. L. Brown, U.S.—6'4 $\frac{3}{4}$"
3. P. Lewden, France—6'3 $\frac{9}{16}$"

Broad Jump
1. W. De Hart Hubbard, U.S.—24'5 $\frac{1}{4}$"
2. E. Gourdin, U.S.—23'10 $\frac{7}{16}$"
3. S. Hansen, Norway—23'9 $\frac{13}{16}$"

Triple Jump
1. A. Winter, Australia—50'11 $\frac{1}{4}$"
2. L. Brunetto, Argentina—50'7 $\frac{1}{8}$"
3. V. Tuulos, Finland—50'5 $\frac{1}{8}$"

Pole Vault
1. L. Barnes, U.S.—12'11 $\frac{1}{2}$"
2. G. Graham, U.S.—12'11 $\frac{1}{2}$"
3. J. Brooker, U.S.—12'9 $\frac{9}{16}$"

Shot Put
1. C. Houser, U.S.—49'2 $\frac{3}{8}$"
2. G. Hartranft, U.S.—49'2"
3. R. Hills, U.S.—48'0 $\frac{3}{8}$"

Discus Throw
1. L. C. Houser, U.S.—151'5 $\frac{5}{16}$"
2. V. Niittymaa, Finland—147'5 $\frac{11}{16}$"
3. T. Lieb, U.S.—147'1"

Hammer Throw
1. F. Tootell, U.S.—174'10 $\frac{1}{4}$"
2. M. McGrath, U.S.—166'9 $\frac{9}{16}$"
3. M. Nokes, Gt. Brit.—160'4 $\frac{3}{16}$"

Javelin Throw
1. J. Myyra, Finland—206'6 $\frac{3}{4}$"
2. G. Lindstrom, Sweden—199'10 $\frac{7}{16}$"
3. E. Oberst, U.S.—191'5 $\frac{1}{4}$"

Decathlon

1. H. Osborn, U.S.
2. E. Norton, U.S.
3. A. Kolmpere, Estonia

Pentathlon

1. E. R. Lehtonen, Finland
2. E. Somfay, Hungary
3. R. Legendre, U.S.

SWIMMING AND DIVING—MEN

100 Metres Free-Style

1. J. Weissmuller, U.S.—59.0
2. D. Kahanamoku, U.S.—1:01.4
3. S. Kahanamoku, U.S.—1:01.8

100 Metres Backstroke

1. W. Kealoha, U.S.—1:13.2
2. P. Wyatt, U.S.—1:15.4
3. C. Bartha, Hungary—1:17.8

400 Metres Free-Style

1. J. Weissmuller, U.S.—5:04.2
2. A. Borge, Sweden—5:05.6
3. A. Charlton, Australia—5:06.6

800 Metres Relay

1. U.S.—9:53.4
2. Australia—10:02.2
3. Sweden—10:06.8

1,500 Metres Free-Style

1. A. Charlton, Australia—20:06.6
2. A. Borg, Sweden—20:41.4
3. F. Beaurepaire, Australia—20:48.4

Platform Diving

1. A. White, U.S.
2. D. Fall, U.S.
3. C. Pinkston, U.S.

Springboard Diving

1. A. White, U.S.
2. P. Desjardins, U.S.
3. C. Pinkston, U.S.

200 Metres Breast Stroke

1. R. Skelton, U.S.—2:56.6
2. J. de Combe, Belgium—2:59.2
3. W. Kirschbaum, U.S.—3:01.0

Plain Diving

1. R. Eve, Australia
2. J. Jansson, Sweden
3. H. Clarke, Great Britain

SWIMMING AND DIVING—WOMEN

100 Metres Free-Style

1. E. Lackie, U.S.—1:12.4
2. M. Wehselau, U.S.—1:12.8
3. G. Ederle, U.S.—1:14.2

400 Metres Free-Style Relay

1. U.S.—4:58.8
2. Great Britain—5:17.0
3. Sweden—5:35.8

400 Metres Free-Style

1. M. Norelius, U.S.—6:02.2
2. H. Wainwright, U.S.—6:03.8
3. G. Ederle, U.S.—6:04.8

Platform Diving

1. C. Smith, U.S.
2. E. Becker, U.S.
3. H. Topel, Sweden

200 Metres Breast Stroke

1. L. Morton, Great Britain—3:33.2
2. A. Geragnty, U.S.—3:34.0
3. G. Carson, Great Britain—3:35.4

Springboard Diving

1. E. Becker, U.S.
2. A. Riggin, U.S.
3. C. Fletcher, U.S.

100 Metres Back Stroke

1. S. Bauer, U.S.—1:23.2
2. P. Harding, Great Britain—1:27.4
3. A. Riggin, U.S.—1:28.2

Fancy Diving

1. E. Becker, U.S.
2. A. Riggin, U.S.
3. C. Fletcher, U.S.

BOXING

Flyweight

1. F. La Barba, U.S.
2. J. McKenzie, Great Britain
3. R. Fee, U.S.

Welterweight

1. J. Delarge, Belgium
2. H. Mendez, Argentina
3. D. Lewis, Canada

Bantamweight

1. W. Smith, South Africa
2. S. Tripoli, U.S.
3. J. Ces, France

Middleweight

1. H. Mallin, Great Britain
2. J. Elliott, Great Britain
3. J. Beecken, Belgium

Featherweight

1. J. Fields, U.S.
2. J. Salas, U.S.
3. P. Quartucci, Argentina

Light-Heavyweight

1. H. Mitchell, Great Britain
2. T. Petersen, Denmark
3. S. Sorsdal, Norway

Lightweight

1. H. Nielsen, Denmark
2. A. Copello, Argentina
3. F. Boylstein, U.S.

Heavyweight

1. O. Von Porat, Norway
2. S. Petersen, Denmark
3. A. Porzio, Argentina

WRESTLING

Free-Style—Bantamweight

1. K. Pihlajamaki, Finland
2. K. Makinen, Finland
3. B. Hines, U.S.

Free-Style—Featherweight

1. R. Reed, U.S.
2. C. Newton, U.S.
3. K. Naitoh, Japan

Free-Style—Lightweight

1. R. Vis, U.S.
2. V. Wickstrom, Finland
3. A. Haavisto, Finland

Free-Style—Welterweight

1. H. Genri, Switzerland
2. E. Leino, Finland
3. A. Muller, Switzerland

Free-Style—Middleweight

1. F. Haggmann, Switzerland
2. P. Olivier, Belgium
3. V. Pekkala, Finland

Free-Style—Light-Heavyweight

1. J. Spellman, U.S.
2. R. Svensson, Sweden
3. C. Courant, Switzerland

Free-Style—Heavyweight

1. H. Steele, U.S.
2. H. Wernli, Switzerland
3. A. McDonald, Great Britain

Greco-Roman—Bantamweight

1. E. Putsep, Estonia
2. A. Ahlfors, Finland
3. V. Ilkonen, Finland

Greco-Roman—Featherweight

1. K. Anttila, Finland
2. A. Toivola, Finland
3. E. Malmberg, Sweden

Greco-Roman—Lightweight

1. O. Friman, Finland
2. L. Keresztes, Hungary
3. K. Westerlund, Finland

Greco-Roman—Middleweight

1. E. Westerlund, Finland
2. A. Lindfors, Finland
3. R. Steinberg, Estonia

Greco-Roman—Light-Heavyweight

1. C. Westergren, Sweden
2. R. Svensson, Sweden
3. O. Pellinen, Finland

Greco-Roman—Heavyweight

1. H. Deglane, France
2. E. Rosenquist, Finland
3. R. Bado, Hungary

WEIGHT-LIFTING

Featherweight

1. P. Gabetti, Italy—887¼ lb.
2. A. Stadler, Austria—848¾ lb.
3. A. Reinmann, Switz.—843¼ lb.

Lightweight

1. E. Decottignies, France—970 lb.
2. A. Zwerzina, Austria—942½ lb.
3. B. Durdys, Czechoslovakia—937 lb.

Middleweight

1. C. Galimberti, Italy—1,085¾ lb.
2. A. Newland, Estonia—1,002 lb.
3. J. Kikkas, Estonia—992 lb.

Light-Heavyweight

1. C. Rigoulot, France—1,107¾ lb.
2. F. Hunenberger, Switzerland—1,080¼ lb.
3. L. Friedrich, Austria—1,080¼ lb.

Heavyweight

1. G. Tonani, Italy—1,140¾ lb.
2. F. Aigner, Austria—1,135¼ lb.
3. H. Tammer, Estonia—1,096¾ lb.

CYCLING

1,000 Metres Sprint

1. L. Michard, France
2. J. Meyer, Netherlands
3. J. Cugnot, France

2,000 Metres Tandem

1. J. Cugnot/L. Choury, France
2. E. Hansen/W. Falck-Hansen, Denmark
3. M. Peeters/B. van Drakesstein, Netherlands

4,000 Metres Team Pursuit

1. Italy—5:12.0 2. Poland 3. Belgium

50 Kilometres Track

1. J. Willems, Netherlands
2. C. A. Alden, Great Britain
3. F. H. Wyld, Great Britain

Road Race—Individual

1. A. Blanchonnet, France—6:20:48.0
2. H.Hoevenaers,Belgium—6:30:27.0
3. R. Hamel, France—6:30:51.6

Road Race—Team

1. France—19:30:14.0
2. Belgium—19:46:55.4
3. Sweden—19:59:41.6

EQUESTRIAN SPORTS

Grand Prix Jumping—Individual
1. A. Gemuseus, Switzerland
2. T. Lequio, Italy
3. A. Krolikiewicz, Poland

Grand Prix Jumping—Team
1. Sweden
2. Switzerland
3. Portugal

Grand Prix Dressage—Individual
1. E. Linder, Sweden
2. B. Sandstrom, Sweden
3. F. Lesage, France

Three-Day Event—Individual
1. A. van Zijp, Netherlands
2. F. Kirkjeberg, Denmark
3. S. Doak, U.S.

Three-Day Event—Team
1. Netherlands
2. Sweden
3. Italy

FENCING—MEN

Foil—Individual
1. R. Ducret, France
2. P. Cattiau, France
3. M. van Damme, Belgium

Foil—Team
1. France
2. Belgium
3. Hungary

Epée—Individual
1. C. Delport, Belgium
2. R. Ducret, France
3. N. Hellsten, Sweden

Epée—Team
1. France
2. Belgium
3. Italy

Sabre—Individual
1. S. Posta, Hungary
2. R. Ducret, France
3. J. Garai, Hungary

Sabre—Team
1. Italy
2. Hungary
3. Netherlands

FENCING—WOMEN

Foil—Individual
1. E. Osiier, Denmark
2. G. Davis, Great Britain
3. G. Heckscher, Denmark

GYMNASTICS—MEN

Combined Exercises—Individual
1. L. Stukelj, Yugoslavia
2. R. Prazak, Czechoslovakia
3. B. Supcik, Czechoslovakia

Combined Exercises—Team
1. Italy 2. France
3. Switzerland

Horizontal Bar
1. L. Stukelj, Yugoslavia
2. J. Gutweniger, Switzerland
3. A. Higelin, France

Parallel Bars
1. A. Guttinger, Switzerland
2. R. Prazak, Czechoslovakia
3. G. Zampori, Italy

Pommelled Horse
1. J. Wilhelm, Switzerland
2. J. Gutweniger, Switzerland
3. A. Rebetez, Switzerland

Long Horse Vault
1. F. Kriz, U.S.
2. J. Koutny, Czechoslovakia
3. B. Morkovsky, Czechoslovakia

Rings
1. F. Martino, Italy
2. R. Prazak, Czechoslovakia
3. L. Vacha, Czechoslovakia

Rope Climbing
1. B. Supcik, Czechoslovakia
2. A. Seguin, France

Side Horse Vault
1. A. Seguin, France
2. J. Gounot, France

ROWING

Single Sculls

1. J. Beresford, Great Britain—7:49.2
2. W. Garrett-Gilmore, U.S.—7:54.0
3. J. Schneider, Switzerland—8:01.0

Double Sculls

1. J. Kelly/P. Costello, U.S.—6:34.0
2. J. Stock/M. Detton, France—7:54.8
3. R. Bosshard/H. Thoma, Switz.

Coxswainless Pairs

1. W. Rosingh/A. Beynen, Netherlands—8:19.4
2. J. Bouton/R. Piot, France—8:21.6

Coxed Pairs

1. Switzerland—8:39.0
2. Italy—8:39.1
3. U.S.

Coxswainless Fours

1. Great Britain—7:08.6 (Trinity B.C. Cambridge)
2. Canada
3. Switzerland

Coxed Fours

1. Switzerland—7:18.4
2. France—7:21.6
3. U.S.

Eights

1. U.S. (Yale B.C.)—6:33.4
2. Canada(Toronto B.C.)—6:49.0
3. Italy (Zara B.C.)

YACHTING

Monotype

1. Belgium   2. Norway   3. Finland

6 Metres

1. Norway   2. Denmark   3. Netherlands

8 Metres

1. Norway   2. Great Britain   3. France

SHOOTING

Automatic Pistol

1. H. Bailey, U.S.
2. W. Carlberg, Sweden
3. L. Hannelius, Finland

Free Rifle

1. M. Fisher, U.S.
2. C. Osburn, U.S.
3. N. Larsen, Denmark

Miniature Rifle, 50 Metres—Team

1. France
2. Denmark
3. Switzerland

Rifle, Three Distances—Team

1. U.S.
2. France
3. Haiti

Revolver, 25 Metres—Team

1. U.S.
2. Sweden
3. Argentina

Running Deer, Single Shot—Individual

1. J. K. Boles, U.S.
2. C. W. Mackworth-Praed, Gt. Brit.
3. O. M. Olsen, Norway

Running Deer, Single Shot—Team

1. Norway
2. Sweden
3. U.S.

Running Deer, Double Shot—Individual

1. O. A. L. Olsen, Norway
2. C. W. Mackworth-Praed, Gt. Brit.
3. A. G. A. Swahn, Sweden

Running Deer, Double Shot—Team

1. Great Britain
2. Norway
3. U.S.

Small-Bore Rifles—Prone

1. C. C. de Lisle, France
2. M. Dinwiddie, U.S.
3. J. Hartmann, Switzerland

Clay Pigeon—Individual

1. G. Halasy, Hungary
2. K. Hubert, Finland
3. F. Hughes, U.S.

Clay Pigeon—Team

1. U.S.
2. Canada
3. Finland

MODERN PENTATHLON

1. B. Lindman, Sweden   2. G. Dryssen, Sweden   3. B. Uggla, Sweden

RUGBY—FOOTBALL

1. U.S.   2. France   3. Roumania

SOCCER

1. Uruguay   2. Switzerland   3. Sweden

LAWN TENNIS—MEN

Singles
1. V. Richards, U.S.
2. H. Cochet, France
3. Baron de Morpurgo, Italy

Doubles
1. V. Richards/F. T. Hunter, U.S.
2. H. Cochet/J. Brugnon, France
3. J. Borotra/R. Lacoste, France

LAWN TENNIS—WOMEN

Singles
1. H. Wills, U.S.
2. M. Vlasto, France
3. Miss McKane, Great Britain

Doubles
1. Miss H. Wills/Mrs. S. Wightman, U.S.
2. Mrs. E. Covell/Miss K. McKane, Great Britain
3. Mrs. Sheppard-Barron/Miss S. Colyer, Great Britain

POLO

1. Argentina   2. U.S.   3. Great Britain

WATER POLO

1. France   2. Belgium   3. U.S.

Chapter 9

THE IX OLYMPIAD

Amsterdam, 1928

Amsterdam had been trying to get the Olypmpic Games since 1912. In 1920, it withdrew its application in favor of Antwerp. It was selected for the 1924 Games, but withdrew again because Baron de Coubertin wanted Paris to be host on the 30th anniversary of the modern Olympics. Antwerp almost lost the 1928 Olympics too because of financial difficulties. But these were resolved at the last moment when Dutch municipalities and citizens from as far away as the East Indies contributed sufficient funds to insure the success of the IX Olympiad.

The United States won the combined track and field championship with eight gold medals to five for Finland, but the American runners were a major disappointment, winning only three of the 12 races.

A 19-year-old Canadian, Percy Williams, became the only non-American runner to win both the sprints. (Others: Archie Hahn 1904, Ralph Craig 1912, Eddie Tolan 1932, Jesse Owens 1936, Bobby Morrow 1956.) Williams' double surprised everyone but his coach, Bob Granger, who had been predicting that he would be an Olympic champion since he had watched him in a Vancouver high school track meet two years earlier. Williams, who had been told when he was 15 to avoid strenuous exercise because he had had rheumatic fever, did not look strong enough to run a city block. He weighed 126 pounds, the lightest Olympic sprint champion in history. He equalled the Olympic record of 10.6 in a quarter final but finished second to Bob McAllister of the U.S. in the 100 metre semifinal. In the final, he beat Jack London of Great Britain by almost a yard.

In the 200 metres, Williams came within two yards of being eliminated in a trial heat but won the semifinal with little trouble. In the final, he was running even with Helmut Koernig of Germany who had beaten him in the preliminary, but the German faded to finish third in a tie with defending champion Jackson Scholz of the United States behind Walter Rangeley of Great Britain. Koernig was awarded the bronze medal when Scholz refused to meet him in a match race four days later.

The only American runner to win an individual gold medal at Amsterdam was Ray Barbuti, and he was almost caught by James Ball of Canada. Barbuti salvaged victory by lunging at the tape and sprawling on the cinder track. Barbuti, George Baird, Fred Alderman and Emerson Spencer set a world record 3:14.2 in the 1,600 metres relay in which the German and Canadian teams also broke the former record. In the 400 metres relay, the U.S. team of Frank Wykoff, James Quinn, Charles Borah and Henry Russell equalled the world record of 41 seconds.

Defending champion Douglas Lowe of Great Britain was not expected to win again in the 800 metres, but he did, mainly because co-world record holders Lloyd Hahn of the United States and Sera Martin of France finished fifth and sixth.

Harri Larva, a 22-year-old watchmaker from Paavo Nurmi's home town of Avo, cut two fifths of a second off Nurmi's 1924 record in the 1,500 metres, beating co-favored Jules Ladoumegue in the stretch. The Frenchman started to sprint too soon and was too tired to shake off Larva's last minute charge. Nurmi defeated compatriot Ville Ritola by three fifths of a second in the 10,000 metres, but Ritola beat Nurmi by two seconds in the 5,000 metres. Nurmi also had to settle for a silver in the 3,000 metre steeplechase. He was beaten by another Finn, Toivo Loukola, who cut nearly 12 seconds off the Olympic record.

Nurmi's performance was the major disappointment of the IX Olympiad. He had not been defeated in competition for eight years. The task of running five distance races in seven days proved too much for a man of 32.

There was also an upset in the marathon. El Ouafi, a French Foreign Legionnaire from Morocco and Algeria, had never won a race in his life. He was far back after eight miles, and did not start to improve his position until the 15-mile mark. With six miles to go, he was closing on the leaders, Chicago taxi-driver Joie Ray, Kanematsu Yamada of Japan and Martii Maltelinen of Finland. El Ouafi finally got ahead of them with a mile to go, but he finished only 26 seconds ahead of Santiago newsboy Miguel Plaza who also overtook the leaders. Plaza was so excited about winning a silver medal that he grabbed a Chilean flag from an official and ran an extra lap around the track with it. Maltelinen came third ahead of Ray who pulled a muscle during the last lap around the stadium.

There were major upsets in the hurdle races. Sid Atkinson, a second stringer on the South African team, won the 110 metres by flinging himself between Stephen Anderson and John Collier of the United States at the finish. The favoured George Weightman-Smith of South Africa, who had set an Olympic record of 14.6 in the preliminaries, was a poor fifth in the final in which both Atkinson and Anderson were clocked in 14.8, a tenth of a second ahead of Collier. Lord Burghley of Britain passed the co-favored Frank Cuhel and F. Morgan Taylor of the United States in the stretch to win the 400 metres hurdles. Taylor, the defending Olympic champion, also held the world record.

Defending discus champion Bud Houser of the U.S. almost failed to qualify for the final, fouling his first attempt and losing control of the disc on his second. But he qualified on his third and final try and went on to lower his own Olympic record by 3'10''.

Mikio Oda gave Japan its first Olympic track and field gold medal, beating Levi Casey of the U.S. by 1¼" in the triple jump. Vilho Tuulos of Finland was third once again.

In the decathlon, Akilles Jaervinen, whose father Werner had won Finland's first gold medal by winning the Greek style javelin in 1906, finished second to countryman Paavo Yrjola.

American shot putter John Kuck set a world record 52'0$\frac{13}{16}$''. Emil Hirschfield of Germany, who had broken Ralph Rose's record of 19 years standing a few months earlier, was third behind Hollywood movie star Bruce Bennett, who competed under his real name, Herman Brix.

ATHENS, 1896. Start of the 100 metres race won by Thomas Burke of the U.S.

DORANDO PIETRI of Italy being helped across the finish line in the marathon. London. 1908. Pietri was therefore disqualified for receiving this aid, and the gold medal went to Johnny Hayes of the U.S.

JIM THORPE won both the pentathlon and the decathlon for the U.S. in the 1912 Stockholm Olympics. Later when it was discovered that Thorpe had been paid for making summer baseball appearances, his medals and titles were confiscated.

PAAVO NURMI. The Flying Finn won six gold medals for distances from 1,500 metres to 10,000 metres in the Olympic Games of 1920, 1924 and 1928.

EDDIE TOLAN and *RALPH METCALFE. Tolan (right) won the 100 and 200 metres in Los Angeles. 1932. Metcalfe came second in the 100 metres and third in the 200 metres.*

BE DIDRIKSON. The lanky can set world records for the metres hurdles and the jave- and missed another when was disaualified and placed nd in the high jump. 1932 mpic Games. Los Angeles.

JUAN CARLOS ZABALA. *The Argentinian distance runner*
celebrated his 20th birthday by winning the marathon at Los
Angeles. 1932.

JESSE OWENS. Probably the most famous of all U.S. sprinters. His four gold medals at Berlin in 1936 astounded Adolf Hitler.

*GLENN MORRIS of the
.U.S. won a gold medal
in the decathlon. Berlin.
1936.*

*CORNELIUS JOHNSON.
The Negro high jumper
was the first American to
win a gold medal at Berlin
in 1936.*

FANNY BLANKERS - KOEN won four gold medals for the Netherlands in London. 1948.

B MATHIAS of the U.S. The only 1 to win the Olympic decathlon e. He won in London, 1948, and Helsinki, 1952.

EMIL ZATOPEK. The great Czech distance runner leadin.
Herbert Schade in the 10,000 metres. Helsinki. 1952.

Women competed for the first time in track and field at Amsterdam, although they had been entered in other sports in previous Olympics. Elizabeth Robinson of the United States set a world record of 12.2 seconds for the 100 metres. The Canadians thought Fanny Rosenfeld had won but their protest was disallowed. However, Miss Rosenfeld, Florence Bell, Ethel Smith and Myrtle Cook set a world record of 48.4 seconds in beating the United States in the 400 metre relay.

Another Canadian, Ethel Catherwood, fulfilled her pre-game promise to set a world record by high jumping $5'2\frac{9}{16}''$. Mildred Wiley of the U.S. and Carolina Gisolf of Holland were tied for second at $5'1\frac{7}{16}''$.

The United States scored well in rowing, with the University of California beating the Thames Rowing Club by three quarters of a length in the eights, Charles McIlvaine and Paul Costello defeating Jack Guest and Joe Wright of Canada in the double skulls, and the Pennsylvania Barge Club defeating Cambridge in the fours.

Soccer was the most popular spectator sport, contributing more than a third of the total receipts. Defending champion Uruguay retained the title with a 2-1 victory over Argentina in a playoff after they had tied 1-1 in regular competition.

India started a streak of six straight field hockey championships by winning all five games without being scored against. More than 42,000 people watched India beat Holland 3-0 in the final game.

Sven Thofelt of Sweden defeated defending champion Bo Lindman in the modern pentathlon without winning any of the five events. He beat Lindman, also of Sweden, by three points with a second in swimming, fourth in fencing, sixth in shooting, 14th in riding and 21st in running.

The Americans won the swimming honors against stiff competition from Japan, Argentina, Sweden, Holland and Germany. Johnny Weissmuller was a repeat winner in the 100 metres freestyle and anchored the U.S. team victory in the 800 metres relay giving him five gold medals in two Olympics. Peter Desjardins of the United States won both diving competitions.

Versatile Marie Braun of The Netherlands won a gold medal for the 100 metres backstroke and then switched to freestyle to win a silver medal in the 400 metres behind defending champion Martha Norelius of the U.S.

OFFICIAL IX OLYMPIAD RESULTS

Amsterdam, 1928

TRACK AND FIELD—MEN

100 Metres
1. P. Williams, Canada—10.8
2. J. London, Great Britain
3. G. Lammers, Germany

200 Metres
1. P. Williams, Canada—21.8
2. W. Rangeley, Great Britain
3. H. Koernig, Germany

400 Metres
1. R. Barbuti, U.S.—47.8
2. J. Ball, Canada—48.0
3. J. Buchner, Germany—48.2

800 Metres
1. D. Lowe, Great Britain—1:51.8
2. E. Byhlen, Sweden—1:52.8
3. H. Engelhardt—Germany—1:53.2

1,500 Metres
1. H. Larva, Finland—3:53.2
2. J. Ladoumegue, France—3:54.0
3. E. Purje, Finland—3:57.0

5,000 Metres
1. V. Ritola, Finland—14:38.0
2. P. Nurmi, Finland—14:40.0
3. E. Wide, Sweden—14:40.2

10,000 Metres
1. P. Nurmi, Finland—30:18.8
2. V. Ritola, Finland—30:19.4
3. E. Wide, Sweden—31:04.0

Marathon
1. E. Ouafi, France—2:32:57.0
2. M. Plaza, Chile—2:33:32.0
3. M. Maltelinen, Finland—2:35:02.0

110 Metres Hurdles
1. S. Atkinson, So. Africa—14.8
2. S. Anderson, U.S.—14.8
3. J. Collier, U.S.—14.9

400 Metres Hurdles
1. Lord Burghley, Gt. Brit.—53.4
2. F. Cuhel, U.S.—53.6
3. F. M. Taylor, U.S.—53.8

3,000 Metres Steeplechase
1. T. Loukola, Finland—9:21.8
2. P. Nurmi, Finland—9:32.6
3. O. Andersen, Finland—9:35.2

400 Metres Relay
1. U.S.—41.0
2. Germany—41.2
3. Great Britain—41.4

1,600 Metres Relay
1. U.S.—3:14.2
2. Germany—3:14.6
3. Canada—3:15.0

High Jump
1. R. King, U.S.—6′4⅜″
2. B. Hedges, U.S.—6′3 3/16″
3. C. Menard, France—6′3 1/16″

Broad Jump
1. E. Hamm, U.S.—25′4 8/16″
2. S. Cator, Haiti, 24′10 1/16″
3. A. Bates, U.S.—24′3 8/16″

Triple Jump
1. M. Oda, Japan—49′10 11/16″
2. L. Casey, U.S.—49′9¼″
3. V. Tuulos, Finland—49′6⅞″

Pole Vault
1. S. Carr, U.S.—13′9⅜″
2. W. Droegemuller, U.S.—13′5⅜″
3. C. McGinnis, U.S.—12′11½″

Shot Put
1. J. Kuck, U.S.—52′0 11/16″
2. H. Brix, U.S.—51′8 1/16″
3. E. Hirschfield, Germany—51′6⅞′

Discus Throw
1. L. C. Houser, U.S.—155′3″
2. A. Kivi, Finland—154′11 7/16″
3. J. Corson, U.S.—154′6 1/16″

Hammer Throw
1. P. O'Callaghan, Ireland—168′7¼
2. O. Skiold, Sweden—168′3¼″
3. E. Black, U.S.—161′8 11/16″

Javelin Throw
1. E. Lundquist, Sweden—218′6 1/16″
2. B. Szepes, Hungary—213′10 11/16″
3. O. Sunde, Norway—209′7¾″

Decathlon
1. P. Yrjola, Finland
2. A. Jaervinen, Finland
3. K. Doherty, U.S.

TRACK AND FIELD—WOMEN

100 Metres
1. E. Robinson, U.S.—12.2
2. F. Rosenfeld, Canada—12.2
3. E. Smith, Canada—12.2

400 Metres Relay
1. Canada—48.4
2. U.S.—48.8
3. Germany—49.0

800 Metres
1. L. Radke, Germany—2:16.8
2. K. Hitomi, Japan—2:17.5
3. I. Gentzel, Sweden—2:17.8

High Jump
1. E. Catherwood, Canada—5'2 $\frac{9}{16}$"
2. { C. Gisolf, Neth.—5'1 $\frac{7}{16}$"
   { M. Wiley, U.S.—5'1 $\frac{7}{16}$"

Discus Throw
1. H. Konopacka, Poland—129'11 $\frac{13}{16}$"
2. L. Copeland, U.S.—121'7⅞"
3. R. Svedberg, Sweden—117'10 $\frac{9}{16}$"

SWIMMING AND DIVING—MEN

100 Metres Free-Style
1. J. Weissmuller, U.S.—58.6
2. I. Barany, Hungary—59.8
3. K. Takaishi, Japan—1:00.0

200 Metres Breast Stroke
1. Y. Tsuruta, Japan—2:48.8
2. E. Rademacher, Germ.—2:50.6
3. T. Yldefonso, Philippines—2:56.4

400 Metres Free-Style
1. A. Zorilla, Argentina—5:01.6
2. A. Charlton, Australia—5:03.6
3. A. Borg, Sweden—5:04.6

800 Metres Relay
1. U.S.—9:36.2
2. Japan—9:41.4
3. Canada—9:47.8

1,500 Metres Free-Style
1. A. Borg, Sweden—19:51.8
2. A. Charlton, Australia—20:02.6
3. C. Crabbe, U.S.—20:28.8

Platform Diving
1. P. Desjardins, U.S.
2. F. Simaika, Egypt
3. M. Galitzen, U.S.

100 Metres Backstroke
1. G. Kojac, U.S.—1:08.2
2. W. Laufer, U.S.—1:10.0
3. P. Wyatt, U.S.—1:12.0

Springboard Diving
1. P. Desjardins, U.S.
2. M. Galitzen, U.S.
3. F. Simaika, Egypt

SWIMMING AND DIVING—WOMEN

100 Metres Free-Style
1. A. Osipowich, U.S.—1:11.0
2. E. Garatti, U.S.—1:11.4
3. M. Cooper, Gt. Brit.—1:13.6

100 Metres Backstroke
1. M. Braun, Netherlands—1:22.0
2. E. King, Great Britain—1:22.2
3. M. Cooper, Great Britain—1:22.8

400 Metres Free-Style
1. M. Norelius, U.S.—5:42.8
2. M. Braun, Netherlands—5:57.8
2. J. McKim, U.S.—6:00.2

400 Metres Free-Style Relay
1. U.S.—4:47.6
2. Great Britain—5:02.8
3. South Africa—5:13.4

200 Metres Breast Stroke
1. H. Schrader, Germany—3:12.6
2. M. Baron, Netherlands—3:15.2
3. L. Muhe-Hildensheim, Germany—3:17.6

Platform Diving
1. B. Pinkston, U.S.
2. G. Coleman, U.S.
3. L. Sjoquist, Sweden

Springboard Diving
1. H. Meany, U.S.
2. D. Poynton, U.S.
3. G. Coleman, U.S.

BOXING

Flyweight
1. A. Kocsis, Hungary
2. A. Apell, France
3. C. Cavagnoli, Italy

Featherweight
1. L. van Klaveren, Netherlands
2. V. Peralta, Argentina
3. H. Devine, U.S.

Bantamweight
1. V. Tamagnini, Italy
2. J. Daley, U.S.
3. H. Isaacs, South Africa

Lightweight
1. C. Orlandi, Italy
2. S. Halaiko, U.S.
3. G. Berggren, Sweden

Welterweight
1. E. Morgan, New Zealand
2. P. Landini, Argentina
3. R. Smillie, Canada

Middleweight
1. P. Toscani, Italy
2. J. Hermanek, Czechoslovakia
3. L. Steyaert, Belgium

Light-Heavyweight
1. V. Avendano, Argentina
2. E. Pistula, Germany
3. K. Miljon, Netherlands

Heavyweight
1. A. R. Jurado, Argentina
2. N. Ramm, Sweden
3. M. Michaelsen, Denmark

WRESTLING

Free-Style—Bantamweight
1. K. Makinen, Finland
2. E. Spapen, Belgium
3. J. Trifonou, Canada

Free-Style—Featherweight
1. A. Morrison, U.S.
2. K. Pihlajamaki, Finland
3. H. Minder, Switzerland

Free-Style—Lightweight
1. O. Kapp, Estonia
2. C. Pacome, France
3. E. Leino, Finland

Free-Style—Welterweight
1. A. Haavisto, Finland
2. L. Appleton, U.S.
3. M. Letchford, Canada

Free-Style—Middleweight
1. E. Kyburz, Switzerland
2. D. Stockton, Canada
3. S. Rabin, Great Britain

Free-Style—Light-Heavyweight
1. T. Sjostedt, Sweden
2. A. Bogli, Switzerland
3. H. Lefebre, France

Free-Style—Heavyweight
1. J. Richthoff, Sweden
2. A. Sihvola, Finland
3. E. Dame, France

Greco-Roman—Bantamweight
1. K. Leucht, Germany
2. J. Maudr, Czechoslovakia
3. G. Gozzi, Italy

Greco-Roman—Featherweight
1. V. Vali, Estonia
2. E. Malmberg, Sweden
3. G. Quaglia, Italy

Greco-Roman—Lightweight
1. L. Keresztes, Hungary
2. E. Sperling, Germany
3. E. Westerlund, Finland

Greco-Roman—Middleweight
1. V. Kokkinen, Finland
2. L. Papp, Hungary
3. A. Kusnetz, Sweden

Greco-Roman—Light-Heavyweight
1. I. Moustafa, Egypt
2. A. Rieger, Germany
3. Onni Pellinen, Finland

Greco-Roman—Heavyweight
1. R. Svensson, Sweden
2. H. Nystrom, Finland
3. G. Gehring, Germany

WEIGHT-LIFTING

Featherweight
1. F. Andryzek, Austria—633¾ lb.
2. P. Gabetti, Italy—622¾ lb.
3. H. Wolpert, Germany—622¾lb.

Lightweight
1. K. Helbig, Germany—711 lb.
2. H. Haas, Austria—711 lb.
3. F. Arnout, France—667 lb.

Middleweight
1. R. Francois, France—738½ lb.
2. C. Galimberti, Italy—733 lb.
3. A. Scheffer, Netherlands—722 lb.

Light-Heavyweight
1. S. Nosseir, Egypt—782½ lb.
2. L. Hostin, France—777 lb.
3. J. Verheyen, Netherlands—744 lb.

Heavyweight
1. J. Strassberger, Germany—810 lb.
2. A. Luhaar, Estonia—793½ lb.
3. J. Skobla, Czechoslovakia—788 lb.

CYCLING

1,000 Metres Sprint
1. R. Beaufrand, France
2. A. Mazairac, Netherlands
3. W. Falck-Hansen, Denmark

1,000 Metres Time-Trial
1. W. Falck-Hansen, Den.—1:14.2
2. B. van Drakesstein, Neth.—1:15.2
3. E. Gray, Australia—1:15.6

2,000 Metres Tandem
1. B. Leene/D. van Dijk, Neth.
2. J. Sibbit/E. Chambers, Gt. Brit.
3. Bernhardt/Kother, Germany

4,000 Metres Team Pursuit
1. Italy—5:01.8
2. Netherlands—5:06.2
3. Great Britain

Road Race—Individual
1. H. Hanson, Denmark
2. F. Southall, Great Britain
3. Gosta Carlsson, Sweden

Road Race—Team
1. Denmark
2. Great Britain
3. Sweden

EQUESTRIAN SPORTS

Grand Prix Jumping—Individual
1. F. Ventura, Czechoslovakia—
   0 faults
2. M. L. M. Bertran, France—
   2 faults
3. C. Kuhn, Switzerland—4 faults

Grand Prix Jumping—Team
1. Spain—4 faults.
2. Poland—8 faults
3. Sweden—10 faults

Grand Prix Dressage—Individual
1. C. von Langen, Germany
2. C. Marion, France
3. R. Olsson, Sweden

Grand Prix Dressage—Team
1. Germany
2. Sweden
3. Netherlands

Three-Day Event—Individual
1. F. de Mortanges, Netherlands
2. G. P. de Kruyff, Netherlands
3. B. Neumann, Germany

Three-Day Event—Teams
1. Netherlands
2. Norway
3. Poland

FENCING—MEN

Foil—Individual
1. L. Gaudin, France
2. E. Casmir, Germany
3. G. Gaudini, Italy

Foil—Team
1. Italy
2. France
3. Argentina

Epée—Individual
1. L. Gaudin, France
2. G. Buchard, France
3. G. Calnan, U.S.

Epée—Team
1. Italy
2. France
3. Portugal

Sabre—Individual
1. O. Tersztyanszky, Hungary
2. A. Petschauer, Hungary
3. Bini, Italy

Sabre—Team
1. Hungary
2. Italy
3. Poland

FENCING—WOMEN

Foil—Individual
1. H. Mayer, Germany
2. M. Freeman, Great Britain
3. O. Oelkers, Germany

GYMNASTICS—MEN

Combined Exercises—Individual
1. G. Miez, Switzerland
2. H. Hanggi, Switzerland
3. L. Stukelj, Yugoslavia

Combined Exercises—Team
1. Switzerland
2. Czechoslovakia
3. Yugoslavia

Horizontal Bar
1. G. Miez, Switzerland
2. R. Neri, Italy
3. E. Mack, Switzerland

Parallel Bars
1. L. Vacha, Czechoslovakia
2. J. Primozic, Yugoslavia
3. H. Hanggi, Switzerland

Pommelled Horse
1. H. Hanggi, Switzerland
2. G. Miez, Switzerland
3. H. Savolainen, Finland

Long Horse Vault
1. E. Mack, Switzerland
2. E. Loffler, Czechoslovakia
3. S. Drganc, Yugoslavia

Rings
1. L. Stukelj, Yugoslavia
2. L. Vacha, Czechoslovakia
3. E. Loffler, Czechoslovakia

GYMNASTICS—WOMEN

Combined Exercises—Team
1. Netherlands
2. Italy
3. Great Britain

ROWING

Single Sculls
1. H. Pearce, Australia—7:11.0
2. K. Myers, U.S.—7:20.8
3. T. D. Collet, Great Britain—7:19.8

Double Sculls
1. C. McIlvaine/P. Costello, U.S.— 6:41.4
2. J. Guest/J. Wright, Canada
3. V. Flessel/L. Losert, Austria

Coxswainless Pairs
1. B. Muller/K. Moeschter, Germany —7:06.4
2. R. A. Nisbet/T. O'Brien, Great Britain—7:08.8
3. J. Schmitt/P. McDowell, U.S.— 7:20.4

Coxed Pairs
1. Switzerland—7:42.6
2. France—7:48.4
3. Belgium—7:59.4

Coxswainless Fours
1. Great Britain—6:36.0
2. U.S.—6:37.0
3. Italy—6:37.0

Coxed Fours
1. Italy—6:47.8
2. Switzerland—7:03.4
3. Poland—7:12.8

Eights
1. U.S. (University of Calif.)—6:03.2
2. Great Britain (Thames R.C.)— 6:05.6
3. Canada

YACHTING

8 Metres
1. France
2. Holland
3. Sweden

6 Metres
1. Norway
2. Denmark
3. Estonia

Monotype
1. S. G. Thorell, Sweden
2. H. Robert, Norway
3. B. Broman, Finland

MODERN PENTATHLON
1. S. Thofelt, Sweden
2. B. Lindman, Sweden
3. H. Kahl, Germany

FIELD HOCKEY
1. India
2. Netherlands
3. Germany

SOCCER
1. Uruguay
2. Argentina
3. Italy

WATER POLO
1. Germany
2. Hungary
3. France

Chapter 10

THE X OLYMPIAD

Los Angeles, 1932

PAAVO Nurmi went to Los Angeles hoping to add a marathon win to his illustrious career. But even before the Finnish team had departed from Helsinki, his amateur status had been under investigation because he had been accused of padding his expense account during a European tour. When the International Amateur Athletic Federation ruled at Los Angeles that Nurmi could not compete in the Olympics the rest of the Finnish team threatened to withdraw. And when the Finns did not go through with their threat, thousands of demonstrators marched to the headquarters of the Finnish Olympic Association to protest.

Nurmi, who knew that at the age of 36 he would never have another chance at the Olympics, was a sad and disillusioned spectator at Los Angeles. His enforced retirement from amateur competition left him with a 15 year career of 19 world records for distances between 1,500 and 20,000 metres, and seven gold and three silver medals in 10 Olympic races in which he set four records.

His disqualification was also a major setback to Olympic organizers who had been relying on him as a drawing card to boost lagging advance ticket sales. Because of the depression, newspapers had been speculating that the Games would flop and there were rumours from abroad that many countries could not afford the long trip to Los Angeles. But when the first overseas athletes did arrive, the gloomy atmosphere changed almost overnight. There was a box office rush and the 105,000 seats at Olympic stadium were sold out for the opening ceremonies.

With Nurmi out of action, a scrawny tomboy from Beaumont, Texas, became the major attraction of the 1932 Olympic Games. Mildred Babe Didrikson set four world records, although one was disallowed on a technicality. The Babe set her first records on her initial Olympic appearance. She pitched the javelin like a catcher pegging off a runner at second base. The spear never went higher than 10 feet but it landed 143'3$\frac{11}{16}$" away, breaking the previous record by 11 feet. In a trial heat of the 80 metre hurdles she lowered the world record by 1.4 seconds to 11.8. She knocked another tenth of a second off that time in the final. Never before had any athlete broken two world records in an Olympic debut.

However, the Babe set her sights on another record in the high jump and probably she could have set a record in any of the other events if the Olympic rules of the time had not limited her to three events.

The world record high jump was 5'3⅛". Babe beat this easily by clearing 5'5", but so did teammate Jean Shiley. Miss Shiley then cleared 5'5½" and Miss Didrikson knocked down the bar on her first try but cleared it on her second. They both failed at 5'5¾" but the officials awarded them one more attempt to break the tie. Miss Shiley missed. Miss Didrikson cleared the bar with four inches to spare but her foot caught the vertical support bar on her descent and shook the horizontal bar off the supports. The bar was lowered half an inch. They both jumped the height but the officials disqualified Miss Didrikson's jump because her head had gone over before her feet. The "no diving" rule, incidentally, was rescinded a year later but it cost her a possible gold medal and world record.

The Babe was prepared to enter three more events but the Olympic rules restricted her to two gold medals and a silver. After the Games, however, she unofficially equalled or broke every Olympic track and field record for women. Babe Didrikson's hopes of returning for the 1936 Olympic Games were shattered shortly after the Los Angeles Games when the Amateur Athletic Union declared she was a professional because her picture appeared in a car advertisement. So she took up golf and won 17 straight amateur tournaments and then earned more than $1,000,000 in sports, mostly golf, until cancer claimed her life at the age of 42.

In other women's track and field events at Los Angeles, Stanislawa Waladiewicz, a Polish girl whose name was anglicized to Stella Walsh in U.S. press

72

reports, beat Hilda Strike of Canada by a foot in the 100 metres dash setting a world record of 11.9 seconds.

Ruth Osborn of the U.S. thought she had the discus gold medal until teammate Lilian Copeland, the silver medallist in 1928, beat her on her last toss of 133'1⅝", a foot and a half better than Miss Osborn's throw.

Eddie Tolan of the U.S. was the only double winner in men's track and field, winning the 100 and 200 metres. Tolan of Michigan and Ralph Metcalfe of Marquette were co-holders with Percy Williams of Canada of the world record in the 100 at 10.3 seconds. They both equalled it again at Los Angeles with Tolan the winner in a photo finish. Metcalfe, Tolan, Carlos Bianchi Luti of Italy and Arthur Jonath of Germany successively broke the world record in the quarter finals of the 200 metres. Tolan lowered it by a fifth of a second to 21.2 in the final, beating George Simpson and Metcalfe for a U.S. sweep. Jonath, overcome with excitement after setting the previous record of 21.4 in the preliminaries, spent the ensuing two days without sleep or food and thus finished last in the final.

The 400 metre final was billed as a grudge match between Bill Carr of Pennsylvania and Ben Eastman of Stanford. Eastman held the world record for half a mile in 1:50 and was prepared for the 800 metres in the Olympics. However, U.S. track coach Dink Templeton entered him in the 400 instead, confident that he could get revenge for two previous losses to Carr at that distance. But Carr sprinted past him with 60 yards to go and won by five yards in a world record 46.2. Eight months later he broke both legs in a car accident and never raced again.

British school teacher Tom Hampson, who had only been running for four years, set a world record 1:49.9 in the 800 metres beating Alex Wilson of Canada by a half stride after running fifth for the first half. Phil Edwards of Canada, who had set the pace most of the way, was third.

Unheralded Luigi Beccali of Italy was lost among the stragglers until the last turn of the 1,500 metres when he began to sprint, passing seven runners to win by six feet over Jerry Cornes of Great Britain who just got by Phil Edwards before the finish. Glenn

Cunningham of the United States, who had set the early pace, faltered to come in fourth. At one point, Cunningham and Edwards had a 12 metre lead until Cornes caught up to them on the last lap. Defending champion Harri Larva of Finland fell back and finished last after making a determined bid to catch up to the leaders.

The only major dispute of the Games occurred in the 5,000 metre race awarded to Lauri Lehtinen of Finland more than an hour after the United States claimed that he had interfered with Ralph Hill in a stretch duel over the last 60 yards. Hill had been on Lehtinen's heels all the way and when he tried to pass him on the outside the Finn swung out and blocked him off. Hill cut back to the inside lane and Lehtinen blocked him again and then made a straight run for the tape with Hill catching up but losing by three inches. They were both clocked in an Olympic record 14:30.

Volmari Iso-Hollo and Lauri Virtanen, who finished third in the 5,000 metres, were expected to keep Finland's unbeaten streak in 10,000 metres intact. The experts laughed when an unknown Pole, Janusz Kusocinski, predicted that they could never catch him. Kusocinski set a fast pace but the two Finns stayed within striking distance and after 16 of the 25 laps, Iso-Hollo caught up to him and passed him with 2,000 metres to go. But the Pole regained the lead in the backstretch and beat Iso-Hollo by 10 yards in an Olympic record 30:11.4 with Virtanen third.

Iso-Hollo won the 3,000 metre steeplechase but he had to run an extra lap because an official forgot to wave the flag signalling the last lap. On the extra lap, Tom Evenson of Great Britain passed Joe McCluskey of the United States but McCluskey declined to accept the silver medal because he said neither he nor Evenson were aware that they were running an extra 460 metres. The extra lap did not make any difference to Iso-Hollo. He led all the way.

Juan Carlos Zabala, a 19-year-old Argentine schoolboy who trained by running around his newspaper delivery route, won the marathon by 19 seconds over Sam Ferris of Great Britain. Only eight of the 28 starters failed to complete the course and the first four finishers were only 400 yards apart.

After the 110 metre hurdle race, the judges announced that George Saling, Percy Beard and Jack Keller had scored a U.S. sweep but after checking the photos and the electrotimer they gave Donald Finlay of Great Britain the bronze medal. Willi Welscher of Germany had actually finished third but he was disqualified for knocking over four hurdles. Every runner in the race knocked over at least one hurdle.

Ireland's Robert Tisdall set a world record 51.8 in the 400 metre hurdles but it was disallowed because he knocked down the last hurdle. Glen Hardin of the U.S. who finished three feet behind him, was credited with equalling the world record of 52 seconds. The race was supposed to be a match between two former winners, F. Morgan Taylor (1924) and Lord Burghley (1928), but they finished third and fourth.

Canada's Duncan McNaughton broke the American high jumpers' string of victories which started with the Olympic revival in 1896. World record holder George Spitz of the U.S. (6' 8½") was eliminated at 6' 4". McNaughton and Bob Van Osdel of the U.S. both cleared 6' 6" but they couldn't make 6' 7". The jump-off ended when the bar was lowered to 6' $5\frac{9}{16}$". McNaughton cleared it on his second try and Van Osdel missed on all three attempts.

Another world record holder, Chuher Nambu of Japan, failed to win the broad jump, the only track and field event in which no Olympic record was set. Nambu's best mark had been 26' 2 1/7" but he had to settle for third place with his best jump of 24'5¼". U.S. national champion Edward Gordon won at 25' 0¾", an inch and a half better than teammate Lambert Redd.

Nambu redeemed himself, however, by setting a world record 51' 7" in the triple jump, more than five inches better than Mikio Oda's world record set in the 1928 Olympics.

World record pole vaulter Bill Graber, who had set the mark of 14' 4⅜" in the U.S. Olympic trials, could do no better than 13' 7¼" and fourth place. Bill Miller of the U.S. won by brushing over the bar at 14' 1⅞". Shuhei Nishida of Japan, whose best jump before the Olympics had been 13' 9", drew a roar from the crowd of 75,000 as he had one more try. He almost made it, but the bar fell and Miller was the winner.

The jinx on world record holders continued in the shot put. Zygmunt Heljasz of Poland had set the mark of 52' 7⅞" a month earlier but he could not even win a medal at the Games. William Sexton, a 22-year-old, 240-pound New Yorker, won on his last throw of 52' 5$\frac{5}{16}$" to beat team mate Harlow Rothert.

Ville Porhola of Finland, who had won the Olympic shot put gold medal 12 years earlier, competed in the hammer throw this time and looked like an easy winner after his first throw of 171' 6". But defending champion Dr. Patrick O'Callaghan of Ireland beat him by better than five feet on his last throw.

Finland scored a sweep in the javelin with Matti Jaervinen, one of three Jaervinens on the Finnish team whose father had won that country's first gold medal in 1906, beating the former Olympic record by 20 feet.

His brother Akilles held the world record in the decathlon but lost to University of Kansas fullback Jim Bausch. The other brother, Kaarlo, did not place in the shot put.

Japan won every event but one in the men's swimming, Buster Crabbe of the U.S. winning the 400 metre freestyle; and the American women swimmers won everything but the 200 metre breast stroke taken by Clare Dennis of Australia. Helen Madison won the 100 and 400 metres free-style. Harold Smith of the U.S. beat teammate Michael Galitzen in the platform diving. The positions were reversed in the springboard.

Brazil's water polo team was disqualified when three players attacked Hungarian referee Bela Konjati after Germany had beaten them 7-3. The Germans lost the final 6-2 to Hungary.

In rowing, barely a boat length separated the first four finishers in the eights, won again by the United States; and Robert Pearce of Australia successfully defended his single skull championship.

OFFICIAL X OLYMPIAD RESULTS

Los Angeles, 1932

TRACK AND FIELD—MEN

100 Metres
1. E. Tolan, U.S.—10.3
2. R. Metcalf, U.S.—10.3
3. A. Jonath, Germany—10.4

200 Metres
1. E. Tolan, U.S.—21.2
2. G. Simpson, U.S.—21.4
3. R. Metcalfe, U.S.—21.5

400 Metres
1. W. Carr, U.S.—46.2
2. B. Eastman, U.S.—46.4
3. A. Wilson, Canada—47.4

800 Metres
1. T. Hampson, Gt. Brit.—1:49.8
2. A. Wilson, Canada—1:50.0
3. P. Edwards, Canada—1:50.6

1,500 Metres
1. L. Beccali, Italy—3:51.2
2. J. Cornes, Gt. Brit.—3:52.2
3. P. Edwards, Canada—3:52.8

5,000 Metres
1. L. Lehtinen, Finland—14:30.0
2. R. Hill, U.S.—14:30.0
3. L. Virtanen, Finland—14:44.0

10,000 Metres
1. J. Kusocinski, Poland—30:11.4
2. V. Iso-Hollo, Finland—30:12.6
3. L. Virtanen, Finland

Marathon
1. J. C. Zabala, Argentina—2:31:36.0
2. S. Ferris, Great Britain—2:31.55.0
3. A. Toivonen, Finland—2:32.12.0

110 Metres Hurdles
1. G. Saling, U.S.—14.6
2. P. Beard, U.S.—14.7
3. D. Finlay, Great Britain—14.8

400 Metres Hurdles
1. R. Tisdall, Eire—51.8
2. G. Hardin, U.S.—52.0
3. F. M. Taylor, U.S.—52.1

3,000 Metres Steeplechase
1. V. Iso-Hollo, Finland—10:33.4
2. T. Evenson, Great Britain
3. J. McCluskey, U.S.

400 Metres Relay
1. U.S.—40.0
2. Germany—40.9
3. Italy—41.6

1,600 Metres Relay
1. U.S.—3:08.2
2. Great Britain—3:11.2
3. Canada—3:12.8

50,000 Metres Walk
1. T. Green, Great Britain—4:50:10.0
2. J. Balinsh, Latvia—4:57:20.0
3. U. Frigerio, Italy—4:59:06.0

High Jump
1. D. McNaughton, Canada—6'5⅝"
2. R. Van Osdel, U.S.—6'5 7/16"
3. S. Toribio, Philippines—6'5 9/16"

Broad Jump
1. E. Gordon, U.S.—25'0¾"
2. C. L. Redd, U.S.—24'11 3/16"
3. C. Nambu, Japan—24'5 5/16"

Triple Jump
1. C. Nambu, Japan—51'6⅞"
2. E. Svensson, Sweden—50'3⅛"
3. K. Oshima, Japan—49'7¼"

Pole Vault
1. W. Miller, U.S.—14'1⅞"
2. S. Nishida, Japan—14'1 5/16"
3. G. Jefferson, U.S.—13'9⅜"

Shot Put
1. L. Sexton, U.S.—52'5 13/16"
2. H. Rothert, U.S.—51'4 13/16"
3. F. Douda, Czech.—51'2 9/16"

Discus Throw
1. J. Anderson, U.S.—162'4 7/16"
2. H. Laborde, France—159'0¼"
3. P. Winter, France—153'8½"

Hammer Throw
1. P. O'Callaghan, Ire.—176'10 13/16"
2. V. Porhola, Finland—171'5⅞"
3. P. Zaremba, U.S.—165'1½"

Javelin Throw
1. M. Jaervinen, Finland—238'6 9/16"
2. M. Sippala, Finland—229'0"
3. E. Penttila, Finland—225'4¼"

Decathlon
1. B. Bausch, U.S.   2. A. Jaervinen, Finland   3. W. Eberle, Germany

TRACK AND FIELD—WOMEN

100 Metres
1. S. Walasiewicz, Poland—11.9
2. H. Strike, Canada—11.9
3. W. von Bremen, U.S.—12.0

80 Metres Hurdles
1. M. Didrikson, U.S.—11.7
2. E. Hall, U.S.—11.7
3. M. Clark, South Africa—11.8

77

400 Metres Relay
1. U.S.—47.0
2. Canada—47.0
3. Great Britain—47.6

High Jump
1. J. Shiley, U.S.—5'4 $\frac{15}{16}$"
2. M. Didrickson, U.S.—5'4 $\frac{15}{16}$"
3. E. Dawes, Canada—5'2 $\frac{13}{16}$"

Javelin Throw
1. M. Didrickson, U.S.—143'3 $\frac{11}{16}$"
2. E. Braumuller, Germany— 142'8 $\frac{3}{16}$"
3. T. Fleischer, Germany—141'6 $\frac{15}{16}$"

Discus Throw
1. L. Copeland, U.S.—133'1 $\frac{5}{8}$"
2. R. Osborn, U.S.—131'7 $\frac{1}{2}$"
3. J. Wajsowna, Poland—127'1 $\frac{1}{4}$"

SWIMMING AND DIVING—MEN

100 Metres Free-Style
1. Y. Miyazaki, Japan—58.2
2. T. Kawaishi, Japan—58.6
3. A. Schwartz, U.S.—58.8

400 Metres Free-Style
1. C. Crabbe, U.S.—4:48.4
2. J. Taris, France—4:48.5
3. T. Oyokota, Japan—4:52.3

1,500 Metres Free-Style
1. K. Kitamura, Japan—19:12.4
2. S. Makino, Japan—19:14.1
3. J. Christy, U.S.—19:39.5

100 Metres Backstroke
1. M. Kiyokawa, Japan—1:08.6
2. T. Irie, Japan—1:09.8
3. K. Kauatsu, Japan—1:10.0

200 Metres Breast Stroke
1. Y. Tsuruta, Japan—2:45.4
2. R. Koike, Japan—2:46.4
3. T. Yldefonso, Philippines—2:47.1

800 Metres Free-Style Relay
1. Japan—8:58.4
2. U.S.—9:10.5
3. Hungary—9:31.4

Platform Diving
1. H. Smith, U.S.
2. M. Galitzen, U.S.
3. F. Kurtz, U.S.

Springboard Diving
1. M. Galitzen, U.S.
2. H. Smith, U.S.
3. R. Degener, U.S.

SWIMMING AND DIVING—WOMEN

100 Metres Free-Style
1. H. Madison, U.S.—1:06.8
2. W. den Ouden, Neth.—1:07.8
3. E. Saville, U.S.—1:08.2

400 Metres Fee-Style
1. H. Madison, U.S.—5:28.5
2. L. Knight, U.S.—5:28.6
3. J. Maakal, So. Africa—5:47.3

200 Metres Breast Stroke
1. C. Dennis, Australia—3:06.3
2. H. Maehata, Japan—3:06.4
3. E. Jacobson, Denmark—3:07.1

100 Metres Backstroke
1. E. Holm, U.S.—1:19.4
2. P. Mealing, Australia—1:21.3
3. E. Davies, Great Britain—1:22.5

400 Metres Free-Style Relay
1. U.S.—4:38.0
2. Netherlands—4:46.5
3. Great Britain—4:52.4

Platform Diving
1. D. Poynton, U.S.
2. G. Coleman, U.S.
3. M. Roper, U.S.

Springboard Diving
1. G. Coleman, U.S.   2. K. Rawls, U.S.   3. J. Fauntz, U.S.

BOXING

Flyweight
1. S. Enekes, Hungary
2. F. Cabalias, Mexico
3. L. Salica, U.S.

Bantamweight
1. H. Gwynne, Canada
2. H. Ziglarski, Germany
3. J. Villanueva, Philippines

Featherweight
1. C. Robledo, Argentina
2. J. Schleinkofer, Germany
3. C. Carlsson, Sweden

Lightweight
1. L. Stevens, South Africa
2. T. Ahlquist, Sweden
3. N. Bor, U.S.

Welterweight
1. E. Flynn, U.S.
2. E. Campe, Germany
3. B. Ahlberg, Finland

Middleweight
1. C. Barth, U.S.
2. A. Azar, Argentina
3. E. Pierce, South Africa

Light-Heavyweight
1. D. Carstens, South Africa
2. G. Rossi, Italy
3. P. Jorgensen, Denmark

Heavyweight
1. A. Lovell, Argentina
2. L. Rovati, Italy
3. F. Feary, U.S.

WRESTLING

Free-Style—Bantamweight
1. R. Pearce, U.S.
2. O. Zombori, Hungary
3. A. Jaskari, Finland

Greco-Roman—Bantamweight
1. J. Brendel, Germany
2. M. Nizzola, Italy
3. L. Francois, France

Free-Style—Featherweight
1. H. Pihlajamaki, Finland
2. E. Nemir, U.S.
3. E. Karlsson, Sweden

Greco-Roman—Featherweight
1. G. Gozzi, Italy
2. W. Ehrl, Germany
3. L. Koskela, Finland

Free-Style—Lightweight
1. C. Pacome, France
2. K. Karpati, Hungary
3. G. Klaren, Sweden

Greco-Roman—Lightweight
1. E. Malmberg, Sweden
2. A. Kurland, Denmark
3. E. Sperling, Germany

Free-Style—Welterweight
1. J. van Bebber, U.S.
2. D. MacDonald, Canada
3. E. Leino, Finland

Greco-Roman—Welterweight
1. I. Johansson, Sweden
2. V. Kajander-Kajukorpi, Finland
3. E. Gallegatti, Italy

Free-Style—Middleweight
1. I. Johansson, Sweden
2. K. Luukko, Finland
3. J. Tunyogi, Hungary

Greco-Roman—Middleweight
1. V. Kokkinen, Finland
2. J. Foldeak, Germany
3. A. Cadier, Sweden

Free-Style—Light-Heavyweight
1. P. Mehringer, U.S.
2. T. Sjostedt, Sweden
3. E. Scarf, Australia

Greco-Roman—Light-Heavyweight
1. R. Svensson, Sweden
2. O. Pellinen, Finland
3. M. Gruppioni, Italy

Free-Style—Heavyweight
1. J. Richthoff, Sweden
2. J. Riley, U.S.
3. N. Hirschl, Austria

Greco-Roman—Heavyweight
1. C. Westergren, Sweden
2. J. Urban, Czechoslovakia
3. N. Hirschl, Austria

WEIGHT-LIFTING

Featherweight
1. R. Suvigny, France—633¾ lb.
2. H. Wolpert, Germany—622¾ lb.
3. A. Terlazzo, U.S.—617¼ lb.

Middleweight
1. R. Ismayr, Germany—760½ lb.
2. C. Galimberti, Italy—749½ lb.
3. K. Hipfinger, Austria—744 lb.

Lightweight
1. R. Duverger, France—716½ lb.
2. H. Haas, Austria—678 lb.
3. G. Pierini, Italy—667 lb.

Light-Heavyweight
1. L. Hostin, France—804¾ lb.
2. S. Olsen, Denmark—793½ lb.
3. H. Duey, U.S.—727½ lb.

Heavyweight
1. J. Skobla, Czech.—837¾ lb.
2. V. Psenicka, Czech.—832¼ lb.
3. J. Strassberger, Germ.—832¼ lb.

CYCLING

1,000 Metres Sprint
1. J. van Egmond, Netherlands
2. L. Chaillot, France
3. B. Pellizzari, Italy

4,000 Metres Team Pursuit
1. Italy—4:52.9
2. France—4:55.7
3. Great Britain—4:56.0

1,000 Metres Time-Trial
1. E. Gray, Australia—1:13.0
2. J. van Egmond, Neth.—1:13.3
3. C. Rampelberg, France—1:13.4

Road Race—Individual
1. A. Pavesi, Italy—2:28:05.6
2. G. Segato, Italy—2:29:21.4
3. B. Britz, Sweden—2:29:45.2

2,000 Metres Tandem
1. M. Perrin/L. Chaillot, France
2. E. Chambers/S. Chambers, Gt. Br.
3. H. Christensen/W. Gervin, Den.

Road Race—Team
1. Italy—7:27:15.2
2. Denmark—7:38:50.2
3. Sweden—7:39:12.6

EQUESTRIAN SPORTS

Grand Prix Jumping
1. T. Nishi, Japan
2. H. Chamberlin, U.S.
3. C. von Rosen, Sweden

Grand Prix Dressage—Individual
1. F. Lesage, France
2. C. Marion, France
3. H. Tuttle, U.S.

Grand Prix Dressage—Team
1. France
2. Sweden
3. U.S.

Three-Day Event—Individual
1. F. de Mortanges, Netherlands
2. E. Thomson, U.S.
3. C. von Rosen, Sweden

Three-Day Event—Team
1. U.S.   2. Netherlands

FENCING—MEN

Foil—Individual
1. G. Marzi, Italy
2. J. Levis, U S.
3. G. Gaudini, Italy

Foil—Team
1. France
2. Italy
3. U.S.

Epée—Individual
1. G. Medici, Italy
2. G. Buchard, France
3. C. Agostoni, Italy

Epée—Team
1. France
2. Italy
3. U.S.

Sabre—Individual
1. G. Piller, Hungary
2. G. Gaudini, Italy
3. E. Kabos, Hungary

Sabre—Team
1. Hungary
2. Italy
3. Poland

FENCING—WOMEN

Foil—Individual
1. E. Preis, Austria
2. H. Guiness, Great Britain
3. E. Bogen, Hungary

GYMNASTICS

Combined Exercises—Individual
1. R. Neri, Italy
2. I. Pelle, Hungary
3. H. Savolainen, Finland

Combined Exercises—Team
1. Italy
2. U.S.
3. Finland

Floor Exercises
1. I. Pelle, Hungary
2. G. Miez, Switzerland
3. M. Lertora, Italy

Horizontal Bar
1. D. Bixler, U.S.
2. H. Savolainen, Finland
3. E. Terasvirta, Finland

Parallel Bars
1. R. Neri, Italy
2. I. Pelle, Hungary
3. H. Savolainen, Finland

Pommelled Horse
1. I. Pelle, Hungary
2. O. Bonoli, Italy
3. F. Haubold, U.S.

Long Horse Vault
1. S. Guglielmetti, Italy
2. Alfred Jochim, Germany
3. E. Carmichael, U.S.

Rings
1. G. Gulack, U.S.
2. W. Denton, U.S.
3. G. Lattuada, Italy

Rope Climb
1. R. H. Bass, U.S.
2. W. G. Galbraith, U.S.
3. T. F. Connelly, U.S.

Indian Clubs
1. G. Roth, U.S.
2. P. Kronberg, U.S.
3. W. Kuhlemeier, U.S.

Tumbling
1. R. Wolfe, U.S.
2. E. Gross, U.S.
3. W. J. Hermann, U.S.

ROWING

Single Sculls
1. H. Pearce, Australia—7:44.4
2. W. Miller, U.S.—7:45.2
3. G. Douglas, Uruguay—8:13.6

Double Sculls
1. W. Garrett-Gilmour/K. Meyers, U.S.—7:17.4
2. G. Boetzelen/H. Buhtz, Germany—7:22.8
3. N. de Mille/C. Pratt, Canada—7:27.6

Coxswainless Pairs
1. A. Edwards/L. Clive, Great Britain—8:00.0
2. F. Thompson/C. Stiles—New Zealand—8:02.4
3. J. Midolajezyk/H. Budzynski, Poland—8:08.2

Coxed Pairs
1. U.S.—8:25.8
2. Poland—8:31.2
3. France—8:41.2

Coxswainless Fours
1. Great Britain—6:58.2
2. Germany—7:03.0
3. Italy—7:04.0

Coxed Fours
1. Germany—7:19.0
2. Italy—7:19.2
3. Poland—7:26.8

Eights
1. U.S.—6:37.6
2. Italy—6:37.8
3. Canada—6:40.4

YACHTING

Star
1. "Jupiter," U.S.
2. "Joy," Great Britain
3. "Swedish Star," Sweden

Monotype
1. J. Lebrun, France
2. A. L. J. Maas, Netherlands
3. S. A. Cansino, Spain

6 Metres
1. Sweden
2. U.S.A.
3. Canada

8 Metres
1. U.S.
2. Canada

SHOOTING

Free Pistol
1. R. Morigi, Italy
2. H. Hax, Germany
3. D. Matteucci, Italy

Small Bore Rifle—Prone
1. B. Ronmark, Sweden
2. G. Huest, Mexico
3. Z. Hradetsky-Soos, Hungary

MODERN PENTATHLON
1. J. Oxenstierna, Sweden
2. B. Lindman, Sweden
3. R. Mayo, U.S.

FIELD HOCKEY
1. India
2. Japan
3. U.S.

WATER POLO
1. Hungary
2. Germany
3. U.S.

Chapter 11

THE XI OLYMPIAD

Berlin, 1936

THE XI Olympiad was awarded to Berlin before anyone believed that the Nazis would be in power in 1936.

After Adolf Hitler became German Chancellor on January 30, 1932, the Nazi press began a vicious denunciation of the Olympic Games. "An infamous festival dominated by Jews", was the description of Julius Streicher in his weekly *Der Stuermer*.

Dr. Theodor Lewald, president of the Olympic organizing committee and a former German Secretary of State, paid a visit to Hitler which resulted in Der Fuehrer announcing his full support of the Games.

The Nazis, however, insisted on taking over complete control of the Games which were nearly cancelled in 1934. International Olympic Committee president Count Baillet Latour threatened to call them off. Hitler then relented and did everything he could to insure the success of the Olympics.

The luxurious Olympic Village was designed for later use as an army officers' club. All told, the Germans spent about $25,000,000 in building nine arenas. Signs in shop windows barring Jewish customers disappeared during the Games. There was a three-week truce in Hitler's anti-Jewish campaign.

The first winner of the marathon, Spiridon Louis, dressed in his native Greek shepherd's costume, marched into the stadium with the Olympic torch, and the 1936 Olympic Games were declared open.

On the first day of competition, there was an outbreak of nationalistic fervor among the capacity crowd of 110,000 at the Olympic Stadium when shot putter Hans Woellke won the first gold medal of the Games and became the first German in history to win an Olympic track and field championship. Another German, Gerhard Stock, finished third and there was a deafening roar when two German flags were raised on the victory pole. The two German athletes were escorted to Hitler's box to be personally congratulated by Der Fuehrer.

Next, Ilmari Salminen, Arvo Askola and Volmari Iso-Hollo who scored a sweep for Finland in the 10,000 metres, also were invited to receive Hitler's handshake.

The German spectators thundered their approval when their athletes picked up two more opening day medals. Tilly Fleischer and Luise Kruger finished first and second in the women's javelin. Hitler repeatedly shook them by the hand and a beaming Herman Goering slapped them on the back.

However, Hitler had left when Cornelius Johnson, Dave Albritton and Delos Thurber of the United States made a sweep of the high jump late in the afternoon. Johnson and Albritton were Negroes. The ten Negro athletes on the U.S. team were labelled in the Nazi press as "the black auxiliaries". Hitler's hatred for Negroes was almost as vehement as his anti-Jewish bias.

Count Baillet Latour, who had watched Hitler leave during the high jump finals, reminded him that if he was going to honor some winners he should honor them all. Hitler replied that he would refrain from congratulating any more champions.

He kept his promise the next day when Germany picked up its third gold medal. Karl Hein won the hammer throw with an Olympic record 185′ 4″. Another German, Irwin Blask, was second.

On the third day of competition, Jesse Owens added to Hitler's embarrassment by winning the 100-metre dash, the first of four gold medals the Negro sprinter from Ohio State University was to take home from Berlin. Owens, who had picked cotton in Alabama when he was six years old, had set three world records and equalled another in one day in the year preceding the Olympics. He added another world record by winning his semi-final heat of the 100 metres in 10.2 seconds, but it was never made official because of a following wind. In the final, he equalled the Olympic record of 10.3 seconds in beating teammate Ralph Metcalfe, who also finished second in the event at Los Angeles when Eddie Tolan set the record.

The following morning, Owens set a world record for a curved track in winning a trial heat of the 200 metres in 21.1 seconds. He immediately went into the broad jump trials. He held the world record for that, too, but he had trouble qualifying. He only just made it on his last jump.

After lunch, Owens again ran the 200 metres in 21.1 seconds in a quarter final. And then, after a short breather, he returned to the jumping pit and won his second gold medal of the day. His first jump put him ahead but Luz Long of Germany equalled it on his last try. Owens had one jump left; his distance of 26' 5$\frac{5}{16}$" was almost five inches better than Long's. Owens' work was finished for the day. He had broken four former Olympic records.

The following day he won his third gold medal by setting another world record in the 200 metres, beating teammate Mack Robinson by four yards in 20.7 seconds. Hitler watched the race, but left the stadium before Owens was presented with the medal. This time, even the Germans joined in the thunderous applause. Owens by now was clearly the hero of the Games.

On the final day of the Olympics, Owens contributed one more world record and won his fourth gold medal as a member of the winning U.S. 400 metre relay team. Owens and Ralph Metcalfe were last minute replacements for Sam Stoller and Marty Glickman on the team which also included Foy Draper and Frank Wycoff.

Although Owens was without doubt the best individual performer at the Games, the best single performance was turned in by a 130-pound Rhodes scholar medical intern from New Zealand. Dr. Jack Lovelock shaved a full second off the world record by running the 1,500 metres in 3:47.8. Lovelock sprinted the last 300 metres and his great speed carried the next four finishers with him. Glenn Cunningham of the U.S., the world record holder for the mile, defending Olympic champion Luigi Beccali of Italy, Archie San Romani of the U.S. and veteran Canadian Phil Edwards all finished ahead of the former Olympic record.

Archie Williams, a U.S. Negro, won a stretch duel with Arthur Brown of Great Britain to win the 400 metres by a stride; and John Woodruff, another of the American "black auxiliaries", won the 800 metres by breaking most of the fundamentals of the coaching manual. A comparatively inexperienced runner, he had been told to take the lead to avoid interfering with the other competitors, but he found himself blocked by the other runners. He slowed down until everyone had passed him and then began catching them on the outside and went ahead. But Phil Edwards and Mario Lanzi of Italy passed him. Woodruff took another detour around Lanzi and caught Edwards, but his zig-zagging course had taken its toll and Lanzi almost caught him at the tape with Edwards finishing third.

Finland was heading for a sweep of the 5,000 metres when Ilmari Salminen, the 10,000 metre winner, tripped as the closely bunched trio headed into the final lap. That left Gunnar Hoeckert to beat defending champion Lauri Lehtinen with John Henry Jonsson of Sweden finishing third.

Defending champion Juan Zabala of Argentina led the field out of the stadium in the marathon and stayed in front for about 15 miles when he tired and fell out, although he was still ahead. Kitei Son of Japan and Ernest Harper of Great Britain had been jogging along just behind him most of the way. After Zabala's demise, the 21-year-old Japanese student began to run away from Harper, a 29-year-old miner. By the time the Britisher entered the stadium, about two minutes behind Kitei Son, the nonchalant Japanese was already in his dressing room.

Forrest Towns of the United States equalled his own world record of 14.1 seconds in a semi-final heat of the 110-metre hurdles but was one tenth of a second slower in winning the final, and world record holder Glenn Hardin of the U.S. won an easy victory in the 400-metre hurdles in a relatively slow 52.4 seconds.

Gotthardt Handrick of Germany broke Sweden's monopoly in the modern pentathlon.

The Germans dominated most of the events outside of track and field — gymnastics, rowing, canoeing, yachting, equestrian sports and handball. In rowing, they won everything but the double skulls and the eights. British veteran Jack Beresford, competing in his fifth Olympic Games, teamed up with Dick Southwood to win the double skulls. Beresford had won a silver medal in the single skulls in 1920 and a gold for the same in 1924. The United States, represented by a University of Washington crew, continued its mastery in the eight-oared race.

OFFICIAL XI OLYMPIAD RESULTS

Berlin, 1936

TRACK AND FIELD—MEN

100 Metres
1. J. Owens, U.S.—10.3
2. R. Metcalfe, U.S.—10.4
3. M. Osendarp, Netherlands—10.5

200 Metres
1. J. Owens, U.S.—20.7
2. M. Robinson, U.S.—21.1
3. M. Osendarp, Netherlands—21.3

400 Metres
1. A. Williams, U.S.—46.5
2. A. G. Brown, Gt. Brit.—46.7
3. J. LuValle, U.S.—46.8

800 Metres
1. J. Woodruff, U.S.—1:52.9
2. M. Lanzi, Italy—1:53.3
3. P. Edwards, Canada—1:53.6

1,500 Metres
1. J. Lovelock, New Zealand—3:47.8
2. G. Cunningham, U.S.—3:48.4
3. L. Beccali, Italy—3:49.2

5,000 Metres
1. G. Hockert, Finland—14:22.2
2. L. Lehtinen, Finland—14:25.8
3. H. Jonsson, Sweden—14:29.0

10,000 Metres
1. I. Salminen, Finland—30:15.4
2. A. Askola, Finland—30:15.6
3. V. Iso-Hollo, Finland—30:20.2

Marathon
1. K. Son, Japan—2:29:19.2
2. E. Harper, Gt. Brit.—2:31:23.2
3. S. Nan, Japan—2:31:42.0

110 Metres Hurdles
1. F. Towns, U.S.—14.2
2. D. Finlay, Great Britain—14.4
3. F. Pollard, U.S.—14.4

400 Metres Hurdles
1. G. Hardin, U.S.—52.4
2. J. Loaring, Canada—52.7
3. M. White, Philippines—52.8

3,000 Metres Steeplechase
1. V. Iso-Hollo, Finland—9:03.8
2. K. Tuominen, Finland—9:06.8
3. A. Dompert, Germany—9:07.2

400 Metres Relay
1. U.S.—39.8
2. Italy—41.1
3. Germany—41.2

1,600 Metres Relay
1. Great Britain—3:09.0
2. U.S.—3:11.0
3. Germany—3:11.8

50,000 Metres Walk
1. H. Whitlock, Gt. Brit.—4:30:41.1
2. A. Schwab, Switzerland—4:32:09.2
3. A. Bubenko, Latvia—4:32:42.2

High Jump
1. C. Johnson, U.S.—6'8"
2. D. Albritton, U.S.—6'6¾"
3. D. Thurber, U.S.—6'6¾"

Broad Jump
1. J. Owens, U.S.—26'5¼"
2. L. Long, U.S.—25'9¹³⁄₁₆"
3. N. Tajima, Japan—25'4¾"

Triple Jump
1. N. Tajima, Japan—52'5¹⁵⁄₁₆"
2. M. Harada, Japan—51'4⅓"
3. J. Metcalfe, Australia—50'10¼"

Pole Vault
1. E. Meadows, U.S.—14'3¼"
2. S. Nishida, Japan—13'11⁵⁄₁₆"
3. S. Oe, Japan—13'11⁵⁄₁₆"

Shot Put
1. H. Woellke, Germany—53'1¾"
2. S. Barlund, Finland—52'10⅝"
3. G. Stock, Germany—51'4½"

Discus Throw
1. K. Carpenter, U.S.—165'7½"
2. G. Dunn, U.S.—161'11⁵⁄₁₆"
3. G. Oberweger, Italy—161'6⅛"

Hammer Throw

1. K. Hein, Germany—185'4"
2. E. Blask, Germany—180'7"
3. F. Warngard, Sweden—179'10⅝"

Javelin Throw

1. G. Stock, Germany—235'8⅜"
2. Y. Nikkanen, Finland—232'2"
3. K. Toivonen, Finland—232'0¼"

Decathlon

1. G. Morris, U.S.
2. R. Clark, U.S.
3. J. Parker, U.S.

Pentathlon

1. G. Handrick, Germany
2. C. F. Leonard, U.S.
3. S. Abba, Italy

TRACK AND FIELD—WOMEN

100 Metres

1. H. Stephens, U.S.—11.5
2. S. Walasiewicz, Poland—11.7
3. K. Krauss, Germany—11.9

80 Metres Hurdles

1. T. Valla, Italy—11.7
2. A. Steuer, Germany—11.7
3. E. Taylor, Canada—11.7

400 Metres Relay

1. U.S.—46.9
2. Great Britain—47.6
3. Canada—47.8

High Jump

1. I. Csak, Hungary—5'2 15/16"
2. D. Odam, Great Britain—5'2 11/16"
3. E. Kaun, Germany—5'2 11/16"

Javelin Throw

1. T. Fleischer, Germany—148'2 ¾"
2. L. Kruger, Germany—142'0¼"
3. M. Kwasniewska, Poland—137'2"

Discus Throw

1. G. Mauermayer, Germ.—156'3 3/16"
2. J. Wajsowna, Poland—151'7 11/16"
3. P. Mollenhauer, Germ.—130'6⅞"

SWIMMING AND DIVING—MEN

100 Metres Free-Style

1. F. Csik, Hungary—57.6
2. M. Yusa, Japan—57.9
3. S. Arai, Japan—58.0

400 Metres Free-Style

1. J. Medica, U.S.—4:44.5
2. S. Uto, Japan—4:45.6
3. S. Makino, Japan—4:48.1

1,500 Metres Free-Style

1. N. Terada, Japan—19:13.7
2. J. Medica, U.S.—19:34.0
3. S. Uto, Japan—19:34.5

200 Metres Breast Stroke

1. T. Hamuro, Japan—2:42.5
2. E. Sietas, Germany—2:42.9
3. R. Koike, Japan—2:44.2

100 Metres Backstroke

1. A. Kiefer, U.S.—1:05.9
2. A. Van de Weghe, U.S.
3. M. Kiyokawa, Japan

800 Metres Free-Style Relay

1. Japan—8:51.5
2. U.S.—9:03.0
3. Hungary—9:12.3

Platform Diving

1. M. Wayne, U.S.
2. E. Root, U.S.
3. H. Stork, Germany

Springboard Diving

1. R. Degener, U.S.
2. M. Wayne, U.S.
3. A. Greene, U.S.

SWIMMING AND DIVING—WOMEN

100 Metres Free-Style

1. H. Mastenbroek, Neth.—1:05.9
2. J. Campbell, Argentina—1:06.4
3. G. Arendt, Germany—1:06.6

400 Metres Free-Style

1. H. Mastenbroek, Neth.—5:26.4
2. R. Hveger, Denmark—5:27.5
3. L. Wingard, U.S.—5:29.0

200 Metres Breast Stroke

1. H. Maehata, Japan—3:03.6
2. M. Genenger, Germany—3:04.2
3. I. Sorensen, Denmark—3:07.8

100 Metres Backstroke

1. D. Senff, Netherlands—1:18.9
2. H. Mastenbroek, Neth.—1:19.2
3. A. Bridges, U.S.—1:19.4

400 Metres Free-Style Relay

1. Netherlands—4:36.0
2. Germany—4:36.8
3. U.S.—4:40.2

Platform Diving

1. D. Hill, U.S.
2. V. Dunn, U.S.
3. K. Kohler, Germany

Springboard Diving

1. M. Gestring, U.S.
2. K. Rawls, U.S.
3. D. Hill, U.S.

BOXING

Flyweight
1. W. Kaiser, Germany
2. G. Matta, Italy
3. L. Laurie, U.S.

Bantamweight
1. U. Sergo, Italy
2. J. Wilson, U.S.
3. F. Ortiz, Mexico

Featherweight
1. O. Casanova, Argentina
2. C. Catterall, South Africa
3. J. Miner, Germany

Lightweight
1. I. Harangi, Hungary
2. N. Stepulov, Estonia
3. E. Agren, Sweden

Welterweight
1. S. Suvio, Finland
2. M. Murach, Germany
3. G. Petersen, Denmark

Middleweight
1. J. Despeaux, France
2. H. Tiller, Norway
3. R. Villareal, Argentina

Light-Heavyweight
1. R. Michelot, France
2. R. Voigt, Germany
3. F. Risiglione, Argentina

Heavyweight
1. H. Runge, Germany
2. G. Lovell, Argentina
3. E. Nilsen, Norway

WRESTLING

Free-Style—Bantamweight
1. O. Zombori, Hungary
2. R. Flood, U.S.
3. J. Herbert, Germany

Free-Style—Featherweight
1. K. Pihlajamaki, Finland
2. F. Millard, U.S.
3. G. Jonsson, Sweden

Free-Style—Lightweight
1. K. Karpati, Hungary
2. W. Enrl, Finland
3. H. Pihlajamaki, Finland

Free-Style—Welterweight
1. F. Lewis, U.S.
2. T. Andersson, Sweden
3. J. Schleimer, Canada

Free-Style—Middleweight
1. E. Poilve, France
2. R. Voliva, U.S.
3. A. Kirecci, Turkey

Free-Style—Light-Heavyweight
1. K. Fridell, Sweden
2. A. Neo, Estonia
3. E. Siebert, Germany

Free-Style—Heavyweight
1. K. Palusalu, Estonia
2. J. Klapuch, Czechoslovakia
3. H. Nystrom, Finland

Greco-Roman—Bantamweight
1. M. Lorinc, Hungary
2. E. Svensson, Sweden
3. J. Brendel, Germany

Greco-Roman—Featherweight
1. Y. Erkan, Turkey
2. A. Reini, Finland
3. Ł. Karlsson, Sweden

Greco-Roman—Lightweight
1. L. Koskela, Finland
2. J. Herda, Czechoslovakia
3. W. Vali, Estonia

Greco-Roman—Welterweight
1. R. Svedberg, Sweden
2. F. Schafer, Germany
3. E. Virtanen, Finland

Greco-Roman—Middleweight
1. I. Johansson, Sweden
2. L. Schweikert, Germany
3. J. Palotas, Hungary

Greco-Roman—Light-Heavyweight
1. A. Cadier, Sweden
2. E. Bietags, Lithuania
3. A. Neo, Estonia

Greco-Roman—Heavyweight
1. K. Palusalu, Estonia
2. J. Nyman, Sweden
3. K. Hornfischer, Germany

WEIGHT-LIFTING

Featherweight
1. A. Teriazzo, U.S.—689 lb.
2. S. M. Soliman, Egypt—672½ lb.
3. I. Shams, Egypt—661¼ lb.

Lightweight
1. {M. Mesbah, Egypt—755 lb.
   {R. Rein, Austria—755 lb.
3. Karl Jansen, Germany—722 lb.

Middleweight
1. K. El Thouni, Egypt—854¾ lb.
2. R. Ismayr, Germany—777 lb.
3. A. Wagner, Germany—777 lb.

Light-Heavyweight
1. L. Hostin, France—820 lb.
2. E. Deutsch, Germany—804¾ lb.
3. I. Wasif, Egypt—793½ lb.

Heavyweight
1. J. Manger, Austria—903¾ lb.
2. V. Psenicka, Czech.—887¼ lb.
3. A. Luhaar, Estonia—882 lb.

CYCLING

1,000 Metres Sprint
1. T. Merkens, Germany
2. A. van Vliet, Netherlands
3. L. Chaillot, France

1,000 Metres Time-Trial
1. A. van Vliet, Neth.—1:12.0
2. P. Georget, France—1:12.8
3. R. Karsch, Germany—1:13.2

2,000 Metres Tandem
1. E. Ihbe/C. Lorenz, Germ.—11.0
2. B. Leene/H. Ooms, Neth.—11.0
3. P. Georget/G. Maton, France—11.0

4,000 Metres Team Pursuit
1. France—4:45.0
2. Italy—4:51.0
3. Great Britain—4:52.6

Road-Race—Individual
1. R. Charpenier, France—2:33:05.0
2. G. Lapebie, France—2:33:05.2
3. E. Nievergelt, Switz.—2:33:05.8

Road-Race—Team
1. France—7:39:16.2
2. Switzerland—7:39:20.4
3. Belgium—7:39:21.0

EQUESTRIAN SPORTS

Grand Prix Jumping—Individual
1. K. Hasse, Germany
2. H. Rang, Roumania
3. J. Platthy, Hungary

Grand Prix Jumping—Teams
1. Germany
2. Netherlands
3. Portugal

Grand Prix Dressage—Individual
1. H. Pollay, Germany
2. F. Gerhard, Germany
3. A. Podhajsky, Austria

Grand Prix Dressage—Teams
1. Germany
2. France
3. Sweden

Three-Day Event—Individual
1. L. Stubbendorff, Germany
2. E. Thomson, U.S.
3. H. Lunding, Denmark

Three-Day Event—Teams
1. Germany
2. Poland
3. Great Britain

FENCING—MEN

Foil—Individual
1. G. Gaudini, Italy
2. E. Gardere, France
3. G. Bocchino, Italy

Foil—Team
1. Italy
2. France
3. Germany

Epée—Individual
1. F. Riccardi, Italy
2. S. Ragno, Italy
3. G. Medici, Italy

Epée—Team
1. Italy
2. Sweden
3. France

Sabre—Individual
1. E. Kabos, Hungary
2. G. Marzi, Italy
3. A. Gerevich, Hungary

Sabre—Team
1. Hungary
2. Italy
3. Germany

FENCING—WOMEN

Foil—Individual
1. I. Elek, Hungary
2. H. Mayer, Germany
3. E. Preis, Austria

GYMNASTICS—MEN

Combined Exercises—Individual
1. K. Schwarzmann, Germany
2. E. Mack, Switzerland
3. K. Frey, Germany

Combined Exercises—Team
1. Germany
2. Switzerland
3. Finland

Floor Exercises
1. G. Miez, Switzerland
2. J. Walter, Switzerland
3. { K. Frey, Germany
    { E. Mack, Switzerland

Horizontal Bar
1. A. Saarvala, Finland
2. K. Frey, Germany
3. K. Schwarzmann, Germany

Parallel Bars
1. K. Frey, Germany
2. M. Reusch, Switzerland
3. K. Schwarzmann, Germany

Pommelled Horse
1. K. Frey, Germany
2. E. Mack, Switzerland
3. A. Bachmann, Switzerland

Long Horse Vault
1. K. Schwarzmann, Germany
2. E. Mack, Switzerland
3. M. Volz, Germany

Rings
1. A. Hudec, Czechoslovakia
2. L. Stukelj, Yugoslavia
3. M. Volz, Germany

GYMNASTICS—WOMEN

Combined Exercises—Team
1. Germany
2. Czechoslovakia
3. Hungary

ROWING

Single Sculls
1. G. Scnafer, Germany—8:21.5
2. J. Hasenohrl, Austria—8:25.8
3. D. Barrow, U.S.—8:28.0

Double Sculls
1. L. Southwood/J. Beresford, Great Britain—7:20.8
2. J. Pirsch/W. Kaidel, Germany—7:26.2
3. J. Ustupski/R. Verey, Poland—7:36.2

Coxswainless Pairs
1. H. Strauss/W. Eichhorn, Germany—8:16.1
2. H. Larsen/R. Olsen, Denmark—8:19.2
3. J. Curatella/H. Podesta, Argentina—8:23.0

Coxed Pairs
1. Germany—8:36.9
2. Italy—8:49.7
3. France—8:54.0

Coxswainless Fours
1. Germany—7:01.8
2. Great Britain—7:06.5
3. Switzerland—7:10.6

Coxed Fours
1. Germany—7:16.2
2. Switzerland—7:24.3
3. France—7:33.3

Eights
1. U.S.—6:25.4
2. Italy—6:26.0
3. Germany—6:26.4

CANOEING

Kayak Singles—1,000 Metres
1. G. Hradetzky, Austria—4:22.9
2. H. Cammerer, Germany—4:25.6
3. J. Kraaier, Netherlands—4:35.1

Kayak Pairs—1,000 Metres
1. A. Kainz/A. Dorfner, Austria—4:03.8
2. E. Tilker/F. Bondroit, Germany—4:08.9
3. N. Tates/W. van der Kroft, Netherlands—4:12.2

Canadian Singles—1,000 Metres
1. F. Amyot, Canada—5:32.1
2. B. Karlik, Czech.—5:36.9
3. E. Koschik, Germany—5:39.0

Canadian Pairs—1,000 Metres
1. V. Syrovatka/F. Brzak, Czechoslovakia—4:50.1
2. R. Weinstabl/K. Proisl, Austria—4:53.8
3. F. Saker/H. Charters, Canada—4:56.7

Kayak Singles—10,000 Metres
1. G. Hradetzky, Austria—50:1.2
2. H. Eberhardt, France
3. X. Hormann, Germany

Rigid Kayak Pairs—10,000 Metres
1. P. Wevers/L. Landen, Germany—41:45.0
2. V. Kalisch/K. Steinnuber, Austria
3. T. Fahlborg/H. Larsson, Sweden

Rigid Kayak Singles—10,000 Metres
1. E. Krebs, Germany—46:01.6
2. F. Landertinger, Austria
3. E. Riedel, U.S.

Kayak Pairs—10,000 Metres
1. S. Johansson/E. Bladstrom, Sweden—45:48.9
2. W. Horn/E. Hanisch, Germany
3. P. Wijdekop/C. Wijdekop, Neth.

Canadian Pairs—10,000 Metres
1. V. Mottl/Z. Skrdlant, Czechoslovakia—50:33.5
2. F. Saker/H. Charters, Canada
3. R. Weinstabl/K. Proisl, Austria

YACHTING

Star
1. "Wannesee," Germany
2. "Sunshine," Sweden
3. "Bemm II," Netherlands

Monotype
1. "Nurnberg," Netherlands
2. "Rostock," Germany
3. "Potsdam," Great Britain

6 Metres
1. "Lalage," Great Britain
2. "Lully II," Norway
3. "May Be," Sweden

8 Metres
1. "Italia," Italy
2. "Silja," Norway
3. "Germania III," Germany

SHOOTING

Free Pistol
1. T. Ullmann, Sweden
2. E. Krempel, Germany
3. C. des Jammonieres, France

Automatic Pistol (25 Metres)
1. C. van Oyen, Germany
2. H. Hay, Germany
3. T. Ullmann, Sweden

Miniature Rifles (50 Metres)
1. W. Rogeberg, Norway
2. R. Berzsenyi, Hungary
3. W. Karas, Poland

Target Pistol (50 Metres)
1. T. Ullman, Sweden
2. E. Krempel, Germany
3. C. des Jamonniers, France

MODERN PENTATHLON
1. G. Handrick, Germany
2. C. Leonard, U.S.
3. S. Abba, Italy

BASKETBALL
1. U.S.
2. Canada
3. Mexico

HANDBALL
1. Germany
2. Austria
3. Switzerland

FIELD HOCKEY
1. India
2. Germany
3. Netherlands

SOCCER
1. Italy
2. Austria
3. Norway

POLO
1. Argentina
2. Great Britain
3. Mexico

WATER POLO
1. Hungary
2. Germany
3. Belgium

Chapter 12

THE XIV OLYMPIAD

London, 1948

THE Jesse Owens of 1948 was a woman.

Francina Blankers-Koen won four gold medals and became the blonde darling of London. And if the Olympics of 1940 and 1944 had not been cancelled because of the war, she would probably have scored an Olympic record that would have stood for many years.

Fanny Blankers-Koen was competing at London at an age when most track and field athletes are past their prime. She was 30 years old, the wife of the Netherlands track and field coach, and the mother of two boys. She was the oldest competitor at the 1948 Games.

Mrs. Blankers-Koen brought to the Olympics four womens records—the high jump, the broad jump, the 100 metre dash and the 80 metre hurdles. She also belonged to the world champion 440 and 800 metre relay teams.

Her first gold medal performance was no contest. She set an Olympic record of 11.9 in the 100 metres which was run in a cold drizzle before 84,000 spectators huddled behind turned up collars and beneath umbrellas. Three-tenths of a second behind her were Dorothy Manley of Great Britain and Shirley Strickland of Australia.

Next, Fanny Blankers-Koen equalled her own world record of 11.3 in the 80 metre hurdles and then knocked a tenth of a second off that time in winning the final the following day. She was hard pressed by Maureen Gardner of Great Britain who was just inches behind and clocked in the same time, 11.2.

The incredible Dutch blonde then became the first woman to win three individual Olympic track and field gold medals by winning the 200 metre sprint, a new event on the Olympic program. Her time of 24.4 was a tenth of a second off the record she had set in preliminaries. She was an easy winner in the final, beating Audrey Williamson of Great Britain by seven-tenths of a second.

After that race, Mrs. Blankers-Koen had to make a difficult choice. She could have tried for a fourth individual gold medal in the high jump. Instead she decided to save her energy for the 400 metre relay. In that race, the Netherlands team was well beaten until the baton was passed to her on the final leg. She ran the last 100 metres in near-record time to overtake Joyce King of Australia and give the Netherlands team the gold medal by a fifth of a second.

While Mrs. Blankers-Koen won every event on the track program, Micheline Ostermeyer of France was a double winner in the field division, winning the shot put and the discus.

With Fanny Blankers-Koen out of the high jump, Alice Coachman of the United States and Mrs. Dorothy Odam Tyler of Great Britain tied at a record 5′6¼″ with Miss Coachman winning the gold medal because of fewer misses.

The war also delayed the Olympic debut of another great runner, Emil Zatopek, who had been beating all the competition in Czechoslovakia since 1941. The 27-year-old army lieutenant was entered in the 10,000 metres, but nobody really thought he could win it, particularly with world record holder Viljo Heino of Finland in the race. Those who had heard of him thought that 10,000 metres was too far for Zatopek, who did most of his running at the 5,000 metre level.

Heino took the lead while Zatopek jogged along with the stragglers. But close to the halfway mark, Zatopek suddenly sprinted in front of Heino the Finn. The last time anybody had noticed him, he was in 27th place. He stayed with Heino for six laps and then increased his pace again and left Heino so far behind that the world champion quit, even though he was still in second place. Heino simply ran off the track and sat down with his head resting on his hands. With the pressure off, Zatopek still kept up his pace and finished 29:59.6, breaking the Olympic record which Janusz Kusocinski had set 16 years earlier. He finished almost a full lap ahead of Alain Mimoun, an Algerian running for France.

In the 5,000 metres, Zatopek was favored but lost it by a fifth of a second to Gaston Rieff of Belgium. The Czech led for nine laps when Rieff took over the lead. He gradually increased it to 60 yards coming into the final lap. By that time, Zatopek was running third, close behind Willem Slykhuis of The Netherlands. But when he heard the gun warning that the next was the last lap, Zatopek increased his pace. He easily ran down Slykhuis and set his sights on Rieff. Splashing through puddles he was gaining with every stride but failed by two yards.

Sweden made a clean sweep of the 3,000 metre steeplechase, which had been won by Finnish runners since 1924. Tore Sjostrand covered the obstacle course in 9:04.6 with Erik Elmsater and Gote Hagstrom very close behind. The best the Finns could do was fifth place.

The surprise winner of the marathon was 29-year-old Buenos Aires fireman, Delfo Cabrera. He was only considered the third best of three longshot Argentinians in the race. Former Belgian paratrooper Etienne Gailly, 22, held the lead for the first 17 miles, relinquished it to Yun Chil Choi of Korea for the next eight miles, and then went to the front again. However, he was beginning to stagger as he entered the stadium and Cabrera and Tom Richards of Great Britain easily passed him on the final lap around the track. Cabrera beat Richards by a scant 16 seconds and Gailly collapsed after finishing third.

The unexpected also occurred in the 100 metre final. Harrison Dillard, a hurdling specialist who had failed to qualify for the U.S. hurdling team, won it by equalling the Olympic record of 10.3. The 150-pound Dillard had been a mediocre track man at East Tech High School in Cleveland, the same school that produced Jesse Owens. He was not fast enough to be a sprinter there, so he switched to the hurdles.

In the U.S. Olympic trials, Dillard returned to sprinting after falling and being beaten in the hurdles by William Porter, Clyde Scott and Craig Dixon who went on to score a U.S. sweep of the 110 metre hurdles at the Olympics.

Dillard won both his heats in 10.4 seconds in the Olympic preliminaries. Mel Patton's times in the preliminaries were 10.6 and 10.4 and the veteran Barney Ewell, 31, ran both his heats in 10.5. But Patton, who held the world record for 100 yards of 9.3, and Ewell were still the favorites for the final. Dillard, starting from the outside lane, took the lead and never lost it. Ewell, on an inside lane, won a duel with Patton and Lloyd La Beach of Panama and when he felt the finish line thread snap across his chest he thought he had won and did a victory dance until the officials told him that Dillard was the winner. La Beach was third and Patton fifth.

Ewell also lost a close race in the 200 metres. He was beaten by a foot by Patton who had been ahead for the first 150 metres and then raced to the wire in a neck-and-neck duel with Ewell. Both Patton and Ewell were timed in 21.1 seconds with La Beach third again, a tenth of a second behind them.

Arthur Wint, a 6' 4" Jamaican with a stride close to 10 feet, came from behind to defeat countryman Herb McKenley, the world champion quarter miler, in the 400 metres. McKenley, who owned the world record for 400 metres and 440 yards, ran the first 200 metres in 21 seconds, faster than Patton's time for the dash, and had a four yard lead over Wint coming into the stretch. But Wint, a 26-year-old London medical student and Royal Air Force veteran, caught up to McKenley 12 yards from the tape and beat him by two yards, equalling the Olympic record of 46.2 seconds.

Mal Whitfield, who finished third in the 400 metres, beat Wint by two yards in the 800 metres. Robert Chef-D'Hotel of France was first, with Wint second and Whitfield third in the early running. At the halfway mark, Whitfield, a 23-year-old U.S. Army Air Force sergeant, took the lead and Wint dropped back to fifth, seemingly finished. But then he picked up speed again and passed everyone but Whitfield. Both runners broke the former Olympic record while French sportswriter Marcel Hansemme, who finished third, tied t.

One of the worst Olympic mixups occurred in the 400 metre relay. The U.S. team of Ewell, Dillard, Patton and Lorenzo Wright was an easy winner, but the judges disqualified them for illegal baton passing. Coach Dean Cromwell protested, but the gold medal was awarded to the runner-up British team with Italy placing second and Hungary third. Twelve days later, however, the decision was reversed. By that time, the Hungarian team had returned to Budapest with its bronze medals. It had to send them to Italy which had already passed on its silver medals to the British team who had in turn relinquished its gold medals to the U.S.

Wint, running in second place on the third leg of the 1,600 metre relay, collapsed with a cramp, ensuring another gold medal for the United States.

Henri Eriksson won the 1,500 metres although he had never before beaten Lennart Strand, the Swedish co-holder of the world record. The Swedish fireman found the sticky, wet track to his liking and passed Strand at the 1,000 metre mark and then wore him down in the sprint to the tape.

Roy Cochran, 29, won the 400 metre hurdles by six yards over Duncan White of Ceylon. His time of 51.1 was eight tenths of a second faster than the Olympic record he had posted in the trials the previous day. Rune Larsson of Sweden, who equalled the record in the trials was third.

A 17-year-old boy from Tulare, California, proved himself the most versatile athlete in the world by winning the decathlon. Bob Mathias only won one of the 10 events, the pole vault, but was good enough in the others to score 6,386 points, 122 more than his nearest rival, Ignace Heinrich of France.

On the second day of the two-day test it rained all day. Numerous delays stretched the competition to 12 hours. One delay of more than an hour occurred when officials searched the turf to find the mark where Mathias' discus throw had come down. An official had accidentally picked up the flag which marked it.

Finnish movie actor Tapio Rautavarra won the javelin with a throw of 228'10⅞", beating American osteopath Dr. Steve Seymour by seven feet three inches.

The Americans swept the shot put. Wilbur Thompson won with a toss of 56′ 2″, followed by Jim Delaney and Yale football star Jim Fuchs. All three broke the former Olympic record.

Guinn Smith, a 28-year-old U.S. Army Air Force veteran who ignored medical advice to quit athletics because of a knee injury, won the pole vault with a leap of 14′ 1$\frac{5}{16}$″. The vaulters were severely handicapped by rain and huddled in a tunnel between jumps.

High jump champion John Winter pulled a back muscle when he cleared 6′ 4¾″. But the 22-year-old Australian bank clerk recovered to clear 6′ 6″, win, and beat three Americans who had all cleared 6′ 8″ in previous competition.

Capt. William Grut of Sweden won the pentathlon. He was the first athlete to win three events in the competition—riding, fencing and swimming.

Mrs. Vicki Manalo Draves of Pasadena, California, became the first woman to win both the Olympic platform and springboard diving titles.

The United States took 12 of the 16 swimming events. The 800 metre relay team of Wayne Moore, Bill Woolsey, Ford Konno and 17-year-old Jimmy McLane set a world record 8:31.1. McLane also won the 1,500 metres, but lost to Bill Smith of Honolulu in the 400 metres.

With Britain being the home of the famous Henley Regatta, there was more than a casual interest in the rowing events. British veterans John Wilson and Stanley Laurie astonished the experts by defeating Josef and Hans Kalt of Switzerland in the pairs without coxswain. They were both 40 years old and had not been in regular competition since before the war until training started for the Olympics. Almost as unbelievable was the victory of Britishers Dick Burnell and Bert Bushnell in the double skulls. They had rowed together for the first time only a few weeks before the Olympics, but had got along so well together that they beat Age Larsen and Ebbe Parsner of Denmark by one and one half lengths.

A major disappointment was the failure of world champion Jack Kelly, jr., in the single skulls, the event his father had won in 1920. Weakened by a cold, he was beaten by Eduardo Risso of Uruguay in the semifinals. Mervyn Wood of Australia beat Risso in the final.

For a while, there was more fighting among the fans in one of the boxing competitions than there was in the ring. Edward Johnson of the United States had decisioned Ben Alves of Uruguay in a preliminary featherweight bout. The unpopular decision caused 20 minutes of booing and brawling that almost reached riot proportions. Two officials got into a violent argument on the judges' stand and almost came to blows before they were separated by two other officials. Alves' supporters carried him onto the judges' stand to protest the decision. Guards pushed them away, but Alves broke free and ran around the arena, waving to the partisan crowd. Meanwhile, the officials tried to get another bout going, but the boxers were ignored by the shouting crowd.

OFFICIAL XIV OLYMPIAD RESULTS

London, 1948

TRACK AND FIELD—MEN

100 Metres
1. W. H. Dillard, U.S.—10.3
2. H. N. Ewell, U.S.—10.4
3. L. La Beach, Panama—10.4

200 Metres
1. M. Patton, U.S.—21.1
2. N. Ewell, U.S.—21.1
3. L. La Beach, Panama—21.2

400 Metres
1. A. Wint, Jamaica—46.2
2. H. McKenley, Jamaica—46.4
3. M. Whitfield, U.S.—46.9

800 Metres
1. M. Whitfield, U.S.—1:49.2
2. A. Wint, Jamaica—1:49.5
3. M. Hansenne, France—1:49.8

1,500 Metres
1. H. Eriksson, Sweden—3:49.8
2. L. Strand, Sweden—3:50.4
3. W. Slykhuis, Netherlands—3:50.4

5,000 Metres
1. G. Rieff, Belgium—14:17.6
2. E. Zatopek, Czech.—14:17.8
3. W. Slykhuis, Neth.—14:26.8

10,000 Metres
1. E. Zatopek, Czech.—25:59.6
2. A. Mimoun, France—30:47.4
3. B. Albertsson, Sweden—30:53.6

Marathon
1. D. Cabrera, Argentina—2:34:51.6
2. T. Richards, Gt. Brit.—2:35:07.6
3. E. Gailly, Belgium—2:35:33.6

110 Metres Hurdles
1. W. Porter, U.S.—13.9
2. C. Scott, U.S.—14.1
3. C. Dixon, U.S.—14.1

400 Metres Hurdles
1. R. Cochran, U.S.—51.1
2. D. White, Ceylon—51.8
3. R. Larsson, Sweden—52.2

3,000 Metres Steeplechase
1. T. Sjostrand, Sweden—9:04.6
2. E. Elmsater, Sweden—9:08.2
3. G. Hagstrom, Sweden—9:11.8

400 Metres Relay
1. U.S.—40.6
2. Great Britain—41.3
3. Italy—41.5

1,600 Metres Relay
1. U.S.—3:10.4
2. France—3:14.8
3. Sweden—3:16.3

10,000 Metres Walk
1. J. F. Mikaelsson, Sweden—45:13.2

50,000 Metres Walk
1. J. Ljunggren, Sweden—4:41.52.0
2. G. Godel, Switzerland—4:48.17.0
3. T. Johnson, Gt. Brit.—4:48.31.0

High Jump
1. J. Winter, Australia—6'5 15/16"
2. B. Paulsen, Norway—6'4 3/4"
3. G. Stanich, U.S.—6'4 3/4"

Broad Jump
1. W. Steele, U.S.—25'8 1/15"
2. T. Bruce, Australia—24'9 7/16"
3. H. Douglas, U.S.—24'9"

Triple Jump
1. A. Ahman, Sweden—50'6 5/16"
2. G. Avery, Australia—50'5"
3. R. Sarialp, Turkey—49'3 1/2"

Pole Vault
1. O. G. Smith, U.S.—14'1 5/16"
2. E. Kataja, Finland—13'9 3/4"
3. R. Richards, U.S.—13'9 3/8"

Shot Put
1. W. Thompson, U.S.—56'2"
2. J. Delaney, U.S.—54'8 11/16"
3. J. Fuchs, U.S.—53'10 1/2"

Discus Throw
1. A. Consolini, Italy—173'2"
2. G. Tosi, Italy—169'10 1/2"
3. F. Gordien, U.S.—166'6 13/16"

Hammer Throw
1. I. Nemeth, Hungary—183'11 1/2"
2. I. Gubijan, Yugoslavia—178'0 5/8"
3. R. Bennet, U.S.—176'3 3/8"

Javelin Throw
1. T. Rautavaara, Finland—228'10 7/8"
2. S. Seymour, U.S.—221'8"
3. J. Varszegi, Hungary—219'10 11/16"

Decathlon
1. R. Mathias, U.S.
2. I. Heinrich, France
3. F. Simmons, U.S.

TRACK AND FIELD—WOMEN

100 Metres
1. F. Blankers-Koen, Neth.—11.9
2. D. Manley, Great Britain—12.2
3. S. Strickland, Australia—12.2

200 Metres
1. F. Blankers-Koen, Neth.—24.4
2. A. Williamson, Gt. Brit.—25.1
3. A. Patterson, U.S.—25.2

80 Metres Hurdles
1. F. Blankers-Koen, Neth.—11.2
2. M. Gardner, Gt. Brit.—11.2
3. S. Strickland, Australia—11.4

400 Metres Relay
1. Netherlands—47.5
2. Australia—47.6
3. Canada—47.8

High Jump
1. A. Coachman, U.S.—5'6 1/4"
2. D. Tyler, Great Britain—5'6 1/4"
3. M. Ostermeyer, France—5'3 3/8"

Long Jump
1. O. Gyarmati, Hungary—18'8 1/4"
2. S. de Portela, Argentina—18'4 1/2"
3. A. Leyman, Sweden—18'3 1/2"

Javelin Throw
1. H. Bauma, Austria—149'6"
2. K. Parviainen, Finland—143'8"
3. L. Carlstedt, Denmark—140'5"

Shot Put
1. M. Ostermeyer, France—45'1 1/2"
2. A. Piccinini, Italy—42'11 1/2"
3. I. Schaffer, Austria—42'10 1/2"

Discus Throw
1. M. Ostermeyer, France—137'6 3/8"
2. V. E. Cordiale, Italy—135'0 7/8"
3. J. Mazeas, France—132'7 3/8"

SWIMMING AND DIVING—MEN

100 Metres Free-Style
1. W. Ris, U.S.—57.3
2. A. Ford, U.S.—57.8
3. G. Kadas, Hungary—58.1

400 Metres Free-Style
1. W. Smith, U.S.—4:41.0
2. J. McLane, U.S.—4:43.4
3. J. Marshall, Australia—4:47.7

1,500 Metres Free-Style
1. J. McLane, U.S.—19:18.5
2. J. Marshall, Australia—19:31.3
3. G. Mitro, Hungary—19:43.2

200 Metres Breast Stroke
1. J. Verdeur, U.S.—2:39.3
2. K. Carter, U.S.—2:40.2
3. R. Sohl, U.S.—2:43.9

800 Metres Free-Style Relay
1. U.S.—8:46.0
2. Hungary—8:48.4
3. France—9:08.0

Platform Diving
1. S. Lee, U.S.
2. B. Harlan, U.S.
3. J. Capilla, Mexico

Springboard Diving
1. B. Harlan, U.S.   2. M. Anderson, U.S.   3. S. Lee, U.S.

SWIMMING AND DIVING—WOMEN

100 Metres Free-Style
1. G. Andersen, Denmark—1:06.3
2. A. Curtis, U.S.—1:06.5
3. M. Vaessen, Neth.—1:07.6

100 Metres Backstroke
1. K. Harup, Denmark—1:14.4
2. S. Zimmerman, U.S.—1:16.0
3. J. J. Davies, Australia—1:16.7

400 Metres Free-Style
1. A. Curtis, U.S.—5:17.8
2. K. Harup, Denmark—5:21.2
3. C. Gibson, Great Britain—5:22.5

400 Metres Free-Style Relay
1. U.S.—4:29.2
2. Denmark—4:29.6
3. Netherlands—4:31.6

200 Metres Breast Stroke
1. P. van Vliet, Neth.—2:57.2
2. B. Lyons, Australia—2:57.7
3. E. Novak, Hungary—3:00.2

Platform Diving
1. V. Draves, U.S.
2. P. Elsener, U.S.
3. B. Christoffersen, Denmark

Springboard Diving
1. V. Dawes, U.S.   2. Z. A. Olsen, U.S.   3. P. Elsener, U.S.

BOXING

Flyweight
1. P. Perez, Argentina
2. S. Bandinelli, Italy
3. S. A. Han, Korea

Welterweight
1. J. Torma, Czechoslovakia
2. H. Herring, U.S.
3. A. Ottavio, Italy

Bantamweight
1. T. Csik, Hungary
2. G. Zuddas, Italy
3. J. Venegas, Puerto Rico

Middleweight
1. L. Papp, Hungary
2. J. Wright, Great Britain
3. I. Fontana, Italy

Featherweight
1. E. Formenti, Italy
2. D. Shepherd, South Africa
3. A. Antkeiwicz, Poland

Light-Heavyweight
1. G. Hunter, South Africa
2. D. Scott, Great Britain
3. M. Cia, Argentina

Lightweight
1. G. Dreyer, South Africa
2. J. Vissers, Belgium
3. S. Wad, Denmark

Heavyweight
1. R. Iglesias, Argentina
2. G. Nilsson, Sweden
3. J. Arthur, South Africa

WRESTLING

Free-Style—Flyweight
1. L. Viitala, Finland
2. H. Balamir, Turkey
3. T. Johansson, Sweden

Free-Style—Welterweight
1. Y. Dogu, Turkey
2. R. Garrard, Australia
3. L. Mervill, U.S.

Free-Style—Bantamweight
1. N. Akkar, Turkey
2. G. Leeman, U.S.
3. C. Kouyos, France

Free-Style—Middleweight
1. G. Brand, U.S.
2. A. Candemir, Turkey
3. E. Linden, Sweden

Free-Style—Featherweight
1. G. Bilge, Turkey
2. I. Sjolin, Sweden
3. A. Muller, Switzerland

Free-Style—Light-Heavyweight
1. H. Wittenberg, U.S.
2. F. Stockli, Switzerland
3. B. Fahlkvist, Sweden

Free-Style—Lightweight
1. C. Atik, Turkey
2. G. Frandfors, Sweden
3. H. Baumann, Switzerland

Free-Style—Heavyweight
1. G. Bobis, Hungary
2. B. Antonsson, Sweden
3. J. Armstrong, Australia

Greco-Roman—Flyweight
1. P. Lombardi, Italy
2. K. Olcay, Turkey
3. R. Kangasmaki, Finland

Greco-Roman—Bantamweight
1. K. Pettersson, Sweden
2. M. H. Aly, Egypt
3. H. Kaya, Turkey

Greco-Roman—Featherweight
1. M. Oktav, Turkey
2. O. Anderberg, Sweden
3. F. Toth, Hungary

Greco-Roman—Lightweight
1. K. Freij, Sweden
2. A. Eriksen, Norway
3. K. Ferencz, Hungary

Greco-Roman—Welterweight
1. G. Andersson, Sweden
2. M. Szilvasi, Hungary
3. C. Hansen, Denmark

Greco-Roman—Middleweight
1. A. Gronberg, Sweden
2. M. Tavfur, Turkey
3. E. Gallegatti, Italy

Greco-Roman—Light-Heavyweight
1. K. Nilsson, Sweden
2. K. Grondahl, Finland
3. I. Orapi, Egypt

Greco-Roman—Heavyweight
1. A. Kirecci, Turkey
2. T. Nilsson, Sweden
3. G. Fantoni, Italy

WEIGHT-LIFTING

Bantamweight
1. J. de Pietro, U.S.—678 lb.
2. J. Creus, Great Britain—655¾ lb.
3. R. Tom, U.S.—650¼ lb.

Featherweight
1. M. Fayad, Egypt—733 lb.
2. R. Wilkes, Trinidad—700 lb.
3. J. Salmassi, Iran—689 lb.

Lightweight
1. I. Shams, Egypt—793½ lb.
2. A. Hammouda, Egypt—793½ lb.
3. J. Halliday, Gt. Brit.—749½ lb.

Middleweight
1. F. Spellman, U.S.—860 lb.
2. P. George, U.S.—843¼ lb.
3. S. Kim, Korea—837¾ lb.

Light-Heavyweight
1. S. Stanczyk, U.S.—920½ lb.
2. H. Sakata, U.S.—837¾ lb.
3. G. Magnusson, Sweden—826¾ lb.

Heavyweight
1. J. Davis, U.S.—996½ lb.
2. N. Schemansky, U.S.—937 lb.
3. A. Charite, Neth.—909¼ lb.

CYCLING

1,000 Metres Sprint
1. M. Ghella, Italy
2. R. Harris, Great Britain
3. A. Schandorff, Denmark

1,000 Metres Time-Trial
1. J. Dupont, France—1:13.5
2. P. Nihant, Belgium—1:14.5
3. T. Godwin, Gt. Brit.—1:15.0

2,000 Metres Tandem
1. R. Perona/F. Teruzzi, Italy
2. R. Harris/A. Bannister, Gt. Brit.
3. G. Dron/R. Faye, France

4,000 Metres Team Pursuit
1. France—4:57.8
2. Italy—5:36.7
3. Great Britain—5:55.8

Road-Race—Individual
1. J. Beyaert, France—5:18:12.6
2. G. Voorting, Neth.—5:18:16.2
3. L. Wouters, Belgium—5:18:16.2

Road-Race—Team
1. Belgium—15:18:17.4
2. Great Britain—16:03:31.6
3. France—16:08:19.4

EQUESTRIAN SPORTS

Grand Prix Jumping—Individual
1. H. Mariles, Mexico
2. R. Uriza, Mexico
3. J. d'Orgeix, France

Grand Prix Jumping—Team
1. Mexico
2. Spain
3. Great Britain

Grand Prix—Dressage—Individual
1. H. Moser, Switzerland
2. A. Jousseaume, France
3. G. Boltenstern, Sweden

Grand Prix—Dressage—Team
1. France
2. U.S.
3. Portugal

Three-Day Event—Individual
1. B. Chevallier, France
2. F. Henry, U.S.
3. J. R. Selfelt, Sweden

Three-Day Event—Team
1. U.S.
2. Sweden
3. Mexico

FENCING—MEN

Foil—Individual
1. J. Buhan, France
2. C. d'Oriola, France
3. L. Maszlay, Hungary

Foil—Team
1. France
2. Italy
3. Belgium

Epée—Individual
1. L. Cantone, Italy
2. O. Zappelli, Switzerland
3. E. Mangiarotti, Italy

Epée—Team
1. France
2. Italy
3. Sweden

Sabre—Individual
1. A. Gerevich, Hungary
2. V. Pinton, Italy
3. P. Kovacs, Hungary

Sabre—Team
1. Hungary
2. Italy
3. U.S.

FENCING—WOMEN

Foil—Individual
1. I. Elek, Hungary
2. K. Lachmann, Denmark
3. E. Preis, Austria

GYMNASTICS—MEN

Combined Exercises—Individual
1. V. Huhtanen, Finland
2. W. Lehmann, Switzerland
3. P. Aaltonen, Finland

Combined Exercises—Team
1. Finland
2. Switzerland
3. Hungary

Floor Exercises
1. F. Pataki, Hungary
2. J. Mogyorosi, Hungary
3. Z. Ruzicka, Czechoslovakia

Horizontal Bar
1. J. Stalder, Switzerland
2. W. Lehmann, Switzerland
3. V. Huhtanen, Finland

Parallel Bars
1. M. Reusch, Switzerland
2. V. Huhtanen, Finland
3. {C. Kipfer, Switzerland
  {J. Stalder, Switzerland.

Pommelled Horse
1. {P. Aaltonen, Finland
  {V. Huhtanen, Finland
  {H. Savolainen, Finland

Long Horse Vault
1. P. Aaltonen, Finland
2. O. Rove, Finland
3. {J. Mogyorosi, Hungary
  {F. Pataki, Hungary

Rings
1. K. Frei, Switzerland
2. M. Reusch, Switzerland
3. Z. Ruzicka, Czechoslovakia

GYMNASTICS—WOMEN

Combined Exercises—Team
1. Czechoslovakia
2. Hungary
3. U.S.

ROWING

Single Sculls
1. M. Wood, Australia—7:24.4
2. E. Risso, Uruguay—7:38.2
3. R. Catasta, Italy—7:51.4

Double Sculls
1. B. H. Bushnell/R. Burnell, Great Britain—6:51.3
2. A. Larsen/E. Parsner, Denmark—6:55.3
3. J. Rodriguez/W. Jones, Uruguay—7:12.4

Coxswainless Pairs
1. J. Wilson/W. S. Laurie, Great Britain—7:21.1
2. J. Kalt/H. Kalt, Switz.—7:23.9
3. B. Boni/F. Fanetti, Italy—7:31.

Coxed Pairs
1. Denmark—8:00.5
2. Italy—8:12.2
3. Hungary—8:25.2

Coxswainless Fours
1. Italy—6:39.0
2. Denmark—6:43.5
3. U.S.—6:47.7

Coxed Fours
1. U.S.—6:50.3
2. Switzerland—6:53.3
3. Denmark—6:58.6

Eights
1. U.S.—5:56.7
   University of California
2. Great Britain—6:06.9
3. Norway—6:10.3

CANOEING—MEN

Kayak Singles—1,000 Metres
1. G. Frederiksson, Sweden—4:33.2
2. J. Andersen, Denmark—4:39.9
3. H. Eberhardt, France—4:41.4

Canadian Singles—1,000 Metres
1. J. Holecek, Czech.—5:42.0
2. D. Bennett, Canada—5:53.3
3. R. Boutigny, France—5:55.9

Kayak Pairs—1,000 Metres
1. H. Berglund/L. Klungstrom, Sweden—4:07.3
2. E. Hansen/J. Jensen, Denmark—4:07.5
3. T. Axelsson/N. Bjoerkloef, Finland—4:08.7

Canadian Pairs—1,000 Metres
1. J. Brzak/B. Kudrna, Czechoslovakia—5:07.1
2. S. Lysak/S. Macknowski, U.S.—5:08.2
3. G. Dransart/G. Gandil, France—5:15.2

CANOEING—WOMEN

Kayak Singles—500 Metres
1. K. Hoff, Denmark—2:31.9
2. A. V. Anker-Doedans, Netherlands—2:32.8
3. F. Schwingl, Austria—2:32.9

YACHTING

Dragon
1. "Pan," Norway
2. "Slaghoken," Sweden
3. "Snap," Denmark

Star
1. "Hilarius," U.S.
2. "Kurush II," Cuba
3. "Starita," Netherlands

SHOOTING

Free Pistol
1. C. Vasquez, Peru
2. R. Shnyder, Switzerland
3. T. Ullmann, Sweden

Free Rifle
1. E. Grunig, Switzerland
2. P. Janhonen, Finland
3. W. Rogeberg, Norway

Automatic Pistol
1. K. Takacs, Hungary
2. E. D. S. Valiente, Argentina
3. S. Lundquist, Sweden

Small-Bore Rifle—Prone
1. A. Cook, U.S.
2. W. Tomsen, U.S.
3. J. Jonsson, Sweden

MODERN PENTATHLON
1. W. Grut, Sweden
2. G. Moore, U.S.
3. G. Gardin, Sweden

BASKETBALL
1. U.S.
2. France
3. Brazil

SOCCER
1. Sweden
2. Yugoslavia
3. Denmark

FIELD HOCKEY
1. India
2. Great Britain
3. Netherlands

WATER POLO
1. Italy
2. Hungary
3. Netherlands

Chapter 13

THE XV OLYMPIAD

Helsinki, 1952

RUSSIA had not entered Olympic competition since 1912. After World War II, they showed a new interest in athletics, but were reluctant to enter international competitions until they were convinced they could win. They sent observers to the Olympic Games of 1948 in London and by 1952, decided that their government-subsidized athletes had developed sufficiently to defeat the United States.

They almost made it. The Russians were ahead in the unofficial scoring until the last day when the Americans scored 111 points to defeat them 614-553½.

However, it was a Communist from another country who turned in the most remarkable individual performance at Helsinki. Emil Zatopek, who was promoted to captain in the Czechoslovakian army after winning the 10,000 metre race at London, set Olympic records for the 5,000 metres, 10,000 metres and the marathon. Zatopek, by now billed as the "human locomotive" because of his seemingly endless energy and his flailing style, thus inherited Paavo Nurmi's title as the world's greatest distance runner.

Nurmi made a surprise appearance at the opening ceremonies to the delight of the 90,000 spectators who packed the stadium despite a downpour of rain. The Finns went into a frenzy of hysterical adulation when they realized that the man bearing the Olympic torch into the stadium was the still easy striding Nurmi, by now a 56-year-old living legend who had established 19 world records for distances between 1,500 and 20,000 metres and had won seven Olympic gold medals.

The flying Finn ran one lap and then handed the torch to another Finnish hero of the past, Hannes Kolehmainen—the double gold medal winner of 1912 who ignited the Olympic flame. It was a touch of showmanship unmatched in the Olympic Games and the crowd seemed limp from prolonged shouting and applause.

Nurmi watched the Games from a VIP box and saw Zatopek win the three distance races including the marathon, the race that Nurmi had hoped to win in the 1932 Olympics at Los Angeles.

Before Zatopek's first appearance, there had been some doubt about his condition. He had been sick for part of the year and shortly before the Olympics, he was beaten by Vladimir Kazantzev of Russia in a 5,000 metre race. Alain Mimoun, an Algerian representing France who had finished second to Zatopek in the 10,000 at London, and Aleksandr Anufriayev of Russia were expected to be his toughest competitors in the 10,000 metre race. Zatopek did not take the lead until the sixth lap, and later lost it momentarily to British bank clerk Gordon Pirie. When Zatopek regained the lead on the next lap the race was over. Mimoun made a determined bid to catch him towards the end, but the 30-year-old Czech beat him by nearly 100 metres in 29 minutes, 17 seconds. This was 42.6 seconds faster than he had run in the London Olympics. Anufriayev was third, giving Russia its first Olympic track medal.

In a trial heat for the 5,000 metres, Zatopek had the race won easily when he beckoned Anufriayev to pass him and take the race. In another heat, Herbert Schade of Germany broke the Olympic record by more than two seconds in 14:15.4. In the final, Zatopek took the lead and lost it five times. Finally he bounded from fourth place to first in the stretch to win by five yards over Mimoun again. He alternated with Schade in setting the pace for the first half. Gaston Rieff, who had beaten Zatopek in the 5,000 at London, collapsed after trying to keep up with the Czech. Zatopek was in front going into the last lap when Schade, Chris Chataway of Great Britain and Mimoun passed him. On the last turn, Chataway sprinted to the front but tripped, at which point Zatopek sprinted past Mimoun and Schade. Chataway finished fifth.

Shortly after the 5,000 metre race, Zatopek sat on the sidelines and proudly watched his wife, the former Dana Ingrova, throw the javelin almost 20 feet beyond her personal record to set a new Olympic record of 165′ 7″. They had become engaged during the 1948 Olympics and were married shortly afterwards. With Zatopek's 5,000 metre victory and his wife's javelin triumph, they became the only husband and wife team to win Olympic gold medals on the same day.

On the final day of the track and field portion of the Olympics, Zatopek decided to run the marathon, although he had never competed beyond 10,000 metres in his life. The temptation to win a third gold medal was too much and Zatopek was confident his stamina would last the 26 miles. After 10 miles, he overtook Jim Peters of Great Britain, but Peters stayed on his heels for another 10 miles before dropping back. There was no more competition to worry about, but Zatopek kept up his fast pace and won in a world record 2:23:03.2, finishing almost half a mile ahead of Reinaldo Gorno of Argentina. The defending champion, Delfo Cabrera, also of Argentina, was sixth but still ran a faster time than the former Olympic record set by Kitei Son of Japan in 1936.

The 3,000 metre steeplechase, the only distance event that Zatopek did not compete in, seemed to belong to Russia's Vladimir Kazantsev, the world record holder at 8:48.6. In a trial heat, he broke the Olympic record in 8:58. However, Horace Ashenfelter, a 29-year-old FBI agent, lowered the mark to 8:51 in winning his heat.

The Russian, however, was still favoured to win the final as he had not been pressed in his trial heat and Ashenfelter was not considered to be much more than a washed up distance runner who had just recently learned how to negotiate the obstacle course. In the trial, he had been running far above his head and could never do it again, or so they said.

Kazantsev decided that Ashenfelter was the only one he had to worry about and stayed one or two strides behind him, even though the American was far behind the leaders. On the last lap, the Russian passed Ashenfelter and went on to take the lead, but the FBI man stayed close behind him. At the last and most difficult obstacle, the high water jump, Kazantsev jumped into the deepest part of the moat and looked up to see

Ashenfelter make a dry jump right over him. Before the Russian could get out of the water, Ashenfelter had a six yard lead and went on to win by 30 yards and lower his own Olympic record.

Even more of an upset was the victory of 24-year-old Josef Barthel. in the metric mile, giving Luxemburg its first Olympic gold medal. Barthel was considered to be the least likely winner among the eight starters with co-world record holders Werner Lueg, 23, of Germany, and British medical student Roger Bannister the joint favorites. Barthel was last for most of the first half and then shot up to second place behind Lueg who had the lead right from the start. When Barthel started catching up to Lueg, the German turned his head to see why the crowd was making a big noise. He found out when he looked again. Barthel had passed him, and another early straggler, Bob McMillen of the U.S., sprinted the last 100 yards in 10 seconds to finish ahead of Lueg with Bannister fourth. Barthel's time set an Olympic record for the 1,500 metres of 3:45.1 and all eight runners finished ahead of Dr. Jack Lovelock's 1936 record of 3:47.8.

In 1948 at London, Mal Whitfield defeated Arthur Wint of Jamaica in the 800 metres in an Olympic record 1:49.2. And at Helsinki, Whitfield again beat Wint in 1:49.2. This time, the U.S. Air Force sergeant confidently ran in last place for most of the first half and was third behind Wint and Heinz Ulzheimer of Germany after 400 metres. He took the lead going into the final turn.

A few days later, Whitfield tried to win a second gold medal in the 400 metres, but he had been weakened by a cold and finished last behind Wint, the defending champion. World record holder George Rhoden of Jamaica was in front all the way, defeating veteran Herb McKenley, another Jamaican trained in the U.S., in an Olympic record 45.9 seconds. It was the second silver medal in a row for McKenley. He had finished second to Wint in 1948.

The hard luck McKenley also finished second in the 100 metre dash. He beat Lindy Remigino in the semifinal and thought he had beaten him again in the final. But when Remigino was congratulating McKenley, an official told them that the electro-timer had caught Remigino's chest hitting the tape a fraction of an inch ahead of McKenley who had made a finishing dive. The 21-year-old Remigino had never dreamed he would be an Olympic champion. He was at best only the fifth fastest sprinter in the United States and had considered retiring three months before the Games. But coach George Eastman talked him out of it after his two fastest sprinters—Jim Golliday and Andy Stanfield came down with muscle injuries. The third best sprinter, Arthur Bragg, also pulled a muscle in a semifinal and Dean Smith finished fourth in the final, behind McDonald Bailey of Great Britain.

The United States scored a triple in the 200 metres with Andy Stanfield, equalling Jesse Owen's Olympic record of 20.7 seconds. The judges had to study the photo before giving the silver medal to Thane Baker over Jim Gathers.

Stanfield had been groomed as the successor to Owens. He did the same things equally well, sprint and broad jump. But recurring muscle injuries prevented him from reaching his potential and he had to stop broad jumping. He had equalled the world record in the 100 metres but did not compete at that distance in the Olympics because he felt his legs could only stand up for one event.

However, with the United States trailing Russia in points going into the final day, Stanfield was persuaded to run in the 400 metre relay race and he anchored the U.S. team to a victory over Russia.

Wint, McKenley, Rhoden and Leslie Lang gave Jamaica the 1,600 metre relay in a world record 3:03.9, beating the U.S., team, which also bettered the former record, by a tenth of a second.

Harrison Dillard, the champion who failed to make the U.S. hurdling team in 1948 but consoled himself with a 100 metre win, finally won the gold medal in his favorite event—the 110 metres high hurdles. Dillard and teammate Jack Davis were neck and neck until the last jump where Davis tripped the hurdle and lost by inches with Art Barnard third for another U.S. sweep.

In the 400 metre hurdles, Charles Moore of the U.S. had never been beaten. He also had a score to settle for his father, Crip Moore, who had been on the U.S. Olympic team in 1924 but failed to win a medal. Moore set an Olympic record 50.8 in a preliminary heat and the next day he equalled it in winning the final by four yards over Yuriy Lituyev of Russia on a slow track.

Giuseppe Bordoni of Italy set a world record of 4:28:07.8 in the 50 kilometres walk and celebrated by going for a stroll in Helsinki that evening. John Mikaelsson of Sweden, the defending champion, lowered his own Olympic record in the 10,000 metre walk by a fifth of a second.

Bob Mathias, by now a fullback on the Stanford University team, became the first man to win two Olympic decathlon championships. After that, he announced his retirement at the age of 21. Milt Campbell was second and Floyd Simmons was third for a U.S. sweep. Ignace Heinrich of France, who had beaten Simmons for the silver medal in 1948, retired before the end of the 22-hour, two-day competition, although he was fourth at the time.

The United States also finished 1-2-3 in the shot put. Parry O'Brien won it on his first heave of 57' 1½", an Olympic record, but that only beat teammate Darrow Hooper by less than an inch. World record holder Jim Fuchs was third for the second Olympiad in a row.

The defending champion hammer thrower, Imre Nemeth of Hungary, had been tutoring a 20-year-old protégé, and the pupil, Jozsef Czermak, beat the master. Czermak set an Olympic record 187' 8.04" to qualify and then raised it to 197' 11.5" in the final which bettered Nemeth's world record by more than 17 inches. Nemeth finished third behind Karl Storch of Germany.

Cy Young celebrated his 24th birthday by giving the United States its first javelin championship. The California rancher beat U.S. Marine Bill Miller while the Finnish favorite, Toivo Hyytaiainen, was a disappointing third.

Sim Iness, another Californian, broke the Olympic record six times, every throw bettering the previous one, to defeat the defending discus champion, Adolfo Consolino of Italy.

High jump champion Walter Davis' early career was similar to that of Ray Ewry, who won 10 Olympic jumping medals between 1900 and 1905. Like Ewry, Davis took up athletics to build up his strength after a serious illness. He had polio when he was eight years old. By the time he was 10, he had recovered but was weak and began mild exercises. Two years later, he was growing like a weed and took up jumping and basketball to take advantage of his height. He was 21 years old when he competed in the Olympics and jumped three quarters of an inch over his own height of 6' 8" to win the medal.

Pfc. Jerry Biffle of the U.S. Army won the long jump at 24' 10" after compatriot George Brown, who had exceeded 26 feet several times, fouled on all of his three tries.

Adhemar Ferreira da Silva of Brazil smashed his own world record four times in winning the triple jump at 53' $2\frac{9}{16}$", almost half a foot better than the record he had set the previous year.

Rev. Bob Richards, 26, and Don Laz both out of the University of Illinois, battled for the pole vault title after the rest of the competition had been eliminated. When Laz had failed three times at 14' ¼", Richards cleared 14' 11⅛" on his last jump.

Marjorie Jackson, 20, of Australia, was a double winner in the 100 and 200 metre dashes. She equalled the world record of 11.5 seconds in both the semi-final and final of the 100 metres and set a world record of 23.4 seconds in a semi-final of the 200 metres. In the final, her time of 23.7 seconds was still good enough to beat Bertha Brouwer of Holland by half a second.

Another Australian, Shirley Strickland de la Hunty ran the 80 metre hurdles in a world record 10.9, a tenth of a second faster than the world record she had set in the qualifying round. Thirty-four-year-old Fanny Blankers-Koen, who won four gold medals in 1948, equalled her own Olympic record of 11.2 in a qualifying heat, but was among the also-rans in the final.

The Olympic record was broken 21 times in the women's shot put competition, won by Russian giantess

Galina Zybina with a world record 50′ 1½″; and three other Russian amazons made a sweep of the discus won by Nina Romashkova.

In the broad jump, four women broke the record within minutes of each other in the trials. One of them, Yvette Williams of New Zealand, lowered the record to 20′ 5⅝″ to beat Alexandra Chudina of Russia by four inches in the final.

No less than 151 records were broken at Helsinki. In the men's track and field, there were six world records and 19 Olympic records. And the women set eight Olympic records, including four world records.

In swimming, Olympic records were broken in all 14 events. Clarke Scholes of the United States set a record of 57.1 in the preliminaries of the 100 metres but almost lost the final to Hiroshi Suzuki of Japan. Scholes started off too fast and was tiring at the end when Suzuki nearly caught up to him. They were both timed at 57.4 seconds. Gaston Boiteux of France was so excited about his 17-year-old son, Jean, winning the 400 metre free style that he jumped into the pool fully clothed to embrace him. And Ford Konno of the U.S. who finished second to Boiteux in the 400, defeated Shiro Hashisume of Japan by almost nine seconds in the 1,500 metres. Konno then teamed with Jimmy McLane, Bill Woolsey and Wayne Moore to defeat the Japanese team in the 800 metre relay.

Major Sammy Lee, a Korean serving with the U.S. Army Medical Corps, successfully defended his 1948 platform diving championship and Skippy Browning led an American sweep of the springboard diving competition. He defeated Miller Anderson, who had finished second to Bruce Harlan of the U.S. in 1948.

Mrs. Patricia McCormick helped the United States to overhaul Russia's point total on the final day of competition by winning both of the women's diving medals. There was an American sweep in the platform division with Paula Jean Myers and Juno Irwin getting silver and bronze medals.

Hungary won all but one of the gold medals in the women's swimming events with Katalin Szoke winning the 100 metres freestyle, Valeria Gyenge the 400 metres, Eva Szekely the 200 metres breast stroke. Miss

Szoke also anchored the 400 metres relay team to victory. A South African, Joan Harrison, won the 100 metres backstroke.

In rowing, defending champion Mervyn Wood of Australia lost the single skulls to Yuri Tyukalov of Russia. And Chuck Logg, Jr., son of the Rutgers rowing coach, and Tom Price came from behind to upset the Belgian and Swiss pairs without coxswain. A team from the U.S. Naval Academy easily won the eights over a surprising Russian team which upset Australia, Great Britain and Germany.

Ingemar Johansson, later to become world heavyweight boxing champion, was disqualified in the final bout, giving the gold medal to Edward Sanders of the United States.

Floyd Patterson, the man that Johansson later beat for the heavyweight championship, was still a growing middleweight at the Olympics. He won a gold medal beating Vasile Tita of Roumania in the final.

Three other Americans—Nate Brooks, Charles Atkins and Norval Lee—also won gold medals.

George Genereux, 17, gave Canada its first Olympic gold medal since 1936 by winning the trapshooting championship when Sweden's Knut Holmquist missed the 24th of his final shots to lose by one bird. Genereux learned his marksmanship by picking off prairie chickens with his father on their Saskatchewan farm.

The United States and Russia swept the weightlifting competitions, with Pete George, Tommy Kono, Norbert Schemansky and John Davis getting four gold medals and Russia the other three.

The United States won the basketball championship, beating Russia 86-58 and 36-25. Uruguay, which finished third, was involved in the only ugly incident of the Olympics. In its game against France, Wilfredo Palaez hit American referee Vincent Farrell in the eye after he had called a foul on an Uruguayan player and the rest of the South American players and their fans joined in the ensuing melee which police had to break up.

OFFICIAL XV OLYMPIAD RESULTS

Helsinki, 1952

TRACK AND FIELD—MEN

100 Metres
1. L. Remigino, U.S.—10.4
2. H. McKenley, Jamaica—10.4
3. E. M. Bailey, Gt. Brit.—10.4

200 Metres
1. A. Stanfield, U.S.—20.7
2. T. Baker, U.S.—20.8
3. J. Bathers, U.S.—20.8

400 Metres
1. G. Rhoden, Jamaica—45.9
2. H. McKenley, Jamaica—45.9
3. M. Whitfield, U.S.—46.8

800 Metres
1. M. Whitfield, U.S.—1:49.2
2. A. Wint, Jamaica—1:49.4
3. H. Ulzheimer, Germany—1:49.7

1,500 Metres
1. J. Barthel, Luxemburg—3:45.2
2. R. McMillen, U.S.—3:45.2
3. W. Lueg, Germany—3:45.4

5,000 Metres
1. E. Zatopek, Czech.—14:06.6
2. A. Mimoun, France—14:07.4
3. H. Schade, Germany—14:08.6

10,000 Metres
1. E. Zatopek, Czecn.—29:17.0
2. A. Mimoun, France—29:32.8
3. A. Anufriayev, U.S.S.R.—29:48.2

Marathon
1. E. Zatopek, Czech.—2:23:03.2
2. R. Gorno, Argentina—2:25:35.0
3. G. Jansson, Sweden—2:26:07.0

110 Metres Hurdles
1. W. H. Dillard, U.S.—13.7
2. J. Davis, U.S.—13.7
3. A. Barnard, U.S.—14.1

400 Metres Hurdles
1. C. Moore, U.S.—50.8
2. Y. Lituyev, U.S.S.R.—51.3
3. J. Holland, New Zealand—52.2

3,000 Metres Steeplechase
1. H. Ashenfelter, U.S.—8:45.4
2. V. Kazantsev, U.S.S.R.—8:51.6
3. J. Disley, Great Britain—8:51.8

400 Metres Relay
1. U.S.—40.1
2. U.S.S.R.—40.3
3. Hungary—40.5

800 Metres Relay
1. Jamaica—3:03.9
2. U.S.—3:04.0
3. Germany—3:06.6

50,000 Metres Walk
1. G. Bordoni, Italy—4:28:07.8
2. J. Dolezal, Czech.—4:30:17.8
3. A. Roka, Hungary—4:31:27.2

High Jump
1. W. Davis, U.S.—6'8 5/16"
2. K. Wiesner, U.S.—6'8 5/16"
3. J. T. Conceicao, Brazil—6'5 5/16"

Long Jump
1. J. Biffle, U.S.—24'10"
2. M. Gourdine, U.S.—24'8 7/16"
3. O. Foldessy, Hungary—23'11 3/8"

Triple Jump
1. A. F. da Silva, Brazil—53'2 9/16"
2. L.Shcherbakov, U.S.S.R.—52'5 1/8"
3. A. Devonish, Venezuela—50'11 1/4"

Pole Vault
1. R. Richards, U.S.—14'11 1/8"
2. D. Laz, U.S.—14'9 9/16"
3. R. Lundberg, Sweden—14'5 1/4"

Shot Put
1. W. P. O'Brien, U.S.—57'1 7/16"
2. D. Hooper, U.S.—57'0 5/8"
3. J. Fuchs, U.S.—55'11 6/16"

Discus Throw
1. S. Iness, U.S.—180'6 1/2"
2. A. Consolini, Italy—176'5 5/16"
3. J. Dillion, U.S.—174'9 5/8"

Hammer Throw
1. J. Csermak, Hungary—197'11 9/16"
2. K. Storch, Germany—193'1 5/8"
3. I. Nemeth, Hungary—189'5 1/4"

Javelin Throw
1. C. Young, U.S.—242'0 3/4"
2. W. Miller, U.S.—237'8 3/4"
3. T. Hyytiainen, Finland—235'10 5/16"

Decathlon
1. R. Mathias, U.S.   2. M. Campbell, U.S.   3. F. Simmons, U.S.

TRACK AND FIELD—WOMEN

100 Metres
. M. Jackson, Australia—11.5
. D. Hasenjager, S. Africa—11.8
. S. Strickland, Australia—11.9

200 Metres
1. M. Jackson, Australia—23.7
2. B. Brouwer, Holland—24.2
3. N. Khnykina, U.S.S.R.—24.2

80 Metres Hurdles

1. S. Strickland, Australia—10.9
2. M. Golubnichaya, U.S.S.R.—11.1
3. M. Sander, Germany—11.1

400 Metres Relay

1. U.S.—45.9
2. Germany—45.9
3. Great Britain—46.2

High Jump

1. E. Brand, South Africa—5'5¾"
2. S. Lerwill, Great Britain—5'4 $\frac{15}{16}$"
3. A. Chudina, U.S.S.R.—5'4 $\frac{5}{16}$"

Broad Jump

1. Y. Williams, N. Zeal.—20'5 $\frac{11}{16}$"
2. A. Chudina, U.S.S.R.—20'1 $\frac{3}{4}$"
3. S. Cawley, Gt. Brit.—19'5 $\frac{1}{16}$"

Javelin Throw

1. D. Zatopkova, Czech.—165'7"
2. A. Chudina, U.S.S.R.—164'0⅞"
3. Y. Gorchakova, U.S.S.R.—163'3 $\frac{1}{16}$"

Shot Put

1. G. Zybina, U.S.S.R.—50'1½"
2. M. Werner, Germany—47'9⅝"
3. K. Tochenova, U.S.S.R.—47'6 $\frac{9}{16}$"

Discus Throw

1. N. Romashkova, U.S.S.R.—168'8 $\frac{7}{16}$"
2. Y. Bagryantseva, U.S.S.R.—154'5 $\frac{9}{16}$"
3. N. Dumbadze, U.S.S.R.—151'10 $\frac{1}{16}$"

SWIMMING AND DIVING—MEN

100 Metres Free-Style

1. C. C. Scholes, U.S.—57.4
2. H. Suzuki, Japan—57.4
3. G. Larsson, Sweden—58.2

400 Metres Free-Style

1. J. Boiteux, France—4:30.7
2. F. Konno, U.S.—4:31.3
3. P. Ostrand, Sweden—4:35.2

1,500 Metres Free-Style

1. F. Konno, U.S.—18:30.0
2. S. Hashizume, Japan—18:41.4
3. T. Okamoto, Brazil—18:51.3

200 Metres Breast Stroke

1. J. Davies, Australia—2:34.4
2. B. Stassforth, U.S.—2:34.7
3. H. Klein, Germany—2:35.9

800 Metres Free-Style Relay

1. U.S.—8:31.1
2. Japan—8:33.5
3. France—8:45.9

Platform Diving

1. S. Lee, U.S.
2. J. Capilla, Mexico
3. G. Haase, Germany

Springboard Diving

1. D. Browning, U.S.
2. M. Anderson, U.S.
3. R. Clotworthy, U.S.

SWIMMING AND DIVING—WOMEN

100 Metres Free-Style

1. K. Szoke, Hungary—1:06.8
2. J. Termeulen, Neth.—1:07.0
3. J. Temes, Hungary—1:07.1

400 Metres Free-Style

1. V. Gyenge, Hungary—5:12.1
2. E. Novak, Hungary—5:13.7
3. E. Kawamoto, U.S.—5:14.6

200 Metres Breast Stroke

1. E. Szekely, Hungary—2:51.7
2. E. Novak, Hungary—2:54.4
3. H. Gordon, Great Britain—2:57.6

100 Metres Backstroke

1. J. Harrison, South Africa—1:14.3
2. G. Wielema, Netherlands—1:14.
3. J. Stewart, New Zealand—1:15.8

400 Metres Free-Style Relay

1. Hungary—4:24.4
2. Netherlands—4:29.0
3. U.S.—4:30.1

Platform Diving

1. P. McCormick, U.S.
2. P. J. Myers, U.S.
3. J. Irwin, U.S.

Springboard Diving

1. P. McCormick, U.S.
2. M. Moreau, France
3. Z. A. Jensen, U.S.

BOXING

Flyweight
1. N. Brooks, U.S.
2. E. Basel, Germany
3. {A. Bulakov, U.S.S.R.
   {William Towell, South Africa

Bantamweight
1. P. Hamalainen, Finland
2. J. McNally, Eire
3. {G. Garbuzov, U.S.S.R.
   {J. Kang, South Korea

Featherweight
1. J. Zachara, Czechoslovakia
2. S. Caprari, Italy
3. {J. Ventaja, France
   {L. Leisching, South Africa

Lightweight
1. A. Bolognesi, Italy
2. A. Antkiewicz. Poland
3. {G. Fiat, Roumania
   {E. Pakkanen, Finland

Light-Welterweight
1. C. Adkins, U.S.
2. V. Mednov, U.S.S.R.
3. {E. Malenius, Finland
   {B. Visintin, Italy

Welterweight
1. Z. Chychia, Poland
2. S. Shcherbakov, U.S.S.R.
3. {V. Jorgensen, Denmark
   {G. Heidemann, Germany

Light-Middleweight
1. L. Papp, Hungary
2. T. Van Schalkwyk, South Africa
3. {B. Tishin, U.S.S.R.
   {E. Herrera, Argentina

Middleweight
1. F. Patterson, U.S.
2. V. Tita, Roumania
3. {B. Nikolov, Bulgaria
   {K. Sjolin, Sweden

Light-Heavyweight
1. N. Lee, U.S.
2. A. Pacenza, Argentina
3. {A. Perov, U.S.S.R.
   {H. Siljander, Finland

Heavyweight
1. E. Sanders, U.S.
2.
3. {Andries Nieman, South Africa
   {I. Koski, Finland

WRESTLING

Free-Style—Flyweight
1. H. Gemici, Turkey
2. Y. Kitano, Japan
3. M. Mollaghassemi, Iran

Free-Style—Bantamweight
1. S. Ishii, Japan
2. R. Mamedbekov, U.S.S.R.
3. K. Jadav, India

Free-Style—Featherweight
1. B. Sit, Turkey
2. N. Guivethchi, Iran
3. J. Henson, U.S.

Free-Style—Lightweight
1. O. Anderberg, Sweden
2. T. Evans, U.S.
3. D. Torfighe, Iran

Free-Style—Welterweight
1. W. Smith, U.S.
2. P. Berlin, Sweden
3. A. Modjtavabi, Iran

Free-Style—Middleweight
1. D. Cimakuridze, U.S.S.R.
2. G. Takhti, Iran
3. G. Gurics, Hungary

Free-Style—Light-Heavyweight
1. W. Palm, Sweden
2. H. Wittenberg, U.S.
3. A. Atan, Turkey

Free-Style—Heavyweight
1. A. Mekokishvili, U.S.S.R.
2. H. Antonsson, Sweden
3. K. Richmond, Great Britain

Greco-Roman—Flyweight
1. B. Gurevicn, U.S.S.R.
2. I. Fabra, Italy
3. L. Honkala, Finland

Greco-Roman—Bantamweight
1. I. Hodos, Hungary
2. Z. Khihab, Lebanon
3. A. Teryan, U.S.S.R.

Greco-Roman—Featherweight
1. Y. Punkin, U.S.S.R.
2. I. Polyak, Hungary
3. A. Rashed, Egypt

Greco-Roman—Lightweight
1. K. Safin, U.S.S.R.
2. K. Freij, Sweden
3. M. Athanasov, Czechoslovakia

Greco-Roman—Welterweight
1. M. Szilvasi, Hungary
2. G. Andersson, Sweden
3. K. Taha, Lebanon

Greco-Roman—Middleweight
1. A. Gronberg, Sweden
2. K. Rauhala, Finland
3. N. Belov, U.S.S.R.

Greco-Roman—Light-Heavyweight
1. K. Grondahl, Finland
2. S. Shikhaladze, U.S.S.R.
3. K. Nilsson, Sweden

Greco-Roman—Heavyweight
1. J. Kotkas, U.S.S.R.
2. J. Ruzicka, Czechoslovakia
3. T. Kovanen, Finland

WEIGHT-LIFTING

Bantamweight
1. I. Udodov, U.S.S.R.—694½ lb.
2. M. Namdjou, Iran—678 lb.
3. A. Mirzai, Iran—661¼ lb.

Featherweight
1. R. Chimishkyan, U.S.S.R.—774 lb.
2. N. Saksonov, U.S.S.R.—733 lb.
3. R. Wilkes, Trinidad—711 lb.

Lightweight
1. T. Kono, U.S.—799 lb.
2. Y. Lopatin, U.S.S.R.—771½ lb.
3. V. Barberis, Australia—771½ lb.

Middleweight
1. P. George, U.S.—882 lb.
2. G. Gratton, Canada—860 lb.
3. S. Kim, South Korea—843¼ lb.

Light-Heavyweight
1. T. Lomakin, U.S.S.R.—920½ lb.
2. S. Staczyk, U.S.—915 lb.
3. A. Vorobyev, U.S.S.R.—898¼ lb.

Middle-Heavyweight
1. N. Schemansky, U.S.—981 lb.
2. G. Novak, U.S.S.R.—903¾ lb.
3. L. Kilgour, Trinidad—887¼ lb.

Heavyweight
1. J. Davis, U.S.—1,014 lb.
2. J. Bradford, U.S.—964½ lb.
3. H. Selvetti, Argentina—953½ lb.

CYCLING

1,000 Metres Sprint
1. E. Sacchi, Italy—12.0
2. L. Cox, Australia
3. W. Potzernheim, Germany

1,000 Metres Time-Trial
1. R. Mockridge, Australia—1:11.1
2. M. Morettini, Italy—1:12.7
3. R. Robinson, S. Africa—1:13.0

2,000 Metres Tandem
1. R. Mockridge/L. Cox,
   Australia—11.0
2. R. Robinson/T. Shardelow,
   South Africa
3. A. Maspes/C. Pinarello, Italy

4,000 Metres Team Pursuit
1. Italy—4:46.1
2. South Africa—4:53.6
3. Great Britain

Road-Race—Individual
1. A. Noyelle, Belgium—5:06:03.4
2. R. Grondelaers, Belg.—5:06:51.2
3. E. Ziegler, Germany—5:07:47.5

Road-Race—Team
1. Belgium—15:20:46.6
2. Italy—15:33:27.3
3. France—15:38:58.1

EQUESTRIAN SPORTS

Jumping Grand Prix—Individual
1. P. J. d'Oriola, France
2. O. Cristi, Chile
3. F. Thiedemann, Germany

Jumping Grand Prix—Team
1. Great Britain
2. Chile
3. U.S.

Grand Prix—Dressage—Individual
1. H. St. Cyr, Sweden
2. L. Hartel, Denmark
3. A. Jousseaume, France

Grand Prix—Dressage—Teams
1. Sweden
2. Switzerland
3. Germany

Three-Day Event—Individual
1. H. von Blixen-Finecke, Sweden
2. G. Lefrant, France
3. W. Bussing, Germany

Three-Day Event—Team
1. Sweden
2. Germany
3. U.S.

FENCING—MEN

Foil—Individual
1. C. d'Oriola, France
2. E. Mangiarotti, Italy
3. M. di Rosa, Italy

Foil—Team
1. France
2. Italy
3. Hungary

Epée—Individual
1. E. Mangiarotti, Italy
2. D. Mangiarotti, Italy
3. O. Zappelli, Switzerland

Epée—Team
1. Italy
2. Sweden
3. Switzerland

Sabre—Individual
1. P. Kovacs, Hungary
2. A. Gerevich, Hungary
3. T. Berczelly, Hungary

Sabre—Team
1. Hungary
2. Italy
3. France

FENCING—WOMEN

Foil—Individual

1. I. Camber, Italy   2. I. Elek, Hungary   3. K. Lachmann, Denmark

GYMNASTICS—MEN

Combined Exercises—Individual

1. V. Chukarin, U.S.S.R.
2. G. Shaginyan, U.S.S.R.
3. J. Stalder, Switzerland

Combined Exercises—Team

1. U.S.S.R.
2. Switzerland
3. Finland

Floor Exercises

1. K. Thoresson, Sweden
2. { T. Uesako, Japan
   { Jerzy Jokiel, Poland

Horizontal Bar

1. J. Gunthard, Switzerland
2. { J. Stalder, Switzerland
   { K. Schwarzmann, Germany

Parallel Bar

1. H. Eugster, Switzerland
2. V. Chukarin, U.S.S.R.
3. J. Stalder, Switzerland

Pommelled Horse

1. V. Chukarin, U.S.S.R.
2. { Y. Korolkov, U.S.S.R.
   { G. Shaginyan, U.S.S.R.

Long Horse Vault

1. V. Chukarin, U.S.S.R.
2. M. Takemoto, Japan
3. { T. Uesako, Japan
   { T. Ono, Japan

Rings

1. G. Shaginyan, U.S.S.R.
2. V. Chukarin, U.S.S.R.
3. { H. Eugster, Switzerland
   { D. Leonkin, U.S.S.R.

GYMNASTICS—WOMEN

Combined Exercises—Individual

1. M. Gorokhovskaya, U.S.S.R.
2. N. Bocharyova, U.S.S.R.
3. M. Korondi, Hungary

Combined Exercises—Team

1. U.S.R.R.
2. Hungary
3. Czechoslovakia

Beam

1. N. Bocharyova, U.S.S.R.
2. M. Gorokhovskaya, U.S.S.R.
3. M. Korondi, Hungary

Uneven Bars

1. M. Korondi, Hungary

Parallel Bars

1. M. Korondi, Hungary
2. M. Gorokhovskaya, U.S.S.R.
3. A. Keleti, Hungary

Horse Vault

1. Y. Kalinchuk, U.S.S.R.
2. M. Gorokhovskaya, U.S.S.R.
3. G. Minaycheva, U.S.S.R.

Floor Exercises

1. A. Keleti, Hungary
2. M. Gorokhovskaya, U.S.S.R.
3. M. Korondi, Hungary

Team Drill

1. Sweden

ROWING

Single Sculls

1. Y. Tyukalov, U.S.S.R.—8:12.8
2. M. Wood, Australia—8:14.5
3. T. Kocerka, Poland—8:19.4

Double Sculls

1. T. Copozzo/E. Guerrero,
   Argentina—7:32.2
2. G. Zilin/I. Emchuk, U.S.S.R.—
   7:38.3
3. M. Seijas/J. Rodriguez,
   Uruguay—7:43.7

Coxswainless Pairs

1. C. Logg/T. Price, U.S.—8:20.7
2. M. Knuysen/R. Baetens,
   Belgium—8:23.5
3. K. Schmid/H. Kalt,
   Switzerland—8:32.7

Coxed Pairs

1. France—8:28.6
2. Germany—8:32.1
3. Denmark—8:34.9

Coxswainless Fours

1. Yugoslavia—7:16.0
2. France—7:18.9
3. Finland—7:32.3

Coxed Fours

1. Czechoslovakia—7:33.4
2. Switzerland—7:36.5
3. U.S.—7:37.0

Eights

1. U.S. (Navy)—6:25.9
2. U.S.S.R.—6:31.2
3. Australia—6:33.1

CANOEING—MEN

Kayak Singles—1,000 Metres
1. G. Frederiksson, Sweden—4:07.9
2. T. Stromberg, Finland—4:09.7
3. L. Gantois, France—4:20.1

Kayak Pairs—1,000 Metres
1. K. Wires/Y. Kietanen, Finland—3:51.1
2. L. Glasser/H. Hedberg, Sweden—3:51.1
3. M. Raub/H. Wiedermann, Austria—3:51.4

Canadian Singles—1,000 Metres
1. J. Holecek, Czech.—4:56.3
2. J. Parti, Hungary—5:03.6
3. O. Ojanpera, Finland—5:08.5

Canadian Pairs—1,000 Metres
1. B. Rasch/F. Haunstoft, Denmark—4:38.3
2. J. Brzak/B. Kudrna, Czechoslovakia—4:42.9
3. E. Drews/W. Soltau, Germany—4:48.3

CANOEING—WOMEN

Kayak Singles—500 Metres
1. S. Saimo, Finland—2:18.4
2. G. Liebhart, Austria—2:18.8
3. N. Savina, U.S.S.R.—2:21.6

YACHTING

5.5 Metres
1. "Complex II," U.S.
2. "Encore," Finland
3. "Hojwa," Sweden

Dragon
1. "Pan," Norway
2. "Tornado," Sweden
3. "Gustel X," Germany

Star
1. "Merope," Italy
2. "Comanche," U.S.
3. "Espadarte," Portugal

SHOOTING

Free Pistol (50 Metres)
1. H. Benner, U.S.
2. A. Leon, Spain
3. A. Balogh, Hungary

Automatic Pistol (25 Metres)
1. K. Takacs, Hungary
2. S. Kun, Hungary
3. G. Lichiardopol, Roumania

Free Rifle (300 Metres)
1. A. Bogdanov, U.S.S.R.
2. R. Burchler, Switzerland
3. L. Vainshtein, U.S.S.R.

Small-Bore Rifles—Prone (50 Metres)
1. J. Sarbu, Roumania
2. B. Andreyev, U.S.S.R.
3. A. Jackson, U.S.

Small-Bore Rifles—Three Positions (Combined)
1. E. Kongshaug, Norway
2. V. Ylonen, Finland
3. B. Andreyev, U.S.S.R.

Clay Pigeon
1. G. Genereux, Canada
2. K. Holmqvist, Sweden
3. H. Liljedahl, Sweden

MODERN PENTATHLON

Individual
1. L. Hall, Sweden
2. G. Benedek, Hungary
3. I. Szondi, Hungary

Team
1. Hungary
2. Sweden
3. Finland

BASKETBALL
1. U.S.
2. U.S.S.R.
3. Uruguay

SOCCER
1. Hungary
2. Yugoslavia
3. Sweden

FIELD HOCKEY
1. India
2. Netherlands
3. Great Britain

WATER POLO
1. Hungary
2. Yugoslavia
3. Italy

Chapter 14

THE XVI OLYMPIAD

Melbourne, 1956

The Olympic Games are supposed to be above and beyond political considerations, but politics, both domestic and international, almost crippled the 1956 games at Melbourne, Australia.

First, there was a growing sentiment in the United States to prevent Russia from competing. This appeared to have something to do with the fact that the Russian athletes very nearly defeated the Americans at Helsinki. But the true reason was that the Russians were subsidized by their government and were therefore almost, if not professionals. One of the chief anti-Russian exponents was Republican Senator John Marshall Butler of Maryland who urged Congress to "keep out Russia and her barbaric goon squads." Congress wisely ignored the senator and others who wanted Russia out.

Russian Sports Minister Nikolai Romanov emphasized even more strongly then that Russia did, indeed, intend to win everything it could get its hands on at Melbourne. And after the Russians had won the unofficial point total in the winter games, Romanov boasted: "We came here expecting triumphs in our strong events and expecting to gain experience in others. We did both, and we're going to be away out front in Melbourne."

But Melbourne, even in early February of 1956, did not appear to be ready for the Russians or anyone else.

The first sign of trouble came in 1950 when the trustees of the Melbourne Cricket Ground, heeding the complaints of cricketers and football officials, refused to permit modernization of the grounds. It took two years before the International Olympic Committee finally persuaded them that the Olympic Games were more important than the cricketers. Even as late as 1953, nothing much had been accomplished in the way of Olympic preparation and IOC president Avery Brundage threatened to switch the games to Rome which had advanced further than Melbourne in getting ready for the 1964 games.

The Australian government and the state government of Victoria were feuding about financing the Games. Finally, in 1954, the Federal Government resolved the dispute by loaning the state government $4,500,000 to construct an Olympic Village, which was later used to relieve a chronic housing shortage.

The next problem involved a six month quarantine before horses could be admitted to Australia. The equestrian events were therefore shifted to Stockholm where the Swedes won three of the six events.

Brundage went to Australia in 1955 and the laborers called a strike at the construction site of Olympic Village and the cricket grounds conversion.

"The world thinks we made a mistake in giving the games to Melbourne," Brundage bristled, and the remark seemed to prick the Australians' pride as they belatedly got on with the job.

On the eve of the Games, the Hungarian revolt and the Suez crisis caused more serious disruptions. Egypt, Lebanon and Iraq withdrew to protest the British and French move on the Suez Canal area. Israel reduced its 20-man team to three. Holland withdrew in protest of Russia's use of tanks and guns in Hungary. Switzerland also withdrew and then changed its mind too late to send any athletes to Australia. Communist China, who had 92 athletes ready to go to Melbourne, withdrew when it learned that the International Committee had accepted a 46-member team from Nationalist China.

When the trouble started in Hungary, part of the Hungarian team was already en route to the Olympics. Seventeen of them were aboard a Russian merchant ship with 90 Russian athletes. The rest of the Hungarian athletes were either in Czechoslovakia or still at home many fighting the Russians.

When they arrived at the Melbourne airport a crowd of more than 1,000 was on hand to greet them. A small group of Russians who had come in on another plane were jeered. Some of the Hungarian athletes were wearing black mourning bands.

At the Olympic Village, the Hungarians flew their traditional flag, saying they would not compete under the Communist banner. The head of the Hungarian squad ordered it replaced by the Communist flag, but two Hungarian athletes climbed up the flag pole at night and tore it down again.

The Hungarians' hatred for Russia was obvious whenever athletes from the two countries competed against each other in the Olympics, and it almost broke out into open warfare in a swimming pool when, during the Russia-Hungary water polo game, Russia's Valentin Prokopov butted Ervin Zador of Hungary with his head and Zador was dragged out of the water with a deep gash over his eye. The players began to brawl in the pool and at the water's edge and the Hungarian spectators jumped over the wall to tackle the Russians. Police had to intervene to prevent a riot. The game was called with only a few seconds left and Hungary ahead 4-0. The Hungarians went on to win the championship by beating Yugoslavia 2-1. Yugoslavia won the silver medal by downing Russia 3-2.

Of the Hungarian delegation of 140 athletes and 30 officials an estimated 100 did not go home, including Janos Somogyi, a former world record holder for the 50 kilometer walk, who went into hiding in Melbourne.

The Olympic flame was taken by a relay of 350 runners from Olympia to Athens, put in a fireproof steel box and flown to Cairns, Australia, where an aborigine ran the first one-mile leg of the 2,750 mile relay to Melbourne. Nineteen-year-old Ron Clark, the Australian junior mile champion who had failed to make the Olympic team, brought it into the Melbourne Cricket Grounds, ending the longest journey in history for the Olympic flame.

George Roubanis, a Greek pole vaulter who trained at the University of California, led the 4,000 athletes from 67 countries in the opening parade. Roubanis got a bronze medal, behind Bob Gutowski of the United States and Rev. Bob Richards, who had been within one jump of being eliminated at 13' 1½". He went on to break his own Olympic record of 14' 11¼" by a quarter of an inch. Richards was one of three track and field gold medal winners in the 1952 games who repeated their victories at Melbourne.

World record shot putter Parry O'Brien broke his own Olympic record six times, his best heave travelling 60' 11¼". Bill Nieder of the U.S., Jiri Skobla of Czechoslovakia and Ken Batum of the U.S. all bettered O'Brien's former record.

Adhemar Ferreira da Silva broke his own triple jump Olympic record at 53' 7½" and Iceland picked up a silver medal when Vilhjalmur Einarsson also outjumped da Silva's old record.

Milt Campbell of the U.S. Navy, who had finished second to Bob Mathias in the 1952 decathlon, defeated world record holder Rafer Johnson of the U.S. to get a gold medal this time. He set an Olympic record and came within a few points of Johnson's record.

Campbell came first in the 100 metres, 110 metre hurdles and shot put, and second in the high and broad jumps, the discus and the 400 metres. But a disappointing 11' 1¾" in the pole vault cost him the world record. He normally could clear 12' with ease.

Charlie Dumas, who became the world's first seven foot high jumper during the U.S. Olympic trials, won the Olympic gold medal after a 10 hour competition, with Chila Porter of Australia getting the silver medal. The two 19-year-olds had eliminated the 29 other jumpers when the bar was raised to 6' 11½", three inches higher than Porter had ever jumped in his life. They both missed on their first two tries. Dumas cleared the bar on his third and Porter failed. The crowd, which had dwindled from 90,000 to 50,000 during the supper hour, cheered for three minutes.

World record discus thrower Fortune Gordien of the U.S. was conceded an easy victory, particularly after one of his warm-up throws travelled 198 feet. But the Oregon rancher, who had won a bronze medal in 1948 and was competing in his third Olympics, could do no better than 179' 10" when the competition began. Team mate Al Oerter, 20, beat him with a throw of 184' 10½".

Boston school teacher Hal Connolly defeated former world record holders Mikhail Krivonosov of Russia and Imre Nemeth of Hungary in the hammer throw.

Connolly did not start heaving the hammer until he was at Boston College. He took up the sport to strengthen his throwing arm which was four inches shorter than the other and had been broken several times in football and wrestling, which had been his major sports. In the six months before the Olympics, Krivonosov and Connolly kept breaking each other's world records with Connolly going into the games with an unofficial record of 224' 10½". He out-threw Krivonosov by six inches and all six finalists broke the former Olympic record. Nemeth, who won a gold medal in 1948 and bronze in 1952, was fifth.

Egil Danielson, 23, of Norway, set a world record javelin throw of 281' 2¼" despite a gusty wind to defeat the former world record holder, Janusz Sidlo of Poland. Danielson's toss was 32 feet better than the former Olympic record set by Cy Young, who finished 11th this time.

Vladimir Kuts and Bobby Joe Morrow stood out in the track competitions. Kuts, a Russian naval officer, won the 5,000 and 10,000 metres; while Morrow scored the first Olympic sprint double since Jesse Owens in 1936, and added a third gold medal as a member of the U.S. 400 metre relay team.

Kuts, 29, became the first Russian to win a gold medal in track and field with his 10,000 metre victory which drew the loudest ovation from the 100,000 spectators on the first day of competition. It was strictly a two-man race most of the way with Kuts and Gordon Pirie of Great Britain passing the 3,000 and 4,000 metre marks in world record time. Pirie stayed a stride or two behind the Russian who repeatedly tried to shake him off with short bursts of speed. At the halfway point Kuts was still keeping up his break-neck pace, equalling Emil Zatopek's 14:04.6 Olympic record for 5,000 metres. Pirie was still on his heels. On the 20th lap the Russian, still unable to shake Pirie, changed tactics and slowed up, letting Pirie pass him and take the lead for one lap. Then, Kuts sprinted past Pirie again with five laps to go and Pirie, by now exhausted, staggered home eighth with Kuts winning by 50 yards over Jozsef Kovaks of Hungary, who refused to extend the winner the traditional handshake when they received their medals.

Pirie sought revenge in the 5,000 metre race. He held the world record and was the co-favorite with Kuts. As they were lining up at the start, Kuts stood over the crouched Pirie and seemed to say something to him. Pirie, slightly befuddled, got off to a slow start and lost by almost 100 yards. Once again, Kuts set a wicked pace with Chris Chataway and Derek Ibbotson close behind. Chataway made one challenge and then finished 11th with stomach cramps. Pirie came from behind to beat Ibbotson for the silver medal. Kuts broke Zatopek's Olympic record by 27 seconds.

Morrow, the co-world record holder for 100 yards at 9.3 seconds, equalled the Olympic record of 10.3 in two preliminary heats of the 100 metres. Running against a wind in the final, he was slowed down to 10.5 and the judges took 15 minutes to separate him from Thane Baker, also the runner-up at Helsinki. Then he scored the first Olympic sprint double since 1936 when he defeated the defending champion Andy Stanfield in the 200 metres. He also cut a 10th of a second off Owens' 20 year old record.

Morrow got his third gold medal by anchoring the 400 metre relay team to a world record 39.5, three tenths of a second faster than the former record holding team anchored by Owens in 1936.

Charles Jenkins, 22, of the United States was a surprise winner in the 400 metres, beating Karl Haas of Germany by a yard. The strong favorite was another American, Lou Jones, who held the world record, but he set too fast an early pace and did not place.

Tom Courtney of the U.S. took the lead in the 800 metres in the backstretch, lost it to Derek Johnson of Great Britain, but then came on again 10 yards from the finish line to beat Johnson by a yard in 1:47.7. Courtney was so exhausted after the race that the medal ceremony had to be delayed for an hour while he recovered.

In the 1,600 metre relay, Lou Jones gave the U.S. a three-yard lead which Jesse Mashburn held. Jenkins

124

ran the third leg in 45.5 to hand over a 10-yard cushion to Courtney who maintained the margin.

Ron Delany, a 21-year-old Irishman trained at Villanova University in the United States, came from far behind to win the 1,500 metres in 3:41.2, an Olympic record which was only a fifth of a second off the world record. Delany was in tenth place at the start of the final lap. He started catching up at the head of the backstretch and was third going into the final turn. He caught Klaus Richtzenhaim about 100 yards from home and beat him by five feet. Richtzenhaim just managed to hold off a late sprint by John Landy of Australia and both were timed in 3:42.0. Only about seven feet separated Delany from the last place finisher in the field that included five four-minute milers.

Alain Mimoun, who had finished second to Zatopek three times in the Olympics of 1948 and 1952, finally beat the magnificent Czech at Melbourne. The French-Algerian led most of the way in the marathon and finished before second-place Franjo Mihalic of Yugoslavia came into the stadium. Veikko Karvonen of Finland, who was sixth in 1952, came third this time and Zatopek, the defending champion, was sixth.

Dana Zatopekova also failed in her specialty, the javelin. She came fourth and watched Inese Jaunzeme of Russia beat her 1956 record by 11 feet.

The biggest uproar at Melbourne occurred after the 3,000 metre steeplechase which Chris Brasher of Great Britain won by 15 yards over world record holder Sandor Rosznyoi of Hungary. Rosznyoi claimed that he was thrown off stride when Brasher nudged him on a jump. Then, an official accused Brasher of interfering with bronze medallist Ernst Larsen of Norway on the final lap and disqualified him. Later, a jury of appeals disallowed the disqualification and restored Brasher's gold medal.

Jack Davis had set a world record of 13.3 seconds in the 110 metre hurdles ten days before the Games, but he was beaten by a fraction of an inch in the Olympics by Lee Calhoun. Both were timed in an Olympic record 13.5 and Joel Shankle was third for a U.S. sweep.

The Americans also finished 1-2-3 in the 400 metre hurdles, with world record holder Glenn Davis, 21, equalling the Olympic record of 50.1 seconds that 18-year-old Eddie Southern had set in a semi-final in which he beat Davis. Southern was second in the final with Josh Culbreath of the U.S. Marines third.

An 18-year-old Australian girl, Betty Cuthbert, duplicated Bobby Morrow's triple gold medal by winning both sprints and anchoring the winning relay team. In the 200 metres she equalled the world record of 23.4 seconds.

Defending champion Shirley Strickland of Australia, competing in her third Olympics, set a world record 10.7 in the 80 metre hurdles. There was also a world record in the high jump when Mildred McDaniel of the United States cleared 5′ 9¼″.

Seventeen-year-old Elzbieta Krzesinska equalled her own world record of 20′ 10″ in the broad jump. Galina Zybina lost her shot put crown to another Russian giantess, Tamara Tyshkyevich, and Olga Fikotova dethroned the 1952 discus champion, Nina Romaschkova Ponomaryva and beat her Olympic record by eight feet.

The Australians took most of the honors in swimming, winning seven of the 12 events.

Nineteen-year-old Dawn Fraser set a world record 1:02.0 in the 100 metres with Lorraine Crapp and Faith Leech completing an Australian sweep. The three of them plus Sandra Morgan set a 4:17.1 world record in the 400 metre freestyle relay. Miss Crapp, 18, did however defeat Miss Fraser by a length in the 400 metre freestyle. Fourteen-year-old Sylvia Ruuska of the United States was third.

Murray Rose of Australia, Tsuyoshi Yamanaka of Japan and George Breen of the United States finished 1-2-3 in both the 400 and 1,500 metre freestyle. In the 1,500, Breen had set a world record of 17:52.9 in a qualifying heat, but he did not come near that time in the final.

The Australians swept the 100 metre freestyle with 21-year-old Jon Henricks defeating John Devitt and Gary Chapman; and Masura Furuwaka's victory in the

200 metre breast stroke was Japan's first swimming gold medal in 20 years.

Mrs. Patricia McCormick, 26, of the U.S., became the first woman to score repeat Olympic victories in both the platform and springboard diving. In the platform event, she had been trailing teammate Paula Jean Myers until the final day when she made two superb dives to win the gold medal.

Juan Capilla of Mexico, competing in his third Olympics, won the men's platform diving gold medal. He had a bronze medal from 1948 and a silver from 1952. At Melbourne, he won by only 3/100ths of a point over Gary Tobian of the United States. Capilla also won a bronze medal in the springboard diving division, finishing behind Bob Clotworthy and Don Harper of the U.S. Clotworthy had finished third in 1952.

In rowing, the Yale University team had a close call in the eights, being beaten by Australia and Canada in a preliminary heat but qualified by winning an extra heat for losers. In the final, they defeated the unheralded Canadian team from the University of British Columbia by a length to give the United States its eighth gold medal in the event.

In the fours without coxswain, half of the UBC eights crew—Archie McKinnon, Lorne Loomer, Walter d'Hont and Don Arnold—gave Canada its first Olympic rowing gold medal, defeating the U.S. crew by three lengths. The quartet had not even been included in Canada's Olympic team, but a public subscription raised $6,000 in Vancouver to send them to Melbourne.

A 19-year-old Russian, who had been skulling for less than a year shattered the dreams of Jack Kelly, Jr., whose father had won a gold medal in 1920 for the single skulls. For the third time in the Olympics, Kelly lost his bid for a gold medal, fading in the final 500 metres to finish third while Stuart MacKenzie of Australia stole the silver medal from him.

The Russians picked up a mass of points in some of the lesser events—particularly wrestling and gymnastics—and defeated the United States 622-497 in the unofficial points total. They also won 37 gold medals to 32 for the Americans.

OFFICIAL XVI OLYMPIAD RESULTS

Melbourne, 1956

TRACK AND FIELD—MEN

100 Metres
1. B. Morrow, U.S.—10.5
2. W. T. Baker, U.S.—10.5
3. H. Hogan, Australia—10.6

200 Metres
1. B. Morrow, U.S.—20.6
2. A. Stanfield, U.S.—20.7
3. W. T. Baker, U.S.—20.9

400 Metres
1. C. Jenkins, U.S.—46.7
2. K. Haas, Germany—46.8
3. V. Helsten, Finland—47.0

800 Metres
1. T. Courtney, U.S.—1:47.7
2. D. Johnson, Gt. Brit.—1:47.8
3. A. Boysen, Norway—1:48.1

1,500 Metres
1. R. Delany, Eire—3:41.2
2. K. Richtzenhain, Germ.—3:42.0
3. J. Landy, Australia—3:42.0

5,000 Metres
1. V. Kuts, U.S.S.R.—13:39.6
2. G. Pirie, Great Britain—13:50.6
3. D. Ibbotson, Gt. Brit.—13:54.4

10,000 Metres
1. V. Kuts, U.S.—28:45.6
2. J. Kovacs, Hungary—28:52.4
3. A. Lawrence, Australia—28:53.6

Marathon
1. A. Mimoun, France—2:25:00.0
2. F. Mihalic, Yugoslavia—2:26;32.0
3. V. Karvonen, Finland—2:27:47.0

110 Metres Hurdles
1. L. Calhoun, U.S.—13.5
2. J. Davis, U.S.—13.5
3. J. Shankle, U.S.—14.1

400 Metres Hurdle
1. G. Davis, U.S.—50.1
2. S. E. Southern, U.S.—50.8
3. J. Culbreath, U.S.—51.6

3,000 Metres Steeplechase
1. C. Brasher, Great Britain—8:41.2
2. S. Rozsnyoi, Hungary—8:43.4
3. E. Larsen, Norway—8:44.4

400 Metres Relay
1. U.S.—39.5
2. U.S.S.R.—39.8
3. Germany—40.3

1,600 Metres Relay
1. U.S.—3:04.8
2. Australia—3:06.2
3. Great Britain—3:07.2

20,000 Metres Walk
1. L. Spirin, U.S.S.R.—1:31:27.4
2. A. Mikenas, U.S.S.R.—1:32:03.0
3. B. Junk, U.S.S.R.—1:32:12.0

50,000 Metres Walk
1. N. Read, New Zealand—4:30:42.8
2. Y. Maskinskov, U.S.S.R.—4:32:57.0
3. J. Ljunggren, Sweden—4:35:02.0

High Jump
1. C. Dumas, U.S.—6'11¼"
2. C. Porter, Australia—6'10½"
3. I. Kashkarov, U.S.—6'9¾"

Broad Jump
1. G. Bell, U.S.—25'8¼"
2. J. Bennett, U.S.—25'2¼"
3. J. Valkama, Finland—24'6½"

Triple Jump
1. A. F. da Silva, Brazil—53'7½"
2. V. Einarsson, Iceland—53'4"
3. V. Kreyer, U.S.S.R.—52'6½"

Pole Vault
1. R. Richards, U.S.—14'11½"
2. R. Gutowski, U.S.—14'10½"
3. G. Rouboanis, Greece—14'9"

Shot Put
1. W. P. O'Brien, U.S.—60'11"
2. W. Nieder, U.S.—59'7¾"
3. J. Skobla, Czech.—57'10¾"

Discus Throw
1. A. Oerter, U.S.—184'10½"
2. F. Gordien, U.S.—179'9½"
3. D. Koch, U.S.—178'5½"

Hammer Throw
1. H. Connolly, U.S.—207'3¾"
2. M. Krivonosov, U.S.S.R.—206'9½"
3. A. Samaotsvetov, U.S.S.R.—205'3"

Javelin Throw
1. E. Danielsen, Norway—281'2¼"
2. J. Sidlo, Poland—262'4½"
3. V. Tsibulenko, U.S.S.R.—260'9½"

Decathlon
1. M. Campbell, U.S.
2. R. Johnson, U.S.
3. V. Kuznetsov, U.S.S.R.

TRACK AND FIELD—WOMEN

100 Metres
1. B. Cuthbert, Australia—11.5
2. C. Stubnick, Germany—11.7
3. M. Mathews, Australia—11.7

200 Metres
1. B. Cuthbert, Australia—23.4
2. C. Stubnick, Germany—23.7
3. M. Mathews, Australia—23.8

128

80 Metres Hurdles
1. S. Strickland, Australia—10.7
2. G. Kohler, Germany—10.9
3. N. Thrower, Australia—11.0

400 Metres Relay
1. Australia—44.5
2. Great Britain—44.7
3. U.S.—44.9

High Jump
1. M. McDaniel, U.S.—5'9¼"
2. T. Hopkins, Gt. Brit.—5'5¾"
   M. Pisaryeva, U.S.S.R.—5'5¾"

Long Jump
1. E. Krzesinska, Poland—20'10"
2. W. White, U.S.—19'11¾"
3. N. Dvalishvili, U.S.S.R.—19'11"

Javelin Throw
1. I. Jaunzeme, U.S.S.R.—176'8"
2. M. Ahrens, Chile—165'3"
3. N. Konyayeva, U.S.S.R.—164'11½"

Shot Put
1. T. Tyshkyevich, U.S.S.R.—54'5"
2. G. Zybina, U.S.S.R.—54'2¾"
3. M. Werner, Germany—51'2½"

Discus Throw
1. O. Fikotova, Czech.—176'1½"
2. I. Beglyakova, U.S.S.R.—172'4½"
3. N. Ponomaryeva, U.S.S.R.—170'8"

SWIMMING AND DIVING—MEN

100 Metres Free-Style
1. J. Henricks, Australia—55.4
2. J. Devitt, Australia—55.8
3. G. Chapman, Australia—56.7

400 Metres Free-Style
1. M. Rose, Australia—4:27.3
2. T. Yamanaka, Japan—4:30.4
3. G. Breen, U.S.—4:32.5

1,500 Metres Free-Style
1. M. Rose, Australia—17:58.9
2. T. Yamanaka, Japan—18:00.3
3. G. Breen, U.S.—18:08.2

200 Metres Breast Stroke
1. M. Furukawa, Japan—2:34.7
2. M. Yoshimura, Japan—2:36.7
3. K. Yunishev, U.S.S.R.—2:36.8

200 Metres Butterfly
1. W. Yorzyk, U.S.—2:19.3
2. T. Ishimoto, Japan—2:23.8
3. C. Tumpek, Hungary—2:23.9

100 Metres Backstroke
1. D. Thiele, Australia—1:02.2
2. J. Monckton, Australia—1:03.2

800 Metres Free-Style Relay
1. Australia—8:23.6
2. U.S.—8:31.5
3. U.S.S.R.—8:34.7

Platform Diving
1. J. Capilla, Mexico
2. G. Tobian, U.S.
3. R. Connor, U.S.

Springboard Diving
1. R. Clotworth, U.S.
2. D. Harper, U.S.
3. J. Capilla, Mexico

SWIMMING AND DIVING—WOMEN

100 Metres Free-Style
1. D. Fraser, Australia—1:02.0
2. L. Crapp, Australia—1:02.3
3. F. Leech, Australia—1:05.1

400 Metres Free-Style
1. L. Crapp, Australia—4:54.6
2. D. Fraser, Australia—5:02.5
3. S. Ruuska, U.S.—5:07.1

200 Metres Breast Stroke
1. U. Happe, Germany—2:53.1
2. E. Szekely, Hungary—2:54.8
3. E. ten Elsen, Germ.—2:55.1

100 Metres Butterfly
1. S. Mann, U.S.—1:11.0
2. N. J. Ramey, U.S.—1:11.9
3. M. J. Sears, U.S.—1:14.4

100 Metres Backstroke
1. J. Crinham, Gt. Brit.—1:12.9
2. C. Cone, U.S.—1:12.9
3. M. Edwards, Gt. Brit.—1:13.1

400 Metres Free-Style Relay
1. Australia—4:17.1
2. U.S.—4:19.2
3. South Africa—4:25.7

Platform Diving
1. P. McCormick, U.S.
2. J. Irwin, U.S.
3. P. J. Myers, U.S.

Springboard Diving
1. P. McCormick, U.S.
2. J. Stunyo, U.S.
3. I. Macdonald, Canada

BOXING

Flyweight

1. T. Spinks, Great Britain
2. M. Dobrescu, Roumania
3. John Caldwell, Eire
   Rene Libeer, France

Bantamweight

1. W. Behrendt, Germany
2. S. C. Song, Korea
3. F. Gilroy, Eire
   C. Barrientos, Chile

Featherweight

1. V. Safronov, U.S.S.R.
2. T. Nicholls, Great Britain
3. H. Niedzwiedzki, Poland
   P. Hamalainen, Finland

Lightweight

1. R. McTaggart, Great Britain
2. H. Kurschar, Germany
3. A. Byrne, Eire
   A. Laguetko, U.S.S.R.

Light Welterweight

1. V. Jengibarian, U.S.S.R.
2. F. Nenci, Italy
3. H. Loubscher, South Africa
   C. Dumitrescu, Roumania

Welterweight

1. N. Linca, Roumania
2. F. Tiedt, Eire
3. K. Hogarth, Australia
   N. Cargano, Great Britain

Light-Middleweight

1. L. Papp, Hungary
2. J. Torres, U.S.
3. J. McCormack, Great Britain
   Z. Pietrzykowski, Poland

Middleweight

1. G. Schatkov, U.S.S.R.
2. R. Tapia, Chile
3. G. Chapron France
   V. Zalazar

Light-Heavyweight

1. J. Boyd, U.S.
2. G. Negrea, Roumania
3. C. Lucas, Cnile
   R. Morauskas, U.S.S.R.

Heavyweight

1. P. Rademacher, U.S.
2. L. Mukhin, U.S.S.R.
3. D. Bekker, South Africa
   G. Bozzano, Italy

WRESTLING

Free-Style—Flyweight

1. M. Tsalkalamanidze, U.S.S.R.
2. M. Khojastehpour, Iran
3. H. Akbas, Turkey

Free-Style—Bantamweight

1. M. Dagistanli, Turkey
2. M. Yaghoubi, Iran
3. M. Chakhov, U.S.S.R.

Free-Style—Featherweight

1. S. Sasahara, Japan
2. J. Mewis, Belgium
3. E. Penttila, Finland

Free-Style—Middleweight

1. N. Nikolov, Bulgaria
2. D. Hodge, U.S.
3. G. Skritladze, U.S.S.R.

Free-Style—Light-Heavyweight

1. C. Tahkti, Iran
2. B. Koulayev, U.S.S.R.
3. P. Blair, U.S.

Free-Style—Heavyweight

1. H. Kaplan, Turkey
2. H. Alicher, Bulgaria
3. T. Kangasniemi, Finland

Greco-Roman—Flyweight

1. N. Solovyev, U.S.S.R.
2. I. Fabra, Italy
3. D. Egribas, Turkey

Greco-Roman—Bantamweight

1. K. Vyrupayev, U.S.S.R.
2. E. Vesterby, Sweden
3. F. Horvat, Roumania

Greco-Roman—Featherweight

1. R. Makinen, Finland
2. I. Polyak, Hungary
3. R. Dzneladze, U.S.S.R.

Greco-Roman—Lightweight

1. K. Lehtonen, Finland
2. R. Dogan, Turkey
3. C. Toth, Hungary

Greco-Roman—Welterweight

1. M. Bayrak, Turkey
2. V. Maneyev, U.S.S.R.
3. P. Berlin, Sweden

Greco-Roman—Middleweight

1. G. Karozia, U.S.S.R.
2. D. Dobrev, Bulgaria
3. K. Jansson, Sweden

Greco-Roman—Light-Heavyweight

1. V. Nikolayev, U.S.S.R.
2. P. Kirakov, Bulgaria
3. K. Nilsson, Sweden

Greco-Roman—Heavyweight

1. A. Parfenyov, U.S.S.R.
2. W. Dietrich, Germany
3. A. Bulgarelli, Italy

WEIGHT-LIFTING

Bantamweight
1. C. Vinci, U.S.—754½ lb.
2. V. Stogov, U.S.S.R.—743½ lb.
3. M. Namdjou, Iran—731½ lb.

Featherweight
1. I. Berger, U.S.—776½ lb.
2. E. Minayev, U.S.S.R.—754¾ lb.
3. M. Zielinski, Poland—738 lb.

Lightweight
1. I. Rybak, U.S.S.R.—837½ lb.
2. R. Khabutdinov, U.S.S.R.—821 lb.
3. C. H. Kim, Korea—815¼ lb.

Middleweight
1. F. Bagdanovskiy, U.S.S.R.—
   925¾ lb.
2. P. George, U.S.—909 lb.
3. E. Pignatti, Italy—843 lb.

Light-Heavyweight
1. T. Kono, U.S.—986¼ lb.
2. V. Styepanov, U.S.S.R.—942 lb.
3. J. George, U.S.—920¼ lb.

Middle-Heavyweight
1. A. Vorobyev, U.S.—1,019¼ lb.
2. D. Sheppard, U.S.—975¼ lb.
3. J. Debuf, France—936¾ lb.

Heavyweight
1. P. Anderson, U.S.—1,102 lb.
2. H. Selvetti, Argentina—1,102 lb.
3. A. Pigaiani, Italy—997¼ lb.

CYCLING

1,000 Metres Scratch
1. M. Rousseau, France—11.4
2. G. Pesenti, Italy
3. R. Ploog, Australia

1,000 Metres Time-Trial
1. L. Faggin, Italy—1:09.8
2. L. Foucek, Czech.—1:11.4
3. A. Swift, South Africa—1:11.6

2,000 Metres Tandem
1. I. Brown/A. Marchant, Australia
2. V. Machek/L. Foucek, Czech.
3. G. Ogna/C. Pinarello, Italy

4,000 Metres Team Pursuit
1. Italy—4:37.4
2. France—4:39.4
3. Great Britain—4:42.2

Road Race
1. E. Baldini, Italy—5:21:17.0
2. A. Geyre, France—5:23:16.0
3. A. Jackson, Gt. Brit.—5:23:17.0

Road Race—Teams
1. France—5:21:17.0
2. Great Britain
3. Germany

EQUESTRIAN SPORTS (Held at Stockholm)

Jumping Grand Prix
1. H. Winkler, Germany
2. R. d'Inzeo, Italy
3. P. d'Inzeo, Italy

Jumping Grand Prix—Teams
1. Germany
2. Italy
3. Great Britain

Grand Prix—Dressage
1. H. St. Cyr, Sweden
2. L. Hartel, Denmark
3. L. Linsenhoff, Germany

Grand Prix—Dressage—Teams
1. Sweden
2. Germany
3. Switzerland

Three-Day Event
1. P. Kastenman, Sweden
2. A. L. Westhues, Germany
3. F. Weldon, Great Britain

Three-Day Event—Teams
1. Great Britain
2. Germany
3. Canada

FENCING—MEN

Foil—Individual
1. C. d'Oriola, France
2. G. Bergarrini, Italy
3. A. Spallino, Italy

Foil Team
1. Italy
2. France
3. Hungary

Epée—Individual
1. C. Pavesi, Italy
2. G. Delfino, Italy
3. E. Mangiarotti, Italy

Epée—Team
1. Italy
2. Hungary
3. France

Sabre—Individual
1. R. Karpati, Hungary
2. J. Pawlowski, Poland
3. L. Kuznyetsov, U.S.S.R.

Sabre—Team
1. Hungary
2. Poland
3. U.S.S.R.

FENCING—WOMEN

Foil—Individual

1. G. Sheen, Great Britain   2. O. Orban, Roumania   3. R. Garilhe, France

GYMNASTICS—MEN

Combined Exercises—Individual

1. V. Chukarin, U.S.S.R.
2. T. Ono, Japan
3. Y. Titov, U.S.S.R.

Combined Exercises—Team

1. U.S.S.R.
2. Japan
3. Finland

Floor Exercises

1. V. Muratov, U.S.S.R.
2. {N. Aihara, Japan
   { W. Thoresson, Sweden
   { V. Chukarin, U.S.S.R.

Horizontal Bar

1. T. Ono, Japan
2. Y. Titov, U.S.S.R.
3. M. Takemoto, Japan

Parallel Bars

1. V. Chukarin, U.S.S.R.
2. M. Kubota, Japan
3. {T. Ono, Japan
   { M. Takemoto, Japan

Pommelled Horse

1. B. Shakhlin, U.S.S.R.
2. T. Ono, Japan
3. V. Chukarin, U.S.S.R.

Long Horse Vault

1. H. Bantz, Germany
2. {V. Muratov, U.S.S.R.
   { Y. Titov, U.S.S.R.

Rings

1. A. Azarvan, U.S.S.R.
2. V. Muratov, U.S.S.R.
3. {M. Takemoto, Japan
   { M. Kubota, Japan

GYMNASTICS—WOMEN

Combined Exercises—Individual

1. L. Latynina, U.S.S.R.
2. A. Keleti, Hungary
3. S. Muratova, U.S.S.R.

Combined Exercises—Team

1. U.S.S.R.
2. Hungary
3. Roumania

Beam

1. A. Keleti, Hungary
2. {E. Bosakova, Czechoslovakia
   { T. Manina, U.S.S.R.

Parallel Bars

1. A. Keleti, Hungary
2. L. Latynina, U.S.S.R.
3. S. Muratova, U.S.S.R.

Long Horse Vault

1. L. Latynina, U.S.S.R.
2. T. Manina, U.S.S.R.
3. {A. Colling, Sweden
   { O. Tass, Hungary

Free Standing—Individual

1. L. Laytnina, U.S.S.R.
2. A. Keleti, Hungary
3. E. Leusteanu, Roumania

Team

1. Russia   2. Hungary   3. Roumania

ROWING

Single Sculls

1. V. Ivanov, U.S.S.R.—8:02.5
2. S. Mackenzie, Australia—8:07.7
3. J. B. Kelly, U.S.—8:11.8

Double Sculls

1. A. Berkutov/Y. Tyukalov, U.S.S.R.—7:24.0
2. B. Costello/J. Gardiner, U.S.—7:32.2
3. M. Riley/M. Wood, Australia—7:37.4

Coxswainless Pairs

1. J. Fifer/D. Hecht, U.S.—7:55.4
2. I. Buldakov/V. Ivanov, U.S.S.R.—8:03.9
3. J. Kloimstein/A. Sageder, Austria—8:11.8

Coxed Pairs

1. U.S.—8:26.1
2. Germany—8:29.2
3. U.S.S.R.—8:31.0

Coxswainless Fours

1. Canada—7:08.8
2. U.S.—7:18.4
3. France—7:20.9

Coxed Fours

1. Italy—7:19.4
2. Sweden—7:22.4
3. Finland—7:30.9

Eights

1. U.S. (Yale U.)—6:35.2
2. Canada—6:37.1
3. Australia—6:39.2

CANOEING—MEN

Kayak Singles—1,000 Metres
1. G. Fredriksson, Sweden—4:12.8
2. I. Pisaryev, U.S.S.R.—4:15.3
3. L. Kiss, Hungary—4:16.2

Kayak Pairs—1,000 Metres
1. M. Scheuer/M. Miltenberger, Germany—3:49.6
2. M. Kaaleste/A. Demitkov, U.S.S.R.—3:51.4
3. M. Raub/H. Weedermann, Austria—3:55.8

Canadian Singles—1,000 Metres
1. L. Rottman, Roumania—5:05.3
2. I. Hernek, Hungary—5:06.2
3. G. Bukharin, U.S.S.R.—5:12.7

Canadian Pairs—1,000 Metres
1. A. Dumitru/S. Ismailciuc, Roumania—4:47.4
2. P. Kharin/G. Botyev, U.S.S.R.—4:48.6
3. K. Wieland/F. Mohacsi, Hungary—4:54.3

CANOEING—WOMEN

Kayak Singles—500 Metres
1. E. Dementyeva, U.S.S.R.—2:18.9
2. T. Zenz, Germany—2:19.6
3. T. Soby, Denmark—2:22.3

YACHTING

5.5 Metres
1. "Rush V," Sweden
2. "Vision," Great Britain
3. "Buraddoo," Australia

Dragon
1. "Slaghoken II," Sweden
2. "TIP," Denmark
3. "Bluebottle," Great Britain

Star
1. "Kathleen," U.S.
2. "Merope III," Italy
3. "Gem IV," Bahamas

Finn
1. P. Elvstrom, Denmark
2. A. Nelis, Belgium
3. J. Marvin, U.S.

SHOOTING

Free Pistol
1. P. Linnosvuo, Finland
2. M. Oumarov, U.S.S.R.
3. O. Pinion, U.S.

Automatic Pistol
1. S. Petrescu, Roumania
2. E. Tcherkassov, U.S.S.R.
3. G. Lichiardopol, Roumania

Free Rifle
1. V. Borisov, U.S.S.R.
2. A. Erdman, U.S.S.R.
3. V. Ylonen, Finland

Small-Bore Rifles—Prone
1. G. Quellette, Canada
2. V. Borisov, U.S.S.R.
3. G. Boa, Canada

Small-Bore Rifle—Three Positions
1. A. Bogdnov, U.S.S.R.
2. O. Horinek, Czechoslovakia
3. N. Sundverg, Sweden

Clay Pigeon
1. G. Rossini, Italy
2. A. Smelczynski, Poland
3. A. Ciceri, Italy

MODERN PENTATHLON

Individual
1. L. Hall, Sweden
2. O. Mannonen, Finland
3. V. Korhonen, Finland

Teams
1. U.S.S.R.
2. U.S.
3. Finland

BASKETBALL
1. U.S.
2. U.S.S.R.
3. Uruguay

SOCCER
1. U.S.S.R.
2. Yugoslavia
3. Bulgaria

FIELD HOCKEY
1. India
2. Pakistan
3. Germany

WATER POLO
1. Hungary
2. Yugoslavia
3. U.S.S.R.

Chapter 15

THE XVII OLYMPIAD

Rome, 1960

THE official symbol of the 1960 Olympic Games depicted a she-wolf suckling Romulus and Remus, the legendary founders of Rome. Possibly there was no connection, but Olympic officialdom gave all competitors a questionnaire which included an inquiry about their infancy—whether they had been breast or bottle fed.

A heat wave dampened the enthusiasm of the spectators and athletes during the opening ceremonies. Several competitors complained of the heat and excused themselves from the opening parade, and the 82-member Canadian team evoked criticism by doffing their blazers and appearing in shirt sleeves for the march past.

The Nationalist Chinese team marched behind a placard marked Formosa, but one member carried a sandwich board saying "Under Protest". The team had threatened to pull out of the Games unless it was allowed to compete as the official Chinese team. Communist China was not represented.

Cassius Clay, a brash youngster from Louisville, who had won all but eight of his 170 amateur fights by the time he was 18, wanted to turn professional before the Olympics, but his coach, Kentucky patrolman Joe Martin, persuaded him to go to the Olympics instead with the argument: "If you win, you'll be as good as the tenth ranked pro. It can open the door to fame and wealth."

Not yet fully grown, the future world heavyweight champion competed as a light heavy and, after a close decision over Tony Madigan of Australia, won the division over a Pole with the jawbreaking name of Zbigniew Pietryskowski, chasing him around the ring for the first two rounds and then battering him badly in the third. Clay was so proud of his gold medal that he did not take it off for 48 hours, even wearing it to bed for two nights.

The United States and Italy each won three of the 10 Olympic boxing championships. Edward Crook and Wilbert McClure of the U.S. won the middleweight and light-middleweight medals. The Italian victors were heavyweight Franco de Piccoli, welterweight Giovanni Benvenuti and featherweight Francesco Musso.

The Italians, with an eye on the lira, juggled the traditional schedule of the Olympic Games, putting cycling rather than track and field at the opening of the program because the bicycle races would be more likely to attract the partisan fans. It worked. Italians took an early lead in the gold medal race, winning both cycling events of the opening day. The Romans rejoiced, but the joy was tempered by the death of a Danish competitor, 23-year-old Knud Enemark Jensen, in the 100 kilometre team race. Towards the finish, he suddenly fell off his bicycle and died a few hours later in hospital.

"Heat stroke causing a brain hemorrhage," was the diagnosis of the doctor who treated him at the scene.

But a few days later, the death developed into a scandal. Danish team trainer told the Danish Road Cycling Union that he had given Jensen a shot of Ronicol before the race. The drug, also administered to other members of the team, was to intensify blood circulation. Two other Danish cyclists collapsed during the race. A later investigation revealed that many professional cyclists had been taking this kind of drug, but it was the first time that the amateurs had been caught at it.

The Italians took five of the six cycling gold medals with Russian Viktor Kapitonov getting the other in the 109-mile road race. Sante Gaiardoni was a double winner in the 1,000 metre sprint and 1,000 metre time trial.

The athlete who got the most publicity out of the 1960 Games was Wilma Rudolph, a tall Tennessean who became the first American woman to win both Olympic sprint gold medals. The 20-year-old student from Tennessee State, a Negro university, equalled the world's record of 11.3 seconds with ease in a 100 metre semi-final. In the final, she knocked three tenths of a second off that record. However, it was not recognized because of a strong tailwind.

In the 200 metres, the Tennessee tornado, one of 19 children, set an Olympic record of 23.2 seconds in a preliminary heat and then ran away from the field to take the final with ease against a strong headwind which slowed her down to 24 seconds flat. In front all the way, she finished four yards ahead of Jutta Heine of Germany with Dorothy Hyman, the silver medallist in the 100 metres, and Maria Itkina of Russia in an apparent dead heat for third. The judges awarded Miss Hyman the bronze.

Miss Rudolph's double sprint victory was the fourth consecutive time that the same woman had won both dashes. It began in 1948 when the 200 was added to the Olympic program and Fanny Blankers-Koen scored a double, followed by Australians Marjorie Jackson and Betty Cuthbert in 1952 and 1956. She won her third gold medal as a member of the U.S. 400 metre relay team. In spite of a bad baton pass from Barbara Jones, she ran a speedy anchor leg for an easy victory over the German team and another world record in 44.5 seconds.

Russian sisters Irina and Tamara Press shared some of the women's spotlight with Miss Rudolph. Irina won the 80 metre hurdles in 10.8 seconds after setting an Olympic record of 10.6 seconds in the preliminaries.

Then Tamara heaved the nine pound shot 56' 10'' for an Olympic record, beating Johanna Luttge of Germany and Earlene Brown of the United States.

The women's shot put final followed the women's 400 metre relay on the program and Miss Rudolph inspired Mrs. Brown towards the bronze medal. After finishing the final leg, Miss Rudolph walked over to the 226 pound matron who gave the slim sprinter a bearhug and said: "I knew you'd do it. Now old Earlene better get a move on herself." Whereupon Mrs. Brown, who kept the U.S. team spirits up by joking and dancing to rock-and-roll music, tossed the shot 53 10½", a personal record. Tamara Press also won a silver medal in the discus with a throw of 172' 6½".

The veteran Nina Romashkova Ponomaryeva, who had once been accused of shoplifting a hat during a tour of London, won the gold medal and set an Olympic record of 180' 8¼", breaking the former mark of 176' 1½" by Olga Fikotova of Czechoslovakia in 1956. Since that time, Miss Fikotova had married world record hammer thrower Hal Connolly and, competing now for the United States, finished a disappointing seventh.

Married life did not seem to suit the competitive career of Connolly any better than conjugal bliss had helped his bride. The defending champion finished eighth in the 1960 Olympic hammer throw with a distance of 230' 9", more than 20 feet under the world record he had set only a month before. Russian Vasily Rudenkov won at 220' 15", breaking his own Olympic record set in the preliminaries.

Connolly's demise was one of two major upsets for the United States. John Thomas, who had set a world record 7' 3¾" in the U.S. Olympic trials, seemed a certain gold medal winner. But he failed on three tries to clear 7' 1" while two Russians cleared the bar for the final jump-off. Robert Shavlakadze and Valeriy Brumel both jumped 7' 1" but Shavlakadze won the gold medal with fewer misses. The 1956 record holder, Charles Dumas of the U.S., was sixth.

In the broad jump, however, Ralph Boston restored American prestige. A month before the Olympics, the 21-year-old Boston had broken the oldest world record on the books with a leap of 26' 11¼", shattering the 26' 8¾" mark of Jesse Owens which had stood for a quarter of a century. At Rome, he also smashed Owens' 1936 Olympic record of 26' 5¼" with a jump of 26' 7¾". And Owens, who was among the spectators, came down afterwards to congratulate him.

In the triple jump, the first five finishers all bettered the former Olympic record with winner Joszef Schmidt of Poland setting a world record of 55' 1¾".

In the men's track events, the unrelated Davis boys, Glenn and Otis, and Germany's Armin Hary were the only double gold medal winners.

Glenn Davis, Cliff Cushman and Dick Howard gave the U.S. a sweep in the 400 metre hurdles. Davis broke his own Olympic record at 49.3 seconds, just a tenth of a second slower than his world record. In the homestretch, he shot ahead of the front-running Howard who was barely beaten by the fast-closing Cushman for the silver medal. Cushman had to make a dive for the tape and was sprawled in the cinders when Davis turned around and helped him up. The first four finishers all beat Davis' former 50.1 seconds Olympic record at Melbourne.

Glenn and Otis Davis, Jack Yerman and Earl Young later gave the U.S. a gold medal in the 1,600 metre relay in a world record 3:02.2. The second place German team also bettered the former world mark of 3:03.9 with a 3:02.7.

Otis Davis, a rookie quarter miler at age 27, and Karl Kaufman of Germany both set a world record 44.9 seconds in the 400 metre dash, three tenths of a second under the former record of Lou Jones set in the 1956 U.S. Olympic trials. The judges awarded Davis the gold medal after examining an electric timing device which showed he had won by 1/500ths of a second.

The most spectacular race of the 1960 Olympics followed the 400 metres.

Herb Elliott, 22, of Australia cut four tenths of a second off his own 1,500 metre world record of 3:36.0. He stayed in fourth place most of the way and waited until the very last lap to take the lead. Then he saw coach Percy Cerutty, 65, break past a police cordon to wave a white flag at him. That was a pre-arranged signal that Elliott had a chance to set a world record. He sprinted with every ounce of energy he had and finished 15 yards ahead of Michel Jazy of France. The first six of the nine finalists all broke the former Olympic record.

Elliott, who had not competed seriously for the previous two years, said later that he did not realize that he might be on the way to a world record until he saw Cerutty's shirt.

In the 800 metres, a 22-year-old relatively unknown New Zealander named Peter Snell, who had recently recovered from a leg fracture outran world record holder Roger Moens of Belgium to set an Olympic record of 1:46.3. Moens thought he had won the race. Close to the finish line, he looked behind him and did not see anyone on his tail. At the same time Snell passed him on his blind side and when Moens looked ahead, there was the New Zealander showing him his heels. Moens made a desperate effort to catch him, but he was a fifth of a second too slow. George Kerr, who had set a shortlived Olympic record of 1:47.1 in the preliminaries, came third.

On the same day, another New Zealander distance runner won a gold medal. Murray Halberg, 26, held off a challenge by Hans Grodotzki of Germany to win the 5,000 metres.

In the marathon, the laurels went to barefoot Abebe Bikila who ran the 26 miles and 385 yards in a record two hours, 15 minutes and 16.2 seconds. The Ethiopian palace guard sprinted the last quarter mile to pull ahead of Rhadi Ben Abdesselem of Morocco and won by 150 yards.

The United States supremacy in the sprints, which had been held since Percy Williams of Canada scored a double in 1928, was broken by Armin Hary of Germany in the 100 metres and Livio Berutti of Italy in the 200. Hary, a 23-year-old Frankfurt department store clerk, and Dave Sime of the United States were both clocked in an Olympic record 10.2 seconds but Hary's lunge on the last stride gave him a photo-finish gold medal. Harry Jerome of Canada, who shared the world record with Hary of 10 seconds, was not able to compete in the final. He had pulled up lame in the semi-finals. Berutti, a 21-year-old frail looking college student who was dubbed the Turin Express, equalled the world record of 20.5 seconds for a curved track in finishing a yard ahead of American Les Carney. Stone Johnson and Ray Norton, the co-world record holders, were fifth and sixth.

Norton, Johnson, Sime and Frank Budd also spoiled the high hopes of the United States in the 400 metre relay. At the finish of the race, they were posted as the winners but the co-favored German team did the celebrating when the judges went into a huddle and disqualified the American team. Norton had left the 20 yard passing zone before getting the baton from Budd at the start of the second leg. So the German quartet composed of Bernd Cullman, Hary, Walter

Mahlendorf and Martin Lauer was awarded the gold medal with a world record 39.5 seconds, although they had finished a yard behind the Americans.

Defending champion Lee Calhoun led the United States to a sweep for the third consecutive Olympiad in the 110 metre hurdles. But he had to dive at the tape to beat Willie May. Both were clocked at 13.8 seconds, three tenths of a second slower than Calhoun's 1956 Olympic record. Hayes Johnson also had to make a last minute lunge to beat world record holder Martin Lauer of Germany for the bronze medal.

Rafer Johnson of the United States won the decathlon with an Olympic record of 8,392 points although he came first in only one of the 10 events, the shot put. Silver medallist Y. C. Yang of Formosa finished first in four events, but his poor showing in the shot put and discus cost him the gold medal. He wound up with 8,334 points.

In swimming, Christine Von Saltza picked up three gold medals, winning the women's 400 metre freestyle in 4:50.6, breaking the Olympic record she had set in the preliminaries, and as a member of the U.S. 400 metre freestyle and medley relay teams. She missed a fourth gold medal, finishing two yards behind Dawn Fraser in the 100 metre freestyle. The Australian champion matched her own world record of 1:01.2, and later lowered that to 1:00.6 on the first leg of the 400 metre freestyle relay final.

In the relay race the U.S. team set a world record of 4:08.9, nearly nine seconds better than the old mark, but the outcome was in doubt until the last 10 metres. Australia surprised the Americans by giving Miss Fraser the opening instead of the closing leg. The intended strategy was that Dawn should build up an unbeatable lead. But Joan Spillane of the U.S. stayed within a length of Miss Fraser and Ilse Konrads of Australia, swimming against Shirley Stobs, was only able to add a foot to that lead. On the third leg, 14 year-old Carolyn Wood caught up to the veteran Australian Lorraine Crapp and handed over a two-foot lead to Miss Von Saltza who touched home a full length ahead of Alva Calhoun.

In the medley relay, Miss Von Saltza, at 18 the oldest member of the team, also anchored the U.S. to a gold medal in a world record 4:41.1, more than three seconds better than the former mark. The Australians once more had to settle for a silver medal.

Lynne Burke set a world record for the 100 metres backstroke of 1:09 seconds on the opening leg, but she was less than a length ahead of Satoko Tanaka of Japan. Breast stroker Patty Kempner increased the lead to a full length and butterfly artist Carolyn Schuler handed over a length and a half lead to Miss Von Saltza who salted away the gold medal, finishing five lengths ahead of Dawn Fraser. Miss Schuler and Miss Burke also won gold medals in the 100 metre butterfly and breast stroke.

Carolyn Wood had been favored over Miss Schuler in the butterfly. But Miss Wood staggered the U.S. officials by suddenly stopping about 30 metres from the finish and bursting into tears. A spectator impetuously dove fully clothed into the tank thinking she had a cramp. But there was nothing the matter with Miss Wood, except that the pressure of Olympic competition was just too much for the prodigious 14-year-old school girl.

There was a major upset in the 200 metre breast stroke. The favorite was world record holder Wiltrud Urselmann of Germany, but just before the finish, 19-year-old Briton Anita Lonsbrough overtook her and won in the world record time of 2:49.5.

In the men's competitions, Jeff Farrell, who qualified for the U.S. team only six days after an appendectomy, anchored the two U.S. relay teams to world records. Barely an hour after the medley relay, he returned to swim the last leg of the freestyle relay.

The Australian and Japanese teams finished second and third in both events.

Until his operation, Farrell, billed as the fastest swimmer in the world, had been favored to win the 100 metre freestyle. But he failed to qualify by a tenth of a second. John Devitt of Australia won the medal in a surprise decision over Lance Larson of the U.S. Both Devitt and Larson thought Larson had won. Devitt even congratulated the American but while Larson was happily posing for pictures the announcement came that the Australian had been awarded the gold medal. Both were clocked at 55.2 seconds.

In the 1,500 metres freestyle, 18-year-old Jon Konrads of Australia set an Olympic record of 17:19.6, defeating teammate Murray Rose by three yards. Rose had set the previous Olympic mark in a preliminary heat. George Breen of the United States led up to the 1,050 metre mark and then he tired to finish third, 10 lengths behind Rose. Rose, however, won the 400 metre freestyle with an Olympic record 4:18.3 with Konrads third behind Tsuyoshi Yamanaka of Japan who had also finished second to Rose in the event at Melbourne.

Mike Troy of the United States broke his own world record in winning the 200 metre butterfly in 2:12.8. He led all the way, increasing his margin by half a length every 50 metres to beat Neville Hayes of Australia by two lengths. Dave Gillanders of the United States seemed to finish in a dead heat with Hayes for a second place but the judges awarded the Australian the silver medal. All three broke the former Olympic record.

In rowing, the European champion German team broke the American supremacy in the eights. The U.S. had won the event since 1920 but this time it did not even get a medal. The German crew increased its stroke to 46 a minute from the normal 40 after the Canadian crew from the University of British Columbia took a short-lived lead. Czechoslovakia was third.

OFFICIAL XVII OLYMPIAD RESULTS

Rome, 1960

TRACK AND FIELD—MEN

100 Metres
1. A. Hary, Germany—10.2
2. D. Sime, U.S.—10.2
3. P. Radford, Gt. Brit.—10.3

200 Metres
1. L. Berutti, Italy—20.5
2. L. Carney, U.S.—20.6
3. A. Seye, France—20.7

400 Metres
1. O. Davis, U.S.—44.9
2. C. Kaufmann, Germany—44.9
3. M. Spence, South Africa—45.4

800 Metres
1. P. Snell, New Zealand—1:46.3
2. R. Moens, Belgium—1:46.5
3. G. Kerr, Jamaica—1:47.1

1,500 Metres
1. H. Elliott, Australia—3:35.6
2. M. Jazy, France—3:38.4
3. I. Rozsavolgyi, Hungary—3:39.2

5,000 Metres
1. M. Halberg, New Zeal.—13:43.4
2. H. Grodotzki, Germany—13:44.6
3. K. Zimmy, Poland—13:44.8

10,000 Metres

1. P. Bolotnikov, U.S.S.R.—28:32.2
2. H. Grodotski, Germany—28:37.0
3. W. D. Rower, Australia—28:38.2

Marathon

1. A. Bikila, Ethiopia—2:15:16.2
2. R. B. Abdesselem, Morocco—2:15:41.6
3. A. B. Magee, New Zeal.—2:17:18.2

110 Metres Hurdles

1. L. Calhoun, U.S.—13.8
2. W. May, U.S.—13.8
3. H. Jones, U.S.—14.0

400 Metres Hurdles

1. G. Davis, U.S.—49.3
2. C. Cushman, U.S.—49.6
3. R. Howard, U.S.—49.7

3,000 Metres Steeplechase

1. Z. Krzyszkowiak, Poland—8:34.2
2. N. Sokolov, U.S.S.R.—8:36.4
3. S. Rzhishchin, U.S.S.R.—8:42.2

400 Metres Relay

1. Germany—39.5
2. U.S.S.R.—40.1
3. Great Britain—40.2

1,600 Metres Relay

1. U.S.—3:02.2
2. Germany—3:02.7
3. British W.I.—3:04.0

20,000 Metres Walk

1. V. Golubichniy, U.S.S.R.—1:34:07.2
2. N. Freeman, Australia—1:34:16.4
3. S. Vickers, Gt. Brit.—1:34:56.4

50,000 Metres Walk

1. D. Thompson, Gt. Brit.—4:25:30.0
2. J. Ljunggren, Sweden—4:25:47.0
3. A. Pamich, Italy—4:27:55.4

High Jump

1. R. Shavlakadze, U.S.S.R.—7′1″
2. V. Brumel, U.S.S.R.—7′1″
3. J. Thomas, U.S.—7′0¼″

Broad Jump

1. R. Boston, U.S.—26′7¾″
2. I. Roberson, U.S.—26′7¼″
3. I. Ter-Ovanesyan, U.S.S.R.—26′4½″

Triple Jump

1. J. Schmidt, Poland—55′1¾″
2. V. Goryayev, U.S.S.R.—54′6⅝″
3. V. Kreyer, U.S.S.R.—53′10¾″

Pole Vault

1. D. Bragg, U.S.—15′5⅛″
2. R. Morris, U.S.—15′1⅛″
3. E. Landstrom, Finland—14′11⅛″

Shot Put

1. W. Nieder, U.S.—64′6¾″
2. W. P. O'brien, U.S.—62′8½″
3. D. Long, U.S.—62′4½″

Discus Throw

1. A. Oerter, U.S.—194′2″
2. R. Babka, U.S.—190′4¼″
3. R. Cochran, U.S.—187′6⅜″

Hammer Throw

1. V. Rudenkov, U.S.S.R.—220′1⅝″
2. G.Zdivotzky,Hungary—215′10⅛″
3. T. Rut, Poland—215′4¼″

Javelin Throw

1. V. Tsibulenko, U.S.S.R.—277′8⅜″
2. W. Kruger, Germany—260′4⅝″
3. G. Kulcsar, Hungary—257′9⅜″

Decathlon

1. R. Johnson, U.S.
2. Y. C. Yang, Formosa
3. V. Kuznetsov, U.S.S.R.

TRACK AND FIELD—WOMEN

100 Metres

1. W. Rudolph, U.S.—11.0
2. D. Hyman, Gt. Brit.—11.3
3. G. Leone, Italy—11.3

200 Metres

1. W. Rudolph, U.S.—24.0
2. J. Heine, Germany—24.4
3. D. Hyman, Great Britain—24.7

800 Metres

1. L. Shevtsova, U.S.S.R.—2:04.3
2. B. Jones, Australia—2:04.4
3. U. Donath, Germany—2:05.6

80 Metres Hurdles

1. I. Press, U.S.S.R.—10.8
2. C. Quinton, Gt. Brit.—10.9
3. G. Birkemeyer, Germany—11.0

400 Metres Relay

1. U.S.—44.5
2. Germany—44.8
3. Poland—45.0

High Jump

1. I. Balas, Roumania—6′0¾″
2. {J. Jozwiakowska, Poland—5′7⅜″
   D. Shirley, Gt. Brit.—5′7⅜″

Long Jump

1. V. Krepkina, U.S.S.R.—20′10¾″
2. E. Krzesinska, Poland—20′6¾″
3. H. Claus, Germany—20′4½″

Javelin Throw

1. E. Ozolina, U.S.S.R.—183′8″
2. D. Zatopkova, Czech.—176′5¼″
3. B. Kalediene, U.S.S.R.—175′4½″

Shot Put

1. T. Press, U.S.S.R.—56′9⅞″
2. J. Luttge, Germany—54′5⅞″
3. E. Brown, U.S.—53′10⅜″

Discus Throw

1. N. Ponomaryeva, U.S.S.R.—180′9¼″
2. T. Press, U.S.S.R.—172′6½″
3. L. Manoliu, Roumania—171′9⅜″

SWIMMING AND DIVING—MEN

100 Metres Free-Style
1. J. Devitt, Australia—55.2
2. L. Larson, U.S.—55.2
3. M. dos Santos, Brazil, 55.4

400 Metres Free-Style
1. M. Rose, Australia—4:18.3
2. T. Yamanaka, Japan—4:21.4
3. J. Konrads, Australia—4:21.8

1,500 Metres Free-Style
1. J. Konrads, Australia—17:19.6
2. M. Rose, Australia—17:21.7
3. G. Breen, U.S.—17:30.6

200 Metres Breast Stroke
1. W. Mulliken, U.S.—2:37.4
2. Y. Ohsaki, Japan—2:38.0
3. W. Mensonides, Neth.—2:39.7

200 Metres Butterfly
1. M. Troy, U.S.—2:12.8
2. N. Hayes, Australia—2:14.6
3. J. D. Gillanders, U.S.—2:15.3

800 Metres Free-Style Relay
1. U.S.—8:10.2
2. Japan—8:13.2
3. Australia—8:13.8

400 Metres Medley Relay
1. U.S.—4:05.4
2. Australia—4:12.0
3. Japan—4:12.2

Platform Diving
1. R. Webster, U.S.
2. G. Tobian, U.S.
3. B. Phelps, Great Britain

Springboard Diving
1. G. Tobian, U.S.
2. S. Hall, U.S.
3. J. Botella, Mexico

SWIMMING AND DIVING—WOMEN

100 Metres Free-Style
1. D. Fraser, Australia—1:01.2
2. C. von Saltza, U.S.—1:02.8
3. N. Steward, Great Britain—1:03.1

400 Metres Free-Style
1. C. von Saltza, U.S.—4:50.6
2. J. Cederqvist, Sweden—4:53.9
3. T. Lagerberg, Neth.—4:56.9

200 Metres Breast Stroke
1. A. Lonsbrough, Gt. Brit.—2:49.5
2. W. Urselmann, Germ.—2:50.0
3. B. Gobel, Germany—2:53.6

100 Metres Butterfly
1. C. Schuler, U.S.—1:09.5
2. M. Heemskerk, Neth.—1:10.4
3. J. Andrew, Australia—1:12.2

100 Metres Backstroke
1. L. Burke, U.S.—1:09.3
2. N. Steward, Gt. Brit.—1:10.8
3. S. Tanaka, Japan—1:11.4

400 Metres Free-Style Relay
1. U.S.—4:08.9
2. Australia—4:11.3
3. Germany—4:19.7

400 Metres Medley Relay
1. U.S.—4:41.1
2. Australia—4:45.9
3. Germany—4:47.6

Platform Diving
1. I. Kramer, Germany
2. P. J. Pope, U.S.
3. N. Krutova, U.S.S.R.

Springboard Diving
1. I. Kramer, Germany
2. P. J. Pope, U.S.
3. E. Ferris, Great Britain

BOXING

Flyweight
1. G. Torok, Hungary
2. S. Sivko, U.S.S.R.
3. { K. Tanabe, Japan
   { A. Elgvindi, UAR.

Bantamweight
1. O. Grigoryev, U.S.S.R.
2. P. Zamparini, Italy
3. { B. Bendig, Poland.
   { O. Taylor, Australia

Featherweight
1. F. Musso, Italy
2. J. Adamski, Poland
3. { W. Meyers, South Africa
   { J. Limmonen, Finland

Lightweight
1. K. Pazdzior, Poland
2. S. Lopapoli, Italy
3. { R. McTaggart, Great Britain
   { A. Lavdiono, Argentina

Light-Welterweight
1. B. Nemecek, Czechoslovakia
2. C. Quartey, Ghana
3. { Q. Daniels, U.S.
   { M. Kasprzyk, Poland

Welterweight
1. G. Benvenuti, Italy
2. Y. Radnoyak, U.S.S.R.
3. { L. Drogosz, Poland
   { J. Lloyd, Great Britain

VLADIMIR KUTS. The first Russian winner in an Olympic track and field event, won the 5,000 and 10,000 metres in Melbourne, 1956.

HERB ELLIOTT. The great Australian set a world record of 3:35.6 in the 1,500 metres at the 1956 Olympics in Melbourne.

OTIS DAVIS. The U.S. star set a world record of 44.9 seconds in the 400 metres final in Rome. 1960. Carl Kaufmann of Germany won the silver medal.

VALERIY BRUMEL Russian winner of the high jump in Tokyo. 1964.

...TER SNELL of New Zealand ...nning the 800 metres at Tokyo. ...64. Bill Crothers of Canada fin-...ed second and Wilson Kiprugut ...Kenya won the bronze medal.

BOB HAYES. The American football star ran the 100 metres in an Olympic record of 10 seconds flat, and also anchored the winning U.S. 400 metre relay team. Tokyo. 1964.

TAMARA PRESS
The beefy Russian girl won the shot put in the 1960 and 1964 Olympics and the discus in 1964

DON SCHOLLANDER, shown being congratulated by runner-up Leonid Ilyichev of Russia after winning the 100 metres in a post-Olympic meet in Moscow. Schollander won four gold medals for the U.S. in the 1964 Olympics.

Light-Middleweight
1. W. McClure, U.S.
2. C. Bossi, Italy
3. {B. Lagutin, U.S.S.R.
   {W. Fisher, Great Britain

Middleweight
1. E. Crook, U.S.
2. T. Walasek, Poland
3. {I. Monea, Roumania
   {E. Feofanov, U.S.S.R.

Light-Heavyweight
1. C. Clay, U.S.
2. Z. Pietrzykowski, Poland
3. {A. Madigan, Australia
   {G. Saraudi, Italy

Heavyweight
1. F. de Piccoli, Italy
2. D. Bekker, South Africa
3. {J. Nemec, Czechoslovakia
   {G. Siegmund, Germany

WRESTLING

Free-Style—Flyweight
1. A. Bilek, Turkey
2. M. Matsubara, Japan
3. S. Safepour, Iran

Fee-Style—Bantamweight
1. T. McCann, U.S.
2. M. Zalev, Bulgaria
3. T. Trojanowski, Poland

Free-Style—Featherweight
1. M. Dagistanli, Turkey
2. S. Ivanov, Bulgaria
3. V. Rubashvili, U.S.S.R.

Free-Style—Lightweight
1. S. Wilson, U.S.
2. V. Sinyavsky, U.S.S.R.
3. E. Dimov, Bulgaria

Free-Style—Welterweight
1. D. Blubaugh, U.S.
2. I. Ogan, Turkey
3. M. Bashir, Pakistan

Free-Style—Middleweight
1. H. Gungor, Turkey
2. G. Skhirtladze, U.S.S.R.
3. H. Antonsson, Sweden

Free-Style—Light-Heavyweight
1. I. Atli, Turkey
2. C. Tahkhti, Iran
3. A. Albul, U.S.S.R.

Free-Style—Heavyweight
1. W. Dietrich, Germany
2. H. Kaplan, Turkey
3. S. Sarasov, U.S.S.R.

Greco-Roman—Flyweight
1. D. Pirvulescu, Roumania
2. O. Sayed, U.A.R.
3. M. Paziraye, Iran

Greco-Roman—Bantamweight
1. O. Karavayev, U.S.S.R.
2. I. Cernea, Roumania
3. D. Stoikov, Bulgaria

Greco-Roman—Featherweight
1. M. Sille, Turkey
2. I. Polyak, Hungary
3. K. Vyrupayev, U.S.S.R.

Greco-Roman—Lightweight
1. A. Koridze, U.S.S.R.
2. B. Martinovic, Yugoslavia
3. R. Freij, Sweden

Greco-Roman—Welterweight
1. M. Bayrak, Turkey
2. G. Maritschnigg, Germany
3. R. Schiermeyer, France

Greco-Roman—Middleweight
1. D. Dobrev, Bulgaria
2. L. Metz, Germany
3. I. Taranu, Roumania

Greco-Roman—Light-Heavyweight
1. T. Kis, Turkey
2. K. Bimbalov, Bulgaria
3. G. Kartozia, U.S.S.R.

Greco-Roman—Heavyweight
1. I. Bogdan, U.S.S.R.
2. W. Dietrich, Germany
3. K. Kubat, Czechoslovakia

WEIGHT-LIFTING

Bantamweight
1. C. Vinci, U.S.—759 lb.
2. Y. Miyake, Japan, 742½ lb.
3. K. Khan, Iran—726 lb.

Featherweight
1. E. Minayev, U.S.S.R.—819½ lb.
2. I. Berger, U.S.—797½ lb.
3. S. Mannironi, Italy—775½ lb.

Lightweight
1. V. Busheyev, U.S.S.R.—876 lb.
2. T. H. Liang, Korea, 837½ lb.
3. A. W. Aziz, Iraq—837½ lb.

Middleweight
1. A. Kurynov, U.S.S.R.—964¼ lb.
2. T. Kono, U.S.—942 lb.
3. G. Veres, Hungary—895 lb.

Light-Heavyweight
1. I. Palinski, Poland—975¼ lb.
2. J. George, U.S.—947¼ lb.
3. J. Bochenek, Poland—925¾ lb.

Middle-Heavyweight
1. A. Vorobyev, U.S.S.R.—1041¼ lb.
2. T. Lomakin, U.S.S.R.—1,008 lb.
3. L. Martin, Gt. Brit.—980½ lb.

Heavyweight
1. Y. Vlasov, U.S.S.R.—1,184½ lb.
2. J. Bradford, U.S.—1,129½ lb.
3. N. Schemansky, U.S.—1,102 lb.

CYCLING

1,000 Metres Scratch
1. S. Gaiardoni, Italy
2. L. Sterckx, Belgium
3. V. Gasparella, Italy

1,000 Metres Time-Trial
1. S. Gaiardoni, Italy—1:07.27
2. D. Cieseler, Germany—1:08.75
3. R. Vargashkin, U.S.S.R.—1:08.86

2,000 Metres Tandem
1. S. Bianchetto/G. Beghetto, Italy
2. J. Simon/L. Staber, Germany
3. B. Vasiliyev/V. Leonov, U.S.S.R.

4,000 Metres Team Pursuit
1. Italy—4:30.90
2. Germany—4:35.78
3. U.S.S.R.—4:34.06

Road Race
1. V. Kapitonov, U.S.S.R.—4:20:37.0
2. L. Trape, Italy—4:20:37.0
3. W. Van den Bergnen, Belgium—4:20:57.0

Road Team Time Trial
1. Italy—2:14:33.53
2. Germany—2:16:56.31
3. U.S.S.R.—2:18:41.67

EQUESTRIAN SPORTS

Grand Prix Jumping
1. R. d'Inzeo, Italy
2. P. d'Inzeo, Italy
3. D. Broome, Great Britain

Grand Prix Jumping—Teams
1. Germany
2. U.S.
3. Italy

Grand Prix Dressage
1. S. Filatov, U.S.S.R.
2. G. Fischer, Switzerland
3. J. Neckermann, Germany

Three-Day Event
1. L. Morgan, Australia
2. N. Lavis, Australia
3. A. Buhler, Switzerland

Three-Day Event—Teams
1. Australia   2. Switzerland   3. France

FENCING—MEN

Foil—Individual
1. V. Zhdanovich, U.S.S.R.
2. Y. Sisikin, U.S.S.R.
3. A. Axelrod, U.S.

Foil—Team
1. U.S.S.R.
2. Italy
3. Germany

Epée—Individual
1. G. Delfino, Italy
2. A. Jay, Great Britain
3. B. Khabarov, U.S.S.R.

Epée—Team
1. Italy
2. Great Britain
3. U.S.S.R.

Sabre—Individual
1. R. Karpati, Hungary
2. Z. Horvath, Hungary
3. W. Calarese, Italy

Sabre—Team
1. Hungary
2. Poland
3. Italy

FENCING—WOMEN

Foil—Individual
1. H. Schmid, Germany
2. V. Rastvorova, U.S.S.R.
3. M. Vicol, Roumania

Foil—Team
1. U.S.S.R.
2. Hungary
3. Italy

GYMNASTICS—MEN

Combined Exercises—Individual
1. B. Shakhlin, U.S.S.R.
2. T. Ono, Japan
3. Y. Titov, U.S.S.R.

Combined Exercises—Team
1. Japan
2. U.S.S.R.
3. Italy

Free Exercises
1. N. Aihara, Japan
2. Y. Titov, U.S.S.R.
3. F. Menichelli, Italy

Horizontal Bar
1. T. Ono, Japan
2. M. Takemoto, Japan
3. B. Shakhlin, U.S.S.R.

Parallel Bars
1. B. Shakhlin, U.S.S.R.
2. G. Carminucci, Italy
3. T. Ono, Japan

Pommelled Horse
1. { E. Ekman, Finland
   { Boris Shakhlin, U.S.S.R.
3. S. Tsurumi, Japan

Long Horse Vault
1. { T. Ono, Japan
   { B. Shaklin, U.S.S.R.
3. V. Portnoi, U.S.S.R.

Rings
1. A. Azaryan, U.S.S.R.
2. B. Shakhlin, U.S.S.R.
3. { V. Kapsazov, Bulgaria
   { T. Ono, Japan

GYMNASTICS—WOMEN

Combined Exercises—Individual
1. L. Latynin, U.S.S.R.
2. S. Muratova, U.S.S.R.
3. P. Astakhova, U.S.S.R.

Parallel Bars
1. P. Astakhova, U.S.S.R.
2. L. Latynina, U.S.S.R.
3. T. Lyukhina, U.S.S.R.

Combined Exercises—Individual
1. U.S.S.R.
2. Czechoslovakia
3. Roumania

Horse Vault
1. M. Nikolayeva, U.S.S.R.
2. S. Muratova, U.S.S.R.
3. L. Latynina, U.S.S.R.

Beam
1. E. Boskova, Czechoslovakia
2. L. Latynina, U.S.S.R.
3. S. Muratova, U.S.S.R.

Floor Exercises
1. L. Latynina, U.S.S.R.
2. P. Astakhova, U.S.S.R.
3. T. Lyukhina, U.S.S.R.

ROWING

Single Sculls
1. V. Ivanov, U.S.S.R.—7:13.96
2. A. Hill, Germany—7:20.21
3. T. Kocerka, Poland—7:21.26

Coxed Pairs
1. Germany—7:29.14
2. U.S.S.R.—7:30.17
3. U.S.—7:34.58

Double Sculls
1. V. Kozak/P. Schmidt, Czech.— 6:47.50
2. A. Berkutov/Y. Tyukalov, U.S.S.R.—6:50.48
3. E. Huerlimann/R. Larcher, Switzerland—6:50.59

Coxswainless Fours
1. U.S.—6:26.26
2. Italy—6:28.78
3. U.S.S.R.—6:29.62

Coxswainless Pairs
1. V. Boreyko/O. Golovanov, U.S.S.R.—7:02.01
2. J. Kloimstein/A. Sageder, Austria—7:03.69
3. V. Lehtela/T. Pitkanen, Finland— 7:03.80

Coxed Fours
1. Germany—6:39.12
2. France—6:41.62
3. Italy—6:43.12

Eights
1. Germany—5:57.18
2. Canada—6:01.52
3. Czechoslovakia—6:04.84

CANOEING—MEN

Kayak Singles—1,000 Metres
1. E. Hansen, Denmark—3:53.0
2. I. Szoellosi, Hungary—3:54.0
3. G. Fredriksson, Sweden—3:55.8

Canadian Singles—1,000 Metres
1. J. Parti, Hungary—4:33.9
2. A. Silayev, U.S.S.R.—4:34.4
3. L. Rottman, Roumania—4:35.8

Kayak Pairs—1,000 Metres
1. G. Fredriksson/S. Sjodelius, Sweden—3:34.7
2. A. Szente/G. Meszaros, Hungary—3:34.9
3. S. Kaplaniak/W. Zieliski, Poland—3:37.3

Canadian Pairs—10,000 Metres
1. L. Geyshter/S. Makharenko, U.S.S.R.—4:17.9
2. A. Dezi/F. Lamacchia, Italy— 4:20.7
3. I. Farkas/A. Toro, Hungary— 4:20.8

20,000 Metres Relay
1. Germany—7:39.4
2. Hungary—7:44.0
3. Denmark—7:46.0

CANOEING—WOMEN

Kayak Singles—500 Metres

1. A. Seredina, U.S.S.R.—2:08.1
2. T. Zenz, Germany—2:08.2
3. D. Walkowiak, Poland—2:10.4

Kayak Pairs—500 Metres

1. M. Shubina/A. Seredina, U.S.S.R.—1:54.7
2. T. Zenz/I. Hartmann, Germany— 1:56.6
3. V. Egresi/K. Fried, Hungary— 1:58.2

YACHTING

5.5 Metres

1. "Minotaur," U.S.
2. "Web II," Denmark
3. "Ballerina IV," Switzerland

Star

1. "Tornado," U.S.S.R.
2. "Ma' Lindo," Portugal
3. "Shrew II," U.S.

Dragon

1. "Nirefs," Greece
2. "Tango," Argentina
3. "Venilia," Italy

Flying Dutchman

1. "Sirene," Norway
2. "Skum," Denmark
3. "Macky VI," Germany

Finn

1. P. Elvstrom, Denmark
2. A. Tyukelov, U.S.S.R.
3. A. Nelis, Belgium

SHOOTING

Free Pistol

1. A. Gustchin, U.S.S.R.
2. M. Oumarov, U.S.S.R.
3. Y. Yoshikawa, Japan

Small-Bore Rifles—Prone

1. P. Kohnke, Germany
2. J. Hill, U.S.
3. P. Forcella, Venezuela

Automatic Pistol

1. W. McMillan, U.S.
2. P. Linnosvuo, Finland
3. A. Zabelin, U.S.S.R.

Small-Bore Rifle—Three-Positions

1. V. Shamburkin, U.S.S.R.
2. M. Nyesov, U.S.S.R.
3. K. Zaehriger, Germany

Free Rifle

1. H. Mammerer, Austria
2. M. Spillman, Switzerland
3. V. Borisov, U.S.S.R.

Clay Pigeon

1. I. Dumitrescu, Roumania
2. G. Rossini, Italy
3. S. Kalinin, U.S.S.R.

MODERN PENTATHLON

Individual

1. F. Nemeth, Hungary
2. I. Nagy, Hungary
3. R. Beck, U.S.

Teams

1. Hungary
2. U.S.S.R.
3. U.S.

BASKETBALL

1. U.S.
2. U.S.S.R.
3. Brazil

SOCCER

1. Yugoslavia
2. Denmark
3. Hungary

FIELD HOCKEY

1. Pakistan
2. India
3. Spain

WATER POLO

1. Italy
2. U.S.S.R.
3. Hungary

Chapter 16

THE XVIII OLYMPIAD

Tokyo, 1964

PETER Snell, Bob Hayes, Abebe Bikila and the Russian sisters, Tamara and Irina Press are just a few of the track and field athletes who made history at the 1964 Olympic Games in Tokyo.

But it was the swimmers who stole the show.

Olympic records fell in all 18 events and Americans made off with 16 of the 22 swimming and diving competitions, setting 11 world records in the process.

Don Schollander, an 18-year-old student about to enter Yale University, won four gold medals, something no Olympic swimmer had done before. He won the 100 and 400 metres and swam the anchor legs of both the 400 and 800 metre relay teams.

After setting world records in both the 200 and 400 metres four months before the Olympics, Schollander went into a slump and had lost several races, including one in the U.S. Olympic trials. He was so despondent that he wanted to quit the team. But he regained his confidence in the 100 metre final, sprinting the last five metres to beat Don McGregor of Great Britain by a tenth of a second. Next, Schollander, Steve Clark, Mike Austin and Gary Ilman won the 400 metre relay in a world record 3:33.2.

In the 400 metres freestyle, Schollander once again put on an astonishing dash of speed in the last few metres to set a world record 4:12.2. For Schollander, this was strictly a race against the clock. He beat Frank Wiegand of Germany by 2.7 seconds.

Finally, Schollander, Ilman, Clark and Roy Saari combined for another world record 7:52.1 in easily winning the 800 metre relay by better than seven seconds from Germany. Schollander swam the fastest leg in 1:55.6.

Clark, backstroker Harold Mann, breast stroker Bill Craig and butterfly artist Fred Schmidt swam the 400 metre medley relay in a world record 3:58.4 after the second-string U.S. team had set an Olmpic record of 4:05.1 in the preliminaries. Mann, swimming the lead-off leg, was credited with a world record 59.6 seconds, the first time anyone had broken the minute mark at this distance. Schmidt and Clark also swam faster than the existing world record, but were not credited because of the flying starts used in relays.

Jed Graef, a six-and-a-half footer from Princeton, won the first important race of his career and set a world record of 2:10.3 in the 200 metre backstroke while leading Gary Dilley and Robert Bennett to a U.S. sweep.

Seventeen-year-old Dick Roth broke his own world record in winning the 400 metre individual medley relay in 4:45.4 and then went into hospital to have his appendix removed. He had complained of stomach pains before the race and was almost scratched. However, he insisted on swimming before having the operation.

Fifteen-year-old Sharon Stouder, who had finished second to Dawn Fraser in the 100 metre freestyle when the Australian champion won the event for the third time, then joined the 400 metres freestyle relay team which set a world record 4:03.8. Next, she switched strokes to win the 100 metre butterfly in 1:04.7, beating former record holder Ada Kok of Holland by five feet. She swam the butterfly leg for the record setting (4:33.9) 400 metre medley relay team.

Cathy Ferguson, 16, also a member of that team, set an individual world record of 1:07.7 in the 100 metres backstroke in which the next two swimmers, Christine Caron of France and Virginia Duenkel of the United States, also bettered the former record.

Donna de Varona, a member of the freestyle relay team, won a gold medal in the 400 metre individual medley, beating teammates Sharon Finegan and Martha Randall for a grand slam.

Besides Miss Fraser, the only other swimmer to beat the American women was world record holder Galina Prozumenschikova of Russia who defeated 14-year-old Claudia Kolb of the U.S. in the 200 metres breast stroke.

Australians picked up the other three gold medals in men's swimming. Roy Saari of the United States had set a world record 16:58.7 in the trials but finished seventh in the final, won by Bob Windle. Ian O'Brien set a world record 2:27.8 in the 200 metre breast stroke, and Kevin Berry swam the 200 metre butterfly in a world record 2:06.6.

The Americans won three of the four diving medals. Defending champion Bob Webster retained his platform diving championship and Ken Sitzberger led a U.S. sweep in the sprinboard diving division. Leslie Bush, 17, of the United States upset defending champion Ingrid Kramer Engel of Germany in platform diving but Mrs. Engel retained her springboard diving crown.

At Rome, Peter Snell was an unknown New Zealander when he upset Roger Moens of Belgium in the 800 metres. At Tokyo, his name was almost a household word and he lived up to his reputation. Between Olympics he had set world records for the mile and the 800 yards. When he was not competing, he kept in training by running 100 miles a week, usually in the mountains.

At Tokyo, he became the first runner in 44 years to win the Olympic 800 and 1,500 metres In the 800, he was running behind Bill Crothers of Canada going into the last turn when he started his finishing kick about 250 yards from home, passing Crothers. Crothers started his sprint a little late and was catching up to the New Zealander but finished three yards behind Snell who ran the second fastest 800 metres in history —1:45.1, four fifths of a second behind his own world record. In the 1,500 metres, Snell ran the final quarter in a blazing 52.9 seconds and eased up near the finish because he had the others beaten by 10 yards. He did not try for the world record 3:35.6 Australian Herb Elliott had set at the Rome Olympics. When Snell finally retired a year later, he held the world record for 800 metres and half a mile, although his mile record had been broken by Michel Jazy of France.

At Tokyo, Jazy elected not to run against Snell and chose the 5,000 metres instead. He was running second to Australian Ron Clarke most of the way and on the last lap, he passed the tiring Clarke and thought he had won. But a 27-year-old American, Bob Schull, ran up from last place to challenge the Frenchman and passed Jazy just under 100 yards from home. The amazed Jazy fell back to fourth place behind Harold Norpoth of Germany and Bill Dellinger of the United States, the bronze medallist. Schul was the first American ever to win the Olympic 5,000 metres.

The United States also won the 10,000 metres for the first time in Olympic history. The winner was a 26-year-old part Sioux Indian named Billy Mills. Before the race, hardly anybody had heard of him. He had never won a big race in his life. From the beginning, Mills alternated setting the pace with Ron Clarke, the world record holder. On the final lap, Mohamed Gammoudi of Tunisia passed them. Clarke caught up to Gammoudi in the stretch with Mills 10 yards behind him, but then the 155-pounder from Kansas produced an amazing sprint to beat Gammoudi by three yards and set an Olympic record 28:24.4. Ron Clarke was third, and Pyotr Bolotnikov of Russia, who had set the former world record in 1962, was far back in the field of 42 starters.

Abebe Bikila, by now promoted to a sergeant in Haile Selassie's Imperial Guard, became the only man to win an Olympic marathon twice. And this time, at the age of 32, he had an easier time of it than in Rome when he ran barefooted and won by less than a minute. Wearing shoes in Tokyo, he led most of the way and finished better than four minutes ahead of Basil Heatley of Great Britain.

What Bikila had in stamina, Bob Hayes had in speed. The Florida A & M football star ran the 100 metres in 9.9 seconds in a semi-final, but the world record was disallowed because of a favoring wind. In the final, he equalled the world record in 10 seconds flat, easily beating Enrique Figuerola of Cuba. But Hayes saved his most amazing performance for the 400 metre relay when he ran the last leg in 8.6 seconds to overcome a four yard deficit and lead the U.S. team to a three yard victory over Poland in a world record 39 seconds flat. Hayes personal record, though, did not count because of his running start, but it was undoubtedly the fastest 100 metres ever run.

Henry Carr of the United States, set an Olympic record of 20.3 seconds in the 200 metres and only a headwind stopped him from equalling or breaking his own world record of 20.2 seconds. He won by almost five feet over U.S. Army Private Paul Drayton after Livio Berutti, the defending champion from Italy, had taken the early lead.

Mike Larrabee, a 20-year-old mathematics teacher who almost missed the Olympics because of injuries, came from behind to win the 400 metres over the favored Wendell Motley of Trinidad. Larrabee and Carr then helped the United States to a 1,600 metre relay victory in a world record 3:00.7, beating France by five yards.

Hayes Jones, who had finished third in the 110 metre hurdles at Rome, struck gold in Tokyo, defeating U.S. teammate Blaine Lindgren by two feet. They were even until the last hurdle when Lindgren lost his stride.

Warren Cawley, who set a world record of 49.1 seconds in the U.S. Olympic trials, slowed down to 49.6 seconds in the Olympic 400 metre hurdle final, but beat John Cooper of Great Britain by half a second.

In the high jump, defending champion Robert Shavlakadze was eliminated early leaving it up to Valeriy Brumel of Russia and John Thomas of the U.S. who had finished second and third at Rome. Once again, Brumel beat Thomas, but it was an extremely close contest. Brumel cleared 7'1" on his first try, but Thomas missed once, jumping it on his second attempt. Both cleared 7'1¾" at their first attempt, and then they both failed at 7'2½". Brumel thus was awarded the gold medal because of one less failure at the 7'1" level.

In the jumps Lynn Davies of Wales waited for a break in the wind and defeated defending champion and world record holder Ralph Boston by 1¾" in the broad jump. Igor Ter-Ovanesyan of Russia was once again third. Josef Schmidt of Poland successfully defended his triple jump title. And Fred Hansen kept the U.S. unbroken streak in the pole vault intact. The Americans

have not been beaten in this event since the moder
Olympics began in 1896.

In the shot put, Dallas Long, who had finished th
in 1960, won the gold medal with a heave of 66'8'
to break the Olympic record that runner-up Ran
Matson had set a few minutes before. Parry O'E
who had won in 1952 and 1956 and was secor
1960, produced the best throw of his Olympic career,
but only came fourth.

Al Oerter won his third straight gold medal in the
discus. Despite a torn rib cartillage, his throw of
200'1½" produced a new Olympic record.

Willi Holdorf of Germany won the decathlon over
an elite field that included the favored C. K. Yang of
Formosa, the world record holder. Holdorf, 24, defeated Rein Aun of Russia, although he won only two
of the 10 events—the shot put and the 400 metres.
Yang finished fifth.

Abdon Pamich of Italy was leading in the 50 kilometre walk when he had to leave the course to use the
lavatory at a roadside hotel. However, he caught up to
Vince Nihill of Great Britain, set a world record
4:11.12.4, and won the gold medal.

The 20,000 metres walk winner, Ken Matthews of
Great Britain, was held up for a while coming into the
stadium when his excited wife burst through a security
cordon to give him a congratulatory kiss. Then, she
chased him to the finish line with Japanese officials in
pursuit and gave him a two-minute embrace.

The Press sisters took home three gold medals to
Russia. The mammoth Tamara successfully defended
her shot put title and also won the discus throw. She
had won a silver medal for the discus in Rome. Her
sister Irina set a world record in winning the women's
pentathlon. It was the first time that the event—con-
sisting of the 80 metre hurdles, shot put, high jump,
long jump and 200 metres—had been on the Olympic
program.

Michaela Penes of Roumania set a world record
198"7½" in the javelin, and Mary Rand of Great
Britain a world record 22'2¼" in the long jump. Defending champion Iolanda Balas of Roumania again
won the high jump.

Wyomia Tyus of the United States equalled the world record of 11.2 seconds in the 100 metres trials and won the final in 11.4 seconds over Edith McGuire of the U.S. Miss McGuire won the 200 metres. However the two girls missed a baton pass in the 400 metre relay and lost to a Polish team which set a world record of 43.6 seconds.

British school teacher Ann Packer set a world record 2:01.1 for 800 metres.

Taking all events in consideration, the Americans won 26 gold medals to 20 for Russia. But in overall medals, the Russians were ahead 96-90. On orders from the International Olympic Committee, no unofficial point totals were kept.

OFFICIAL XVIII OLYMPIAD RESULTS

Tokyo, 1964

TRACK AND FIELD—MEN

100 Metres

1. R. Hayes, U.S.—10.0
2. E. Figuerola, Cuba—10.2
3. H. Jerome, Canada—10.2

200 Metres

1. H. Carr, U.S.—20.3
2. P. Drayton, U.S.—20.5
3. E. Roberts, Trinidad—20.6

400 Metres

1. M. Larrabee, U.S.—45.1
2. W. Mottley, Trinidad—45.2
3. A. Badenski, Poland—45.6

800 Metres

1. P. Snell, New Zealand—1:45.1
2. W. Crothers, Canada—1:45.6
3. W. Kiprugut, Kenya—1:45.9

1,500 Metres

1. P. Snell, New Zealand—3:38.1
2. J. Odlozil, Czechoslovakia—3:39.6
3. J. Davies, New Zealand—3:39.6

5,000 Metres

1. R. Schul, U.S.—13:48.8
2. H. Norpoth, Germany—13:49.6
3. W. Dellinger, U.S.—13:49.8

10,000 Metres

1. W. Mills, U.S.—28:24.4
2. M. Gammoudi, Tunisia—28:24.8
3. R. Clarke, Australia—28:25.8

Marathon

1. A. Bikila, Ethiopia—2:12:11.2
2. B. Heatley, Gt. Brit.—2:16:19.2
3. K. Tsuburaya, Japan—2:16:22.8

110 Metre Hurdles

1. H. Jones, U.S.—13.6
2. B. Lindgren, U.S.—13.7
3. A. Mikhailov, U.S.S.R.—13.7

400 Metre Hurdles

1. W. Cawley, U.S.—49.6
2. J. Cooper, Great Britain—50.1
3. S. Morale, Italy—50.1

3,000 Metre Steeplechase

1. G. Roelants, Belgium—8:30.8
2. M. Herriott, Great Britain—8:32.4
3. I. Belyayev, U.S.S.R.—8:33.8

400 Metre Relay

1. U.S.—39.0
2. Poland—39.3
3. France—39.3

1,600 Metre Relay

1. U.S.—3:00.7
2. Great Britain—3:01.6

20,000 Metre Walk

1. K. Matthews, Gt. Brit.—1:29:34.0
2. D. Lindner, Germany—1:31:13.2
3. V. Golubnichy, U.S.S.R.—1:31:59.4

50,000 Metre Walk
1. A. Pamich, Italy—4:11:12.4
2. P. Nihill, Gt. Brit.—4:11:31.2
3. I. Pettersson, Sweden—4:14:17.4

High Jump
1. V. Brumel, U.S.S.R.—7'1¾"
2. J. Thomas, U.S.—7'1¾"
3. J. Rambo, U.S.—7'1"

Broad Jump
1. L. Davies, Gt. Brit.—26'5½"
2. R. Boston, U.S.—26'4"
3. I. Ter-Ovanesyan, U.S.S.R.—26'2½"

Triple Jump
1. J. Schmidt, Poland—55'3½"
2. O. Fyedoseyev, U.S.S.R.—54'7¾"
3. V. Kravchenko, U.S.S.R.—54'4½"

Pole Vault
1. F. Hansen, U.S.—16'8¾"
2. W. Reinhardt, Germany—16'6¾"
3. K. Lehnertz, Germany—16'4¾"

Shot Put
1. D. Long, U.S.—66'8½"
2. R. Matson, U.S.—66'3¼"
3. V. Varju, Hungary—63'7¼"

Discus Throw
1. A. Oerter, U.S.—200'1½"
2. L. Danek, Czech.—198'6½"
3. D. Weill, U.S.—195'2"

Hammer Throw
1. R. Klim, U.S.S.R.—228'10½"
2. G. Zsivotsky, Hungary—226'8"
3. U. Beyer, Germany—223'4½"

Javelin Throw
1. P. Nevala, Finland—271'2¼"
2. G. Kulscar, Hungary—270'0¾"
3. J. Lusis, U.S.S.R.—264'2"

Decathlon
1. W. Holdorf, Germany
2. R. Aun, U.S.S.R.
3. H. Walde, Germany

TRACK AND FIELD—WOMEN

100 Metres
1. W. Tyus, U.S.—11.4
2. W. Maguire, U.S.—11.6
3. E. Kobukowska, Poland—11.6

200 Metres
1. E. Maguire, U.S.—23.0
2. I. Kirszenstein, Poland—23.1
3. M. Black, Australia—23.1

400 Metres
1. B. Cuthbert, Australia—52.0
2. A. Packer, Gt. Brit.—52.2
3. J. Amoore, Australia—53.4

800 Metres
1. A. Packer, Gt. Brit.—2:01.1
2. M. Dupureur, France—2:01.9
3. M. Chamberlain, New Zealand—2:02.8

80 Metres Hurdles
1. K. Balzer, Germany—10.5
2. T. Ciepla, Poland—10.5
3. P. Kilborn, Australia—10.5

400 Metres Relay
1. Poland—43.6
2. U.S.—43.9
3. Great Britain—44.0

High Jump
1. I. Balas, Roumania—6'2¾"
2. M. Brown, Australia—5'10¾"
3. T. Chenchik, U.S.S.R.—5'10"

Long Jump
1. M. Rand, Gt. Brit.—22'2½"
2. I. Kirszenstein, Poland—21'7¾"
3. T. Schelkanova, U.S.S.R.—21'0¾"

Javelin Throw
1. M. Penes, Roumania—198'7½"
2. M. Rudasne, Hungary—191'2"
3. Y. Gorchakova, U.S.S.R.—187'2½"

Shot Put
1. T. Press, U.S.S.R.—59'6¼"
2. R. Garisch, Germany—57'9¼"
3. G. Zybina, U.S.S.R.—57'3"

Discus Throw
1. T. Press, U.S.S.R.—187'10¾"
2. I. Lotz, Germany—186'8½"
3. L. Manoliu, Roumania—186'11"

Pentathlon
1. I. Press, U.S.S.R.
2. M. Rand, Great Britain
3. G. Bystrova, U.S.S.R.

SWIMMING AND DIVING—MEN

100 Metres Free-Style
1. D. Schollander, U.S.—53.4
2. R. McGregor, Great Britain—53.5
3. H. Klein, Germany—54.0

400 Metres Free-Style
1. D. Schollander, U.S.—4:12.2
2. F. Wiegand, Germany—4:14.9
3. A. Wood, Australia—4:15.1

1,500 Metres Free-Style
1. R. Windle, Australia—17:01.7
2. J. Nelson, U.S.—17:03.0
3. A. Wood, Australia—17:07.7

200 Metre Breast Stroke
1. I. O'Brien, Australia—2:27.8
2. G. Prokopenko, U.S.S.R.—2:28.2
3. C. Jastremski, U.S.—2:29.6

200 Metres Butterfly
1. K. Barry, Australia—2:06.6
2. C. Robie, U.S.—2:07.5
3. F. Schmidt, U.S.—2:09.3

200 Metre Backstroke
1. J. Graef, U.S.—2:10.3
2. G. Dilley, U.S.—2:10.5
3. R. Bennett, U.S.—2:13.1

400 Metres Individual Medley
1. R. Roth, U.S.—4:45.4
2. R. Saari, U.S.—4:47.1
3. G. Hetz, Germany—4:51.0

400 Metres Free-Style Relay
1. U.S.—7:52.1
2. Germany—7:59.3
3. Japan—8:03.8

800 Metres Medley Relay
1. U.S.—3:58.4
2. Germany—4:01.6
3. Australia—4:02.3

Platform Diving
1. R. Webster, U.S.
2. K. Dibiasi, Italy
3. T. Gompf, U.S.

Springboard Diving
1. K. Sitzberger, U.S.   2. F. Gorman, U.S.   3. L. Andreasen, U.S.

SWIMMING AND DIVING—WOMEN

100 Metres Free-Style
1. D. Fraser, Australia—59.5
2. S. Stouder, U.S.—59.9
3. K. Ellis, U.S.—1:00.8

400 Metres Free-Style
1. V. Duenkel, U.S.—4:43.3
2. M. Ramenofsky, U.S.—4:44.6
3. T. Stickles, U.S.—4:47.2

200 Metres Breast Stroke
1. G. Prozumenschikova, U.S.S.R.—2:46.4
2. C. Kolb, U.S.—2:47.6
3. S. Babanina, U.S.S.R.—2:48.6

100 Metres Butterfly
1. S. Stouder, U.S.—1:04.7
2. A. Kok, Netherlands—1:05.6
3. K. Ellis, U.S.—1:06.0

100 Metres Backstroke
1. C. Fergusson, U.S.—1:07.7
2. C. Caron, France—1:07.9
3. V. Duenkel, U.S.—1:08.0

400 Metres Individual Medley
1. D. De Varona, U.S.—5:18.7
2. S. Finnegan, U.S.—5:24.1
3. M. Randall, U.S.—2:24.2

400 Metres Free-Style Relay
1. U.S.—4:03.8
2. Australia—4:06.9
3. Netherlands—4:12.0

400 Metres Medley Relay
1. U.S.—4:33.9
2. Netherlands—4:37.0
3. U.S.S.R.—4:39.2

Platform Diving
1. L. Bush, U.S.
2. I. Engel, Germany
3. G. Alekseyeva, U.S.S.R.

Springboard Diving
1. I. Engel, Germany
2. J. Collier, U.S.
3. P. Willard, U.S.

BOXING

Flyweight
1. F. Atzori, Italy
2. A. Olek, Poland
3. { R. Carmody, U.S.
   { S. Sorokin, U.S.S.R.

Bantamweight
1. T. Sakurai, Japan
2. S. C. Chung, South Korea
3. { J. Fabila, Mexico
   { W. Rodriguez, Uraguay

Featherweight
1. S. Stepashkin, U.S.S.R.
2. A. Villaneuva, Phillipines
3. { C. Brown, U.S.
   { H. Schultz, Germany

Lightweight
1. J. Grudzien, Poland
2. V. Barannikov, U.S.S.R.
3. { R. Harris, U.S.
   { J. McCourt, Ireland

Light-Welterweight
1. J. Kulej, Poland
2. E. Frolov, U.S.S.R.
3. { E. Blay, Ghana
   { H. Galhia, Tunisia

Welterweight
1. M. Kasprzyk, Poland
2. R. Tamulis, U.S.S.R.
3. { P. Purhonen, Finland
   { S. Bertini, Italy

Light-Middleweight
1. B. Lagutin, U.S.S.R.
2. J. Gonzales, France
3. { N. Maiyegun, Nigeria
   { J. Grzesiak, Poland

Middleweight
1. V. Popenchenko, U.S.S.R.
2. E. Schultz, Germany
3. { F. Valla, Italy
   { T. Walasek, Poland

Light-Heavyweight
1. C. Pinto, Italy
2. A. Kiselyov, U.S.S.R.
3. { A. Nicolov, Bulgaria
   { Z. Pietrzykowski, Poland

Heavyweight
1. J. Frazier, U.S.
2. H. Huber, Germany
3. { G. Ros, Italy
   { V. Yemelyanov, U.S.S.R.

JUDO

Open Class
1. A. Geesink, Netherlands
2. A. Kaminaga, Japan
3. { T. Boronovskis, Austria
   { K. Glahn, Germany

Heavyweight
1. I. Akano, Japan
2. W. Hofmann, Germany
3. { J. Bregman, U.S.
   { E. T. Kim, South Korea

Lightweight
1. T. Nakatani, Japan
2. E. Haenni, Switzerland
3. { O. Styepanov, U.S.S.R.
   { A. Bogulubov, U.S.S.R.

WRESTLING

Free-Style—Flyweight
1. Y. Yoshida, Japan
2. C. Chang, Korea
3. S. A. Haydari, Iran

Free-Style—Bantamweight
1. Y. Uetake, Japan
2. H. Akbas, Turkey
3. A. A. Ogly, U.S.S.R.

Free-Style—Featherweight
1. O. Watanabe, Japan
2. S. Ivanov, Bulgaria
3. N. Khokhashvili, U.S.S.R.

Free-Style—Lightweight
1. E. Dimor, Bulgaria
2. K. Rost, Germany
3. I. Horiuchi, Japan

Free-Style—Welterweight
1. I. Ogan, Turkey
2. G. Sagaradze, U.S.S.R.
3. M. Sanatkaran, Iran

Free-Style—Middleweight
1. P. Gardjer, Bulgaria
2. H. Gungor, Turkey
3. D. Brand, U.S.

Free-Style—Light-Heavyweight
1. A. Medred, U.S.S.R.
2. A. Ayik, Turkey
3. S. Sherifov, Bulgaria

Free-Style—Heavyweight
1. A. Wanitsky, U.S.S.R.
2. L. Djiber, Bulgaria
3. I1. Kaplan, Turkey

Greco-Roman—Flyweight
1. T. Hanahara, Japan
2. A. Kerezov, Bulgaria
3. D. Pirvulesco, Roumania

Greco-Roman—Bantamweight
1. M. Ichiguchi, Japan
2. V. Trostiansky, U.S.S.R.
3. I. Cernea, Roumania

Greco-Roman—Featherweight
1. I. Polyak, Hungary
2. R. Rurua, U.S.S.R.
3. B. Martinovic, Yugoslavia

Greco-Roman—Lightweight
1. K. Ayvaz, Turkey
2. V. Bularca, Roumania
3. D. Gvantseladze, U.S.S.R.

Greco-Roman—Middleweight
1. B. Simic, Yugoslavia
2. J. Kormanik, Czechoslovakia
3. L. Metz, Germany

Greco-Roman—Light-Heavyweight
1. B. Alexandrov, Bulgaria
2. P. Svensson, Sweden
3. H. Kiehl, Germany

Greco-Roman—Heavyweight
1. I. Kosma, Hungary
2. A. Roschin, U.S.S.R.
3. W. Dietrich, Germany

WEIGHT-LIFTING

Bantamweight
1. A. Vakhonin, U.S.S.R.—787¾ lb.
2. I. Foeldi, Hungary—782¼ lb.
3. S. Ichinoseki, Japan—765¾ lb.

Featherweight
1. Y. Miyake, Japan—876 lb.
2. I. Berger, U.S.—842¾ lb.
3. M. Nowak, Poland—832 lb.

Lightweight
1. W. Baszanowski, Poland—953¼ lb.
2. V. Kaplunov, U.S.S.R.—953¼ lb.
3. M. Zielinski, Poland—925½ lb.

Middleweight
1. H. Zdrazila, Czech.—980¾ lb.
2. V. Kurentsov, U.S.S.R.—969¾ lb.
3. M. Ohuchi, Japan—964 lb.

Light-Heavyweight

1. R. Plyukeider, U.S.S.R.—1,046 lb.
2. G. Toth, Hungary—1,030¼ lb.
3. G. Veres, Hungary—1,030 lb.

Middle-Heavyweight

1. V. Golovanov, U.S.S.R.—1,074 lb.
2. L. Martin, Gt. Brit.—1,046½ lb.
3. I. Palinski, Poland—1,030 lb.

Heavyweight

1. L. Zhabotinsky, U.S.S.R.—
   1,262 lb.
2. Y. Vlasov, U.S.S.R.—1,256 lb.
3. N. Schemansky, U.S.—1,184 ¾ lb.

CYCLING

1,000 Metres Scratch

1. G. Pettenella, Italy
2. S. Bianchetto, Italy
3. D. Morelon, France

4,000 Metres Individual Pursuit

1. J. Daler, Czech.—5:04.75
2. G. Ursi, Italy—5:05.96
3. P. Isakssor., Denmark—5:01.90

1,000 Metres Time-Trial

1. P. Sercu, Belgium—1:09.59
2. G. Pettenella, Italy—1:10.09
3. P. Trentin, France—1:10.42

4,000 Metres Team Pursuit

1. Germany—4:35.67
2. Italy—4:35.74
3. Netnerlands—4:38.99

2,000 Metres Tandem

1. S. Bianchetto/A. Damiano, Italy
2. I. Bodniex/V. Logunov, U.S.S.R.
3. W. Fuggerer/K. Kobusch, Germ.

Road Race

1. M. Zanin, Italy—4:39:51.63
2. K. Rodian, Denmark—4:39:51.65
3. W. Godefroot, Belg.—4:39:51.74

Road Race—Team

1. Netherlands—2:26:31.19
2. Italy—2:26:55.39
3. Sweden—2:27:11.52

EQUESTRIAN SPORTS

Jumping Grand Prix

1. P. Jonquieres, France
2. H. Schridde, Germany
3. P. Robeson, Great Britain

Dressage, Grand Prix—Teams

1. Germany
2. Switzerland
3. U.S.S.R.

Jumping Grand Prix, Teams

1. Germany
2. France
3. Italy

Three-Day Event

1. M. Checcoli, Italy
2. C. Moratorio, Argentina
3. F. Ligges, Germany

Dressage—Grand Prix

1. H. Chammartin, Switzerland
2. H. Boldt, Germany
3. S. Filatov, U.S.S.R.

Three-Day Event—Teams

1. Italy
2. U.S.
3. Germany

FENCING—MEN

Foil—Individual

1. E. Franke, Poland
2. J. Magnan, France
3. D. Revenu, France

Epée—Teams

1. Hungary
2. Italy
3. France

Foil—Team

1. U.S.S.R.
2. Poland
3. France

Sabre—Individual

1. T. Psza, Hungary
2. C. Arabo, France
3. U. Mavlikhanov, U.S.S.R.

Epée—Individual

1. G. Kriss, U.S.S.R.
2. W. Hoskyns, Great Britain
3. G. Kostava, U.S.S.R.

Sabre—Teams

1. U.S.S.R.
2. Italy
3. Poland

FENCING—WOMEN

Foil—Individual

1. I. Rejto, Hungary
2. H. Mees, Germany
3. A. Ragno, Italy

Foil—Teams

1. Hungary
2. U.S.S.R.
3. Germany

GYMNASTICS—MEN

Combined Exercises—Individual
1. Y. Endo, Japan
2. S. Tsurumi, Japan
3. {B. Shakhlin, U.S.S.R.
   {V. Lisitsky, U.S.S.R.

Combined Exercises—Team
1. Japan
2. U.S.S.R.
3. Germany

Floor Exercises
1. F. Menicelli, Italy
2. V. Lisitsky, U.S.S.R.
3. Y. Endo, Japan

Horizontal Bar
1. B. Shakhlin, U.S.S.R.
2. Y. Titov, U.S.S.R.
3. M. Cerar, Yugoslavia

Parallel Bars
1. Y. Endo, Japan
2. S. Tsurumi, Japan
3. F. Menicelli, Italy

Pommelled Horse
1. M. Cerar, Yugoslavia
2. S. Tsurumi, Japan
3. Y. Tsapenko, U.S.S.R.

Long Horse Vault
1. H. Yamashita, Japan
2. V. Lisitsky, U.S.S.R.
3. H. Rantakari, Finland

Rings
1. T. Hayata, Japan
2. F. Menicelli, Italy
3. B. Shakhlin, U.S.S.R.

GYMNASTICS—WOMEN

Combined Exercises—Individual
1. V. Caslavska, Czechoslovakia
2. L. Latynina, U.S.S.R.
3. P. Astakhova, U.S.S.R.

Combined Exercises—Team
1. U.S.S.R.
2. Czechoslovakia
3. Japan

Beam
1. V. Caslavska, Czechoslovakia
2. T. Manina, U.S.S.R.
3. L. Latynina, U.S.S.R.

Parallel Bars
1. P. Astakhova, U.S.S.R.
2. K. Makray, Hungary
3. L. Latynina, U.S.S.R.

Long Horse Vault
1. V. Caslavska, Czechoslovakia
2. {L. Latynina, U.S.S.R.
   {B. Radochla, Germany

Free Exercises
1. L. Latynina, U.S.S.R.
2. P. Astakhova, U.S.S.R.
3. D. Janosi, Hungary

ROWING

Single Sculls
1. V. Ivanov, U.S.S.R.—8:22.51
2. A. Hill, Germany—8:26.34
3. G. Kottman, Switz.—8:29.68

Double Sculls
1. O. Tyurin/B. Dubrovsky, U.S.S.R.—7:10.66
2. S. Cromwell/J. Storm, U.S.—7:13.16
3. V. Andrs/P. Hofman, Czechoslovakia—7:14.23

Coxswainless Pairs
1. G. Hungerford/R. Jackson, Canada—7:32.94
2. S. Blaisse/E. Veenemans, Netherlands—7:33.40
3. M. Schwan/W. Hottenrott, Germany—7:38.63

Coxed Pairs
1. U.S.—8:21.33
2. France—8:23.15
3. Netherlands—8:23.42

Coxswainless Fours
1. Denmark—6:59.30
2. Great Britain—7:00.47
3. U.S.—7:01.37

Coxed Fours
1. Germany—7:00.44
2. Italy—7:02.84
3. Netherlands—7:06.46

Eights
1. U.S.—6:18.23
2. Germany—6:23.29
3. Czechoslovakia—6:25.11

CANOEING—MEN

Kayak Singles—1,000 Metres
1. R. Peterson, Sweden—3:57.13
2. M. Hesz, Hungary—3:57.28
3. A. Vernescu, Roumania—4:00.7

Kayak Pairs—1,000 Metres
1. S. Sjoedelius/G. Utterberg, Sweden—3:38.54
2. A. Geurts/P. Heokstra, Netherlands—3:39.30
3. H. Bueker/H. Zander, Germany

Kayak Fours

1. U.S.S.R.—3:14.67
2. Germany—3:15.39
3. Roumania—3:15.51

Canadian Pairs—1,000 Metres

1. A. Khimich/S. Oschepkov,
   U.S.S.R.—4:04.65
2. J. Boudehen/M. Chapuis,
   France—4:06.52
3. P. Nielsen/J. Sorenson,
   Denmark—4:07.48

Canadian Singles—1,000 Metres

1. J. Eschert, Germany—4:35.14
2. A. Igorov, Roumania—4:37.89
3. E. Penyayev, U.S.S.R.—4:38.31

CANOEING—WOMEN

Kayak Singles—500 Metres

1. L. Khvedosink, U.S.S.R.—2:12.87
2. H. Lauer, Roumania—2:15.35
3. M. Jones, U.S.—2:15.68

Kayak Pairs—500 Metres

1. R. Esser/A. Zimmerman,
   Germany—1:56.95
2. F. Fox/G. Perrier, U.S.—1:59.16
3. H. Lauer/C. Sideri, Roumania—
   2:00.25

YACHTING

5.5 Metres

1. "Barrenjoey," Australia
2. "Rush VII," Sweden
3. "Bingo," U.S.

Dragon

1. "White Lady," Denmark
2. "Mutafo," Germany
3. "Aphrodite," U.S.

Star

1. "Gem," Bahamas
2. "Glider," U.S.
3. "Humbig V," Sweden

Flying Dutchman

1. "Pandora," New Zealand
2. "Lady C," Great Britain
3. "Widgeon," U.S.

Finn

1. W. Kuhweide, Germany
2. P. Barrett, U.S.
3. H. Wind, Denmark

SHOOTING

Free Pistol (50 Metres)

1. V. Markkanen, Finland
2. F. Green, U.S.
3. Y. Yoshikawa, Japan

Automatic Pistol (25 Metres)

1. P. Linnosvuop, Finland
2. I. Tripsa, Roumania
3. L. Nacovsky, Czechoslovakia

Free Rifle (300 Metres)

1. G. Anderson, U.S.
2. S. Kveliashvili, U.S.S.R.
3. M. Gunnarson, U.S.

Small-bore Rifles—Combined
(50 Metres)

1. L. Wigger, U.S.
2. V. Hustov, Bulgaria
3. L. Hammerl, Hungary

Small-bore Rifles—Prone
(50 Metres)

range 50 metres, standing, kneeling,
prone

1. L. Hammerl, Hungary
2. L. Wigger, U.S.
3. T. Pool, U.S.

Clay Pigeons

1. E. Mattarelli, Italy
2. P. Senichev, U.S.S.R.
3. W. Morris, U.S.

MODERN PENTATHLON

Individual

1. F. Toerek, Hungary
2. I. Novikov, U.S.S.R.
3. A. Mokeyev, U.S.S.R.

Teams

1. U.S.S.R.
2. U.S.
3. Hungary

BASKETBALL	FIELD HOCKEY	SOCCER
1. U.S.	1. India	1. Hungary
2. U.S.S.R.	2. Pakistan	2. Czechoslovakia
3. Brazil	3. Australia	3. Germany

VOLLEYBALL—MEN	VOLLEYBALL—WOMEN	WATER POLO
1. U.S.S.R.	1. Japan	1. Hungary
2. Czechoslovakia	2. U.S.S.R.	2. Yugoslavia
3. Japan	3. Poland	3. U.S.S.R.

TOMMIE SMITH and JOHN CARLOS raise black-gloved fists (the symbol of Black Power in the United States) following the finals of the 200 metres dash in Mexico 1968. Smith won the gold medal and Carlos the bronze.

DICK FOSBURY's "flop" won the high jump in Mexico for the U.S. He created a new Olympic record by clearing 7'4¼".

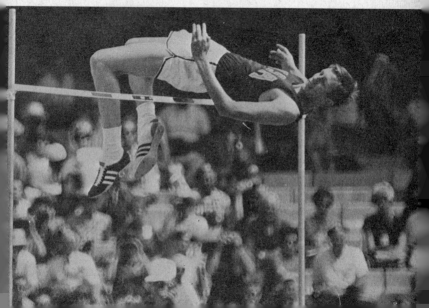

BOB BEAMON's astonishing 29'2½" broad jump broke the existing Olympic and World record by nearly 3 feet. Mexico, 1968.

JIM RYUN (U.S.) leads KIPCHOGE KEINO of Kenya in a 1,500 metres heat. The Kenyan beat Ryun in the final, however, with a new Olympic record. Mexico, 1968.

Chapter 17

THE XIX OLYMPIAD

Mexico, 1968

It was the year of the clenched fist, the symbol of Black Power in the United States used by a few Black athletes to dramatize racial troubles in the country. Sprinters Tommie Smith and John Carlos were suspended by the U.S. Olympic team and ordered out of the Olympic village because they used the defiant gesture while accepting their medals after the 200-metre dash. Smith won and Carlos was third. They raised their black-gloved fists during the playing of the Star Spangled Banner, and they wore Olympic Movement for Human Rights buttons.

"They violated the basic standards of sportsmanship and good manners which are so highly regarded in the U.S.," said the official announcement of the U.S. Olympic Committee.

"We are proud we did it," retorted Carlos.

Lee Evans, also a member of the Santa Clara V.Y.W. track club, who later won the 400-metres, waved from the presentation podium with a closed fist. So did U.S. runners Larry James and Ronald Freeman, runners-up to Evans.

Smith, Carlos, Evans, James and Freeman had earlier supported an Olympic boycott by black athletes. The boycott was eventually withdrawn.

They also ran exceptionally well.

Evans finished the 400 metres in an incredible world record time of 43.8 seconds. Even the fourth-place finisher in the race equalled the listed 45 second world record. In the 200 metres, Smith set a world record 19.8 seconds.

Jim Hines of the United States won the 100-yard dash by equalling the world record of 9.9 seconds. He and silver medallist Charlie Greene made it known they would not accept their medals from International Olympic Committee president Avery Brundage. The presentations were made therefore by Lord Burghley of Great Britain. Hines said they were protesting the committee's indecisive attitude to South Africa's application to participate in the Games. The country was at first approved, but that decision was later reversed because of South Africa's policy of not permitting black and white athletes to compete together. The committee voted South Africa out, 41-13. Russia and the twelve other countries had threatened to withdraw if South Africa had been admitted.

The Mexican Games received more bad publicity when Dan Ferris, secretary emeritus of the U.S. Amateur Athletic Association and a member of the International Amateur Athletic Federation, claimed that athletes from nearly every country represented had accepted kickbacks sometimes totalling as much as $6,000. The athletes, he said, had taken money for wearing particular articles of clothing or using specified equipment. His accusation was partially confirmed by Olga Fikotova Connolly, a Czech gold medalist who had defected to the U.S.

"Everybody in the Olympics does it," she said.

One U.S. athlete even claimed to have found $500 in his track shoe.

To further add to the politically infested Olympics, a Mexican spectator shot himself at the start of a cycling team trial. It was said to be in protest of the Mexican government's treatment of students. The event occurred near an army barracks where hundreds of students had been in custody for inciting riots that had claimed nearly forty lives.

And then the International Swimming Federation protested that 640 female athletes had been subjected to sex tests. All however passed.

In the traditional, unofficial, system of awarding points on a 10-5-4-3-2-1 basis for the first six placings in each event, the United States amassed a total so high that the wire service computer-adding machine came up with conflicting totals. The U.S. athlete won an unprecedented total of 106 medals, including 45 gold medals, to pass the previous Russian record of 103 medals won in Rome in 1960.

There was much talk of the effect of high altitude on the athletes in Mexico City, although Olympic and World records were broken practically every day.

One runner who was obviously at ease in the high altitude was Kipchoge Keino of Kenya who defeated U.S. record holder Jim Ryun with surprising ease in the 1,500 metres. Keino ran the equivalent of a 3:52 mile at 7,500 feet and finished in 3:34.9 seconds to Ryun's 3:37.8. The Kenyan also finished second in the 5,000 metres.

Ralph Doubell of Australia, however, came to Mexico after training at sea level. He equalled New Zealander Peter Snell's world record of 1:44.3 seconds in the 800 metres, and defeated another Kenyan highlander, Wilson Kiprugut for the gold medal.

Mamo Wolbe gave Ethiopia its third straight marathon victory. The man who had won it twice before, Abebe Bikila, dropped out after nearly eleven miles with a broken leg.

Another fallen Olympian was Ron Clarke of Australia, the world 10,000 metres record holder. His demise came on the opening day, October 13th.

Clarke was beaten into submission by Nafali Temu, another Kenyan who finished almost two minutes slower than Clarke's world record time. Temu hadn't even finished the 10,000 metres in Tokyo four years earlier. Perhaps the saddest sight of the Olympic Games in Mexico was of one of the greatest runners in track history sprawled exhausted on the grass, barely a yard beyond the finish line, being administered oxygen. The doctor, Brian Corrigan, was crying. While Clarke was being revived, Temu, Wolbe (the marathon winner) and Mohamed Gamoudi of Tunisia mounted the podium to receive their just awards.

After a four-day rest, Clarke ran the 5,000 metres. Again, he failed to place. It was his final appearance in an Olympic Games. Mohamed Gamoudi, followed by Keino and Temu gave Africa another sweep. Vladimir Kuts of Russia, whose 1956 Olympic record remained unbroken, watched from the press box. It was a sad end for Clarke, a man who had held world records for two, three and six miles, as well as the 5,000 and 10,000 metres, but who never did win an Olympic gold medal.

In the relays, the men's U.S. team of Greene, Pender, Smith and Hines won the 400 metres in a world record 38.2 seconds. Lee Evans anchored the 1,600 metre team for another world mark of 2:56.1 seconds; and the women's sprint relay team, with a magnificent run by Wyomia Tyus, won the 400 metres in 43.4 seconds, another world record. It was the first time any country had scored a triple relay victory since 1932.

The Americans in Mexico, however, were surprisingly upset when David Hemery of Great Britain won the 400 metres hurdles over Gerhard Henning of West Germany in 48.1 seconds and broke the existing world record. Another Briton finished third, thus making it the first time the U.S. had failed to win at least one medal in that event. Willie Davenport made some amends for the U.S. however by winning the 110 metre hurdles.

The American men made no mistakes in the field events.

Nothing in 1968, and not much in Olympic history, has ever matched Bob Beamon's astonishing 29′ 2½″ broad jump on his first attempt. After that, he made a shorter, token jump, and then retired to watch the others fail to reach even 27 feet.

Beamon had broken the world record by almost two feet. Great Britain's Lynn Davies, the 1964 Olympic champion, summed it up for the demoralized also-rans

"I was so shocked, I ceased to become a competitor and became a spectator."

The pole vault provided the narrowest field-even decision. Bob Seagren celebrated the eve of his 22nd birthday by winning with a world record 17′ 8½″. The ordeal took seven hours and Seagren won on a technical decision. He had fewer failures at lower heights than rivals, Claus Schiprowski of West Germany and Wolfgang Nordwig of East Germany, who also broke the world record. All three failed at 17′10½″.

Dick Fosbury won the high jump for the U.S. by going over backwards at an Olympic record 7′ 4¼″. It was called "The Fosbury Flop." After a speedy ap proach, he took off and twisted his body around, going over the bar upside down, and landing with a seemingly uncomfortable thud on his rear end.

"It's the only way I know how," he explained. "It's meditation. I just kind of get the idea of falling over the bar. I don't care what they call it, as long as it gets me across."

Al Oerter, 32, took home his fourth consecutive discuss gold medal with an Olympic record throw of 212' 6½" and Randy Matson won the shotput at 67' 4¾" after setting an Olympic record 67' 10¼" in the qualifying round. The U.S., however, failed to win medals in the javelin, hammer throw or triple jump, in which five men used eight jumps to successively boost Josef Schmidt's eight-year-old Olympic record, Russia's Viktor Saneyev was the eventual winner at 57' 0¾".

Bill Toomey (U.S.) led all the way from the opening 100 metres race (10.4 seconds), to a win in the 1,500 metres in the decathlon. The tired but happy Toomey's only complaint was that after each day, he had to take a dope test that required him to drink 42 glasses of water in the two days to satisfy the doctors.

In women's events, Wyomia Tyus of the United States became the first Olympic runner to retain a 100-metres title. She shaved a 10th. of a second off the world record to finish in a dazzling 11 seconds. In the 200 metres, however, she tired to finish sixth, half a second behind Irene Szewinska of Poland who set a new world record of 22.5 seconds.

Colette Besson of France swept past Great Britain's Lillian Board near the finish of the women's 400 metres event for a very unexpected gold medal; and precocious Maureen Caird of Australia romped over the 80 metres hurdles for an easy win over fellow Australian Pat Kilborn.

Miroslava Rezkova's high jump victory evinced a thunderous ovation, mostly because the 18-year-old Czech defeated two Russians, as well as the favored Rita Schmidt of East Germany who was a disappointing fifth.

Despite a considerable head wind, Viorica Viscopoleanu of Roumania won the women's long jump, beating Mary Rand's world record with a 22'4½" leap on her first attempt, much as Beamon did in the men's event. And then Margitta Gummell made up for many East German disappointments, smashing the world record shotput with a 64'4" toss.

In swimming, the United States won 23 of the 33 events and 58 of the 102 medals. However one of the most outstanding swimmers turned out to be a young East German, Roland Matthews, who won two individual backstroke medals, and then broke his own 100-metres world record in the lead leg of the medley relay to help his team to a silver medal.

Michael Wenden of Australia set a world record of 52.2 seconds in the 100 metres freestyle, but Jan Henne led three American girls to first, second and third places in the women's event — the first time the U.S. had won it since 1932.

Mark Spitz, third to Wenden in the 100 metres, and heralded as a potential six gold medal winner, failed in all three of his individual events, but was on three U.S. team wins in the relays. Team-mate Catie Smith too was a disappointing 5th in the 100 metre breaststroke, and too sick to compete in the 200 metres event. Djurdica Bjedove, 21, won Yugoslavia's first swimming laurels with a gold medal in the 100 metres breaststroke and a silver at 200 metres.

Don Schollander, who won 4 gold medals in the 1964 Olympics met Michael Wenden in the finals of the 200 metres free-style for perhaps the most exciting even in swimming. It was strength and youth versus experience. Wenden, 19, broke the Olympic record he'd set in the heats by 4.1 seconds in finishing in 1:55.2 Schollander was only 6/10ths of a second behind. The other finalists finished in their wakes. Schollander, swimming his last race, said afterwards he thought he coul beat the Australian on the turns, but Wenden, acknowledging a lack of finesse, predicted he'd win just o power. He did.

Felipe "El Tibio" Munez of Mexico defeated worl record holder Vladimir Kosinsky of Russia in the 200 metre breaststroke, although he was never ahead of him until midway through the last lap. It was the first gold medal to be won by a Mexican swimmer.

Felipe Munez delightedly explained his nickname: "My father comes from Aguas Caliente, which means hot water, and my mother comes from Rio Frio, which means cold river. So, they called me El Tibio, which means Lukewarm!"

Debbie Meyer of the United States became the first swimmer to win three individual gold medals. The 16-year-old from Sacramento, Calif., won the 200-, 400- and 800-metre freestyle events. Another American, Kaye Hall, of Tacoma, Washington, upset Elaine Tanner of Canada in winning the 100-metre backstroke in 1:06.2 seconds. Miss Tanner had been expected to win Canada's first swimming gold medal.

Mike Burton of the U.S. upset another Canadian, in winning the 400-metre freestyle in an Olympic record 4:09.0 seconds. The Canadian world record holder (4:06.5), Ralph Hutton, came second in 4:11.7 seconds.

Charles Hickcox of the U.S. did the expected in winning the 400-metre individual medley in 4:48.4. He unhappily pointed out, however, that his time was nearly 10 seconds slower than his world record of 4:39.0 seconds.

Bernie Wrightson gave the United States its 11th consecutive men's springboard diving gold medal; and Klaus Dibiasi, of Italy, performed brilliantly on the platform board to take a gold medal away from Mexico's Alvara Gaxiola in the final. The upset came on the final lay and was a disappointing blow for Mexican President Ordez Diaz who was in the stands. At the same time, however, in a different stadium, two Mexican boxers — flyweight Ricardo Delgado and featherweight Antonio Roldan — came up with two unexpected gold medals, and the President presumably went home somewhat pacified.

Russia won three of the eleven boxing gold medals, but in the heavyweight division, American George Foreman upset the Soviet Union's Iones Chepulis to win a gold medal on a technical knockout in the second round. The only other U.S. boxing gold medallist was lightweight Ronnie Harris who won in an unanimous decision over the defending champion from Poland, Josef Grudzien.

The equestrian honors belonged to Canada. Tom Gaylord, Jim Elder and Jim Day, the Grand Prix jumping team, won Canada's only gold medals in an event their country had never entered before. They beat the French and the West Germans, up to then the best in the world. Elder and his horse *The Immigrant* decided the event eight hours after it began. *The Immigrant* kicked up his heels, galloped sideways and generally misbehaved until Elder muscled him on course and completed the circuit with 16 faults for a total penalty of 27.25 for two rounds. Only David Broome of Great Britain had a better round of eight faults. Before the Games began, the impoverished Canadian team had sent their horses down to Mexico five weeks early to take advantage of cheaper air fares. It was said later that this worked to their considerable advantage as it gave their mounts a chance to get used to the rarified atmosphere.

Marion Coakes, 21, of Great Britain, became the first woman in Olympic history to win an individual medal in equestrian jumping, but she finished second to veteran William Steinkraus of the United States.

Vera Caslavska, 26, who repeated her 1964 performance as overall champion of women's gymnastics, and Josef Odlozil, 1,500 metres silver medallist in Tokyo were married in Mexico, but they had to wait until they returned to Czechoslovakia to celebrate a honeymoon. The Czech team members were sent home as soon as they had completed competing to prevent the possibility of defections. Odlozil's event finished before the gymnastics began and he consequently was sent home early to wait for his bride.

During the opening ceremonies, the 124 Czech competitors received by far the largest ovation of any team other than America's. The team from Russia, which had recently occupied Czechoslovakia, was booed mercilessly. The two countries' gymnastics teams had the closest competition of the games, with Russia finally taking the championship with 382.85 points to the Czechs 382.20.

The story of a nameless British athlete who decided to celebrate after participating in his one event, is still told in many different languages in sporting circles around the athletic world. A sports editor from the United Kingdom invited him to the press centre bar. When it closed at 3 a.m., the journalist helped boost the athlete over the fence to the *Villa Olimpica* to save him a long walk to the gate, and the possible embarrassment of trying to produce his pass before an intolerant guard. The athlete fell to the other side with a thud, but was soon on his feet and the sports editor walked away. A minute later there was a shout in the dark.

"How'd I get over *this* flippin' fence?"

He'd been boosted into the women's quarters, *Stalag Olimpica,* and wasn't heard from for two days!

OFFICIAL XIX OLYMPIAD RESULTS

Mexico City, 1968

TRACK AND FIELD — MEN

100 Metres
1. J. Hines, U.S.—9.9
2. L. Miller, Jamaica—10.0
3. C. Greene, U.S.—10.0

200 Metres
1. T. Smith, U.S.—19.8
2. P. Norman, Australia—20.0
3. J. Carlos, U.S.—20.0

400 Metres
1. L. Evans, U.S.—43.8
2. L. James, U.S.—43.9
3. R. Freeman, U.S.—44.4

800 Metres
1. R. Doubell, Australia—1:44.3
2. W. Kiprugut, Kenya—1:44.5
3. T. Farrell, U.S.—1:45.4

1,500 Metres
1. K. Keino, Kenya—3:34.9
2. J. Ryun, U.S.—3:37.8
3. B. Tummler, W. Germany—3:39.0

5,000 Metres
1. M. Gammoudi, Tunisia—14:05.0
2. K. Keino, Kenya—14:05.2
3. N. Temu, Kenya—14:06.4

10,000 Metres
1. N. Temu, Kenya—29:27.4
2. M. Wolde, Ethiopia—29:28.0
3. M. Gammoudi, Tunisia—29:34.2

Marathon
1. M. Wolde, Ethiopia—2:20:26.4
2. K. Kimihara, Japan—2:23:31.0
3. M. Ryan, New Zealand—2:23:45.0

110 Metre Hurdles
1. W. Davenport, U.S.—13.3
2. E. Hall, U.S.—13.4
3. E. Ottoz, Italy—13.4

400 Metre Hurdles
1. D. Hemery, Great Britain—48.1
2. G. Hennige, W. Germany—49.0
3. J. Sherwood, Great Britain—49.0

3,000 Metre Steeplechase
1. A. Biwott, Kenya—8:51.0
2. B. Kogo, Kenya—8:51.6
3. G. Young, U.S.—8:51.8

400 Metre Relay
1. U.S.—38.2
2. Cuba—38.3
3. France—38.4

1,600 Metre Relay

1. U.S.—2:56.1
2. Kenya—2:59.6
3. W. Germany—3:00.5

20,000 Metre Walk

1. V. Golubnichiy, U.S.S.R.—
   1:33:58.4
2. J. Pedraza, Mexiso—1:34:00.0
3. N. Smaga, U.S.S.R.—1:34:03.4

50,000 Metre Walk

1. C. Hohne, U.S.S.R.—4:20:13.6
2. A. Kiss, Hungary—4:30:17.0
3. L. Young, U.S.—4:31:55.4

High Jump

1. R. Fosbury, U.S.—7'4¼"
2. E. Caruthers, U.S.—7'3½"
3. V. Gavrilov, U.S.S.R.—7'2¾"

Broad Jump

1. R. Beamon, U.S.—29'2½"
2. K. Beer, E. Germany—26'10½"
3. R. Boston, U.S.—26'9¼"

Triple Jump

1. V. Saneyev, U.S.S.R.—57'0¾"
2. N. Prudencio, Brazil—56'8"
3. G. Gentile, Italy—56'6"'

Pole Vault

1. R. Seagren, U.S.—17'8½"
2. C. Schiprowski, W. Germany—
   17'8½"
3. W. Nordwig, E. Germany—
   17'8½"

Shot Put

1. R. Matson, U.S.—67'4¾"
2. G. Woods, U.S.—66'0¼"
3. E. Gushchin, U.S.S.R.

Discus Throw

1. A. Oerter, U.S.—212'6½"
2. L. Milde, E. Germany—
   206'11½"
3. L. Danek, Czechoslovakia—
   206'5"

Hammer Throw

1. G. Zsivotzky, Hungary—240'8"
2. R. Klim, U.S.S.R.—240'5"
3. L. Lovasz, Hungary—228'11"

Javelin Throw

1. J. Lusis, U.S.S.R.—295'7¼"
2. J. Kinnunen, Finland—290'7½"
3. G. Kulcsar, Hungary—285'7½"

Decathlon

1. W. Toomey, U.S.—8,193 pts
2. H. Walde, W. Germany—8,111
   pts.
3. K. Bendlin, W. Germany—8,064
   pts.

TRACK AND FIELD — WOMEN

100 Metres

1. W. Tyus, U.S.—11.0
2. B. Ferrell, U.S.—11.1
3. I. Szewinska, Poland—11.1

200 Metres

1. I. Szewinska, Poland—22.5
2. R. Boyle, Australia—22.7
3. J. Lamy, Australia—22.8

400 Metres

1. C. Besson, France—52.0
2. L. Board, Great Britain—52.1
3. N. Pyechenkina, U.S.S.R.—52.2

800 Metres

1. M. Manning, U.S.—2:00.9
2. I. Silai, Rumania—2:02.5
3. M. Gommers, Netherlands—
   2:02.6

80 Metres Hurdles

1. M. Caird, Australia—10.3
2. P. Kilborn, Australia—10.4
3. Chi Cheng, Formosa—10.4

400 Metres Relay

1. U.S.—42.8
2. Cuba—43.3
3. U.S.S.R.—43.4

High Jump

1. M. Rezkova, Czechoslovakia—
   5'11¾"
2. A. Okorokova, U.S.S.R.—5'11"
3. V. Kozyr, U.S.S.R.—5'11"

Broad Jump

1. V. Viscopoleanu, Rumania—
   22'4½"
2. S. Sherwood, Great Britain—
   21'11"
3. T. Talisheva, U.S.S.R.—
   21'10¼"

Javelin Throw

1. A. Nemeth, Hungary—198'0½"
2. M. Penes, Rumania—196'7"
3. E. Janko, Austria—190'5"

Shot Put

1. M. Gummel, E. Germany—
   64'4"
2. M. Lange, E. Germany—61'7½"
3. N. Chizhova, U.S.S.R.—59'8¼

Discus Throw

1. L. Manoliu, Rumania—191'2½
2. L. Westermann, W. Germany-
   189'6"
3. J. Kleiber, Hungary—180'1½

Pentathlon

1. I. Becker, W. Germany—5,098 pts
2. L. Prokop, Austria—4,966 pts
3. A. Toth Kovacs, Hungary—
   4,959 pts

SWIMMING AND DIVING — MEN

100 Metres Free-Style
1. M. Wenden, Australia—52.2
2. K. Walsh, U.S.—52.8
3. M. Spitz, U.S.—53.0

200 Metres Free-Style
1. M. Wenden, Australia—1:55.2
2. D. Schollander, U.S.—1:55.8
3. J. Nelson, U.S.—1:58.1

400 Metres Free-Style
1. M. Burton, U.S.—4:09.0
2. R. Hutton, Canada—4:11.7
3. A. Mosconi, France—4:13.3

1,500 Metres Free-Style
1. M. Burton, U.S.—16:38.9
2. J. Kinsella, U.S.—16:57.3
3. G. Brough, Australia—17:04.7

100 Metres Backstroke
1. R. Matthes, E. Germany—0:58.7
2. C. Hickcox, U.S.—1:00.2
3. R. Mills, U.S.—1:00.5

200 Metres Backstroke
1. R. Matthes, E. Germany—2:09.6
2. M. Ivey, U.S.—2:10.6
3. J. Horsley, U.S.—2:10.9

100 Metres Breast Stroke
1. D. McKenzie, U.S.—1:07.7
2. V. Kosinsky, U.S.S.R.—1:08.0
3. N. Pankin, U.S.S.R.—1:08.0

200 Metres Breast Stroke
1. F. Munoz, Mexico—2:28.7
2. V. Kosinsky, U.S.S.R.—2:29.2
3. B. Job, U.S.—2:29.9

100 Metres Butterfly
1. D. Russell, U.S.—55.9
2. M. Spitz, U.S.—56.4
3. R. Wales, U.S.—57.2

200 Metres Butterfly
1. C. Robie, U.S.—2:08.7
2. M. Woodroffe, Great Britain—2:09.0
3. J. Ferris, U.S.—2:09.3

200 Metres Individual Medley
1. C. Hickcox, U.S.—2:12.0
2. G. Buckingham, U.S.—2:13.0
3. J. Ferris, U.S.—2:13.3

400 Metres Individual Medley
1. C. Hickcox, U.S.—4:48.4
2. G. Hall, U.S.—4:48.7
3. M. Holthaus, W. Germany—4:51.4

400 Metres Free-Style Relay
1. U.S.—3:31.7
2. U.S.S.R.—3:34.2
3. Australia—3:34.7

800 Meters Free-Style Relay
1. U.S.—7:52.3
2. Australia—7:53.7
3. U.S.S.R.—8:01.6

400 Metres Medley Relay
1. U.S.—3:54.9
2. E. Germany—3:57.5
3. U.S.S.R.—4:00.7

Platform Diving
1. K. Dibiasi, Italy—164.8 pts
2. A. Gaxiola, Mexico—154.49 pts
3. E. Young, U.S.—153.93 pts

Springboard Diving
1. B. Wrighton, U.S.—170.15 pts
2. K. Diabisi, Italy—159.74 pts
3. J. Henry, U.S.—158.09 pts

SWIMMING AND DIVING — WOMEN

100 Metres Free-Style
1. J. Henne, U.S.—1:00.0
2. S. Pedersen, U.S.—1:00.3
3. L. Gustavson, U.S.—1:00.3

200 Metres Free-Style
1. D. Meyer, U.S.—2:10.5
2. J. Henne, U.S.—2:11.0
3. J. Barkman, U.S.—2:11.2

400 Metres Free-Style
1. D. Meyer, U.S.—4:31.8
2. L. Gustavson, U.S.—4:35.5
3. K. Moras, Australia—4:37.0

800 Metres Free-Style
1. D. Meyer, U.S.—9:24.0
2. P. Kruse, U.S.—9:35.7
3. M. Ramirez, Mexico—9:38.5

100 Metres Backstroke
1. K. Hall, U.S.—1:06.2
2. E. Tanner, Canada—1:06.7
3. J. Swaggerty, U.S.—1:08.1

200 Metres Backstroke
1. P. Watson, U.S.—2:24.8
2. E. Tanner, Canada—2:27.4
3. K. Hall, U.S.A.—2:28.9

100 Metres Breast Stroke

1. D. Bejdov, Yugoslavia—1:15.8
2. G. Prozumenshchikova,
   U.S.S.R.—1:15.9
3. S. Wichman, U.S.—1:16.1

200 Metres Breast Stroke

1. S. Wichman, U.S.—2:44.4
2. D. Bejdov, Yugoslavia—2:46.4
3. G. Prozumenschikova, U.S.S.R.
   —2:47.0

100 Metres Butterfly

1. L. McClements, Australia—
   1:05.5
2. E. Daniel, U.S.—1:05.8
3. S. Shields, U.S.—1:06.2

200 Metres Butterfly

1. A. Kok, Netherlands—2:24.7
2. H. Lindner, E. Germany—
   2:24.8
3. E. Daniel, U.S.—2:25.9

200 Metres Individual Medley

1. C. Kolb, U.S.—2:24.7
2. S. Pedersen, U.S.—2:28.8
3. J. Henne, U.S.—2:31.4

400 Metres Individual Medley

1. C. Kolb, U.S.—5:08.5
2. L. Vidali, U.S.—5:22.2
3. S. Steinbach, E. Germany—
   5:25.3

400 Metres Free-Style Relay

1. U.S.—4:02.5
2. E. Germany—4:05.7
3. Canada—4:07.2

400 Metres Medley Relay

1. U.S.—4:28.3
2. Australia—4:30.0
3. West Germany—4:36.4

Platform Diving

1. M. Duchkova, Czechoslovakia
2. N. Lobanova, U.S.S.R.
3. A. Peterson, U.S.

Springboard Diving

1. S. Gossick, U.S.
2. T. Pogoseva, U.S.S.R.
3. K. O'Sullivan, U.S.

BOXING

Light-flyweight

1. F. Rodriquez, Venezuela
2. Yong-Ju Jee, South Korea
3. H. Marbley, U.S.
   H. Skrzypezac, Poland

Flyweight

1. R. Delgado, Mexico
2. A. Olech, Poland
3. S. de Oliveira, Brazil
   L. Rwabogo, Uganda

Bantamweight

1. V. Sokolov, U.S.S.R.
2. E. Mukwanga, Uganda
3. E. Morioka, Japan
   Soon-Kill Chang, South Korea

Featherweight

1. A. Roldan, Mexico
2. A. Robinson, U.S.
3. P. Waruingi, Kenya
   I. Michailov, Bulgaria

Lightweight

1. R. Harris, U.S.
2. J. Grudzien, Poland
3. C. Cutov, Rumania
   Z. Vujin, Yugoslavia

Light-welterweight

1. J. Kulej, Poland
2. E. Regueiferos, Cuba
3. A. Nilsson, Finland
   J. Wallington, U.S.

Welterweight

1. M. Wolke, East Germany
2. J. Bessala, Cameroon
3. V. Musalimov, U.S.S.R.
   M. Guilloti, Argentina

Light-middleweight

1. B. Lagutin, U.S.S.R.
2. R. Garbey, Cuba
3. J. Baldwin, U.S.
   G. Meyer, West Germany

Middleweight

1. C. Finnegan, Great Britain
2. A. Kiselyov, U.S.S.R.
3. A. Zaragoza, Mexico
   A. Jones, U.S.

Light-heavyweight

1. D. Pozdniak, U.S.S.R.
2. I. Monea, Rumania
3. G. Stankov, Bulgaria
   S. Dragan, Poland

Heavyweight

1. G. Foreman, U.S.
2. I. Chepulis, U.S.S.R.
3. G. Bambini, Italy
   J. Rocha, Mexico

WRESTLING

Free-Style Flyweight
1. S. Naata, Japan
2. R. Sanders, U.S.
3. S. Sukhbaatar, Mongolia

Bantamweight
1. Y. Uetake, Japan
2. D. Behm, U.S.
3. A. Gorgoni, Iran

Featherweight
1. M. Kaneko, Japan
2. E. Todorov, Bulgaria
3. S. Seyed-Abassy, Iran

Lightweight
1. A. Movahed, Iran
2. E. Valtchev, Bulgaria
3. S. Danzandarjaa, Mongolia

Welterweight
1. M. Atalay, Turkey
2. D. Robin, France
3. D. Urev, Mongolia

Middleweight
1. B. Gurevich, U.S.S.R.
2. M. Jigjid, Mongolia
3. P. Gardjev, Bulgaria

Light-Heavyweight
1. A. Ayuk, Turkey
2. S. Lomidze, U.S.S.R.
3. J. Csatari, Hungary

Heavyweight
1. A. Medved, U.S.S.R.
2. O. Douraliev, Bulgaria
3. W. Dietrich, West Germany

Greco-Roman Flyweight
1. P. Kirov, Bulgaria
2. V. Balkulin, U.S.S.R.
3. M. Zeman, Czechoslovakia

Bantamweight
1. J. Varga, Hungary
2. I. Baciu, Rumania
3. I. Kochergin, U.S.S.R.

Featherweight
1. R. Rurua, U.S.S.R.
2. H. Fujimoto, Japan,
3. S. Popescu, Rumania

Lightweight
1. M. Munemura, Japan
2. S. Horvat, Yugoslavia
3. P. Galaktopoulos, Greece

Welterweight
1. R. Vester, East Germany
2. D. Robin, France
3. K. Bajko, Hungary

Middleweight
1. L. Metz, East Germany
2. V. Olenik, U.S.S.R.
3. B. Simic, Yugoslavia

Light-Heavyweight
1. B. Radev, Bulgaria
2. N. Yakovenko, U.S.S.R.
3. N. Martinsecu, Rumania

Heavyweight
1. I. Kosma, Hungary
2. A. Roshin, U.S.S.R.
3. P. Kment, Czechoslovakia

WEIGHT-LIFTING

Bantamweight
1. M. Nassiri, Japan—809¾ lb.
2. I. Foldi, Hungary—809¾ lb.
3. H. Trebicki, Poland—788 lb.

Featherweight
1. Yoshinobu Miyake, Japan— 865 lb.
2. D. Shanidze, U.S.S.R.—854 lb.
3. Yoshiyuki, Miyake, Japan— 848½ lb.

Lightweight
1. W. Bsanowski, Poland— 964½ lb.
2. P. Jalayer, Iran—931¼ lb.
3. M. Zielinski, Poland—925½ lb.

Middleweight
1. V. Kurentsov, U.S.S.R.— 1047 lb.
2. M. Oohuchi, Japan—1002¾ lb.
3. K. Bakos, Hungary—969¾ lb.

Light-Heavyweight
1. B. Selitsky, U.S.S.R.— 1,068¾ lb.
2. V. Belyayev, U.S.S.R.— 1,068¾ lb.
3. N. Ozimek, Poland—1,041¼ lb.

Middle-Heavyweight
1. K. Kangasniemi, Finland— 1,140½ lb.
2. Y. Talts, U.S.S.R.—1,118½ lb.
3. M. Golab, Poland—1,090¾ lb.

Heavyweight
1. L. Zhabotinsky, U.S.S.R.— 1,262 lb.
2. S. Reding, Belgium—1,223¼ lb.
3. J. Dube, U.S.—1,223¼ lb.

CYCLING

1,000 Metre Sprint
1. D. Morelon, France
2. G. Turrini, Italy
3. P. Trentin, France

1,000 Metre Time-Trial
1. P. Trentin, France—1:03.91
2. N. Fredborg, Denmark—1:04.61
3. J. Kierzkowski, Poland—
   1:04.63

2,000 Metre Tandem
1. D. Morelon/P. Trentin, France
2. J. Jansen/L. Loevesijn,
   Netherlands
3. D. Goens/R. van Lancker,
   Belgium

Team Pursuit
1. Denmark
2. West Germany
3. Italy

Individual Pursuit
1. D. Rebillard, France
2. M. Frey, Denmark
3. X. Kurmann, Switzerland

Road Time Trial
1. Netherlands—2:7:49.06
2. Sweden—2:9:26.60
3. Italy—2:10:18.74

Road Race
1. P. Vianelli, Italy—4:41:25.24
2. L. Mortensen, Denmark—
   4:42:49.71
3. G. Pettersson, Sweden—
   4:43:15.24

EQUESTRIAN

Grand Prix Individual
1. W. Steinkraus, U.S.
2. M. Coakes, Great Britain
3. D. Broome, Great Britain

Grand Prix Team
1. Canada
2. France
3. West Germany

Three-Day Individual
1. J-J. Guyon, France
2. D. Allhusen, Great Britain
3. M. Page, U.S.

Three-Day Team
1. Great Britain
2. U.S.
3. Australia

Dressage Individual
1. I. Kizimov, U.S.S.R.
2. J. Neckermann, West Germany
3. R. Klimke, West Germany

Dressage Team
1. West Germany
2. U.S.S.R.
3. Switzerland

FENCING

Foil Individual
1. I. Drimba, Rumania
2. J. Kamuti, Hungary
3. D. Revenu, France

Team Foil
1. U.S.S.R.
2. Hungary
3. Rumania

Epée — Individual
1. G. Kulesar, Hungary
2. G. Kriss, U.S.S.R.
3. G. Saccaro, Italy

Epée — Team
1. Hungary
2. U.S.S.R.
3. Poland

Sabre — Individual
1. J. Pawlowski, Poland
2. M. Rakita, U.S.S.R.
3. T. Pezsa, Hungary

Sabre — Team
1. U.S.S.R.
2. Italy
3. Hungary

FENCING — WOMEN

Foil — Individual
1. E. Novikova, U.S.S.R.
2. P. Roldan, Mexico
3. I. Rejto, Hungary

Foil — Team
1. France
2. U.S.S.R.
3. Poland

GYMNASTICS

Individual — Combined
1. S. Kato, Japan
2. M. Voronin, U.S.S.R.
3. A. Nakayama, Japan

Floor
1. S. Kato, Japan
2. A. Nakayama, Japan
3. T. Kato, Japan

Parallel Bars
1. A. Nakayama, Japan
2. M. Voronin, U.S.S.R.
3. Y. Klimenko, U.S.S.R.

Team
1. Japan
2. U.S.S.R.
3. East Germany

Rings
1. A. Nakayama, Japan
2. M. Voronin, U.S.S.R.
3. S. Kato, Japan

Horizontal Bar
1. M. Voronin, U.S.S.R.
2. A. Nakayama, Japan
3. E. Kenmotsu, Japan

Pommelled Horse
1. M. Cerar, Yugoslavia
2. O. Laiho, Finland
3. M. Voronin, U.S.S.R.

Long Horse
1. M. Voronin, U.S.S.R.
2. Y. Endo, Japan
3. S. Diomidov, U.S.S.R.

GYMNASTICS — WOMEN

Individual Combined
1. V. Caslavska, Czechoslovakia
2. Z. Voronina, U.S.S.R.
3. N. Kuchinskaya, U.S.S.R.

Floor
1. V. Caslavska, Czechoslovakia
   L. Petrik, U.S.S.R.
3. N. Kuchinskaya, U.S.S.R.

Horse
1. V. Caslavska, Czechoslovakia
2. E. Zuchold, East Germany
3. Z. Voronina, U.S.S.R.

Asymmetrical Bars
1. V. Caslavska, Czechoslovakia
2. K. Janz, East Germany
3. Z. Voronina, U.S.S.R.

Beam
1. N. Kuchinskaya, U.S.S.R.
2. V. Caslavska, Czechoslovakia
3. L. Petrik, U.S.S.R.

Team
1. U.S.S.R.
2. Czechoslovakia
3. East Germany

ROWING

Single Sculls
1. H. Wienese, Netherlands—
   7:47.80
2. J. Meissner, West Germany—
   7:52.00
3. A. Demiddi, Argentina—
   7:57.19

Double Sculls
1. A. Sass/A. Timoshinin,
   U.S.S.R.—6:51.82
2. L. van Dis/H. Droog,
   Netherlands—6:52.80
3. J. Nunn/W. Maher, U.S.—
   6:54.21

Coxed Pairs
1. Italy—8:04.81
2. Netherlands—8:06.80
3. Denmark—8:08.07

Coxless Pairs
1. J. Lucke/H-J. Bothe, East
   Germany—7:26.56
2. L. Hough/A. Johnson, U.S.—
   7:26.71
3. P. Christiansen/I. Larsen,
   Denmark—7:31.84

Coxed Fours
1. New Zealand—6:45.62
2. East Germany—6:48.20
3. Switzerland—6:49.04

Coxed Fours
1. East Germany—6:39.18
2. Hungary—6:41.64
3. Italy—6:44.01

Eights
1. West Germany—6:07.00
2. Australia—6:07.98
3. U.S.S.R.—6:09.11

CANOEING

Kayak Singles
1. M. Hesz, Hungary—4:2.63
2. A. Shaparenko, U.S.S.R.—4:3.58
3. E. Hansen, Denmark—4:4.39

Kayak Pairs
1. A. Shaparenko/V. Morozov, U.S.S.R.—3:37.54
2. C. Giczi/I. Timar, Hungary—3:38.44
3. G. Seibold/G. Pfaff, Austria—3:40.71

Kayak Fours
1. Norway—3:14.38
2. Rumania—3:14.81
3. Hungary—3:15.00

Canadian Singles
1. T. Tatai, Hungary—4:36.14
2. D. Lewe, West Germany—4:38.31
3. V. Galkov, U.S.S.R.—4:40.42

Canadian Pairs
1. I. Patzaichin/S. Covaliov, Rumania—4:07.18
2. T. Wichmann/G. Petrikovics, Hungary—4:08.77
3. N. Prokupets/M. Zamaton, U.S.S.R.—4:11.30

CANOEING — WOMEN

Kayak Singles
1. L. Pinayeva, U.S.S.R.—2:11.09
2. R. Breuer, West Germany—2:12.71
3. V. Dumitru, Rumania—2:13.22

Kayak Pairs
1. A. Zimmermann/R. Esser, West Germany—1:56.44
2. A. Pfeffer/K. Sagi-Rozsnyoi, Hungary—1:58.60
3. L. Pinayeva/A. Seredina, U.S.S.R.—1:58.61

YACHTING

5.5 Metres
1. Sweden
2. Switzerland
3. Great Britain

Star
1. U.S.
2. Norway
3. Italy

Dragon
1. U.S.
2. Denmark
3. East Germany

Flying Dutchman
1. Great Britain
2. West Germany
3. Brazil

Finn
1. U.S.S.R.
2. Austria
3. Italy

SHOOTING

Free Pistol
1. G. Kosykh, U.S.S.R.
2. H. Mertel, West Germany
3. H. Vollmar, East Germany

Free Rifle
1. G. Anderson, U.S.
2. V. Kornev, U.S.S.R.
3. K. Muller, Switzerland

Rapid Fire Pistol
1. J. Zapedzki, Poland
2. M. Rosca, Rumania
3. R. Suleimanov, U.S.S.R.

Small-Bore Rifle (Prone)
1. J. Kurka, Czechoslovakia
2. L. Hammerl, Hungary
3. I. Ballinger, New Zealand

Small-Bore Rifle
(Three Positions)

1. B. Klinger, West Germany
2. J. Writer, U.S.
3. V. Parkhimovich, U.S.S.R.

Olympic Trench

1. R. Braithwaite, Great Britain
2. T. Garrigus, U.S.
3. K. Czekalla, East Germany

Skeet

1. E. Petrov, U.S.S.R.
2. R. Garagnani, Italy
3. K. Wirnhier, West Germany

MODERN PENTATHLON

1. B. Ferm, Sweden
2. A. Balczo, Hungary
3. P. Lednev, U.S.S.R.

Team

1. Hungary
2. U.S.S.R.
3. U.S.

BASKETBALL

1. U.S.
2. Yugoslavia
3. U.S.S.R.

FIELD HOCKEY

1. Pakistan
2. Australia
3. India

SOCCER

1. Hungary
2. Bulgaria
3. Japan

VOLLEYBALL — MEN

1. U.S.S.R.
2. Japan
3. Czechoslovakia

VOLLEYBALL — WOMEN

1. U.S.S.R.
2. Japan
3. Poland

WATER POLO

1. Yugoslavia
2. U.S.S.R.
3. Poland

THE
WINTER
OLYMPIC
GAMES

BARA ANN SCOTT of *da won the women's figure* *ng title at St. Moritz, 1948.*

SONJA HENIE. The most *famous figure skater of all time* *won Olympic gold medals for* *Norway in 1928, 1932 and* *1936.*

ANDREA MEAD LAWRENCE of the United States won *oth women's slaloms events at Oslo. 1952.*

OTHMAR SCHNEIDER of Austria finishing his winning slalom race in Oslo. 1952.

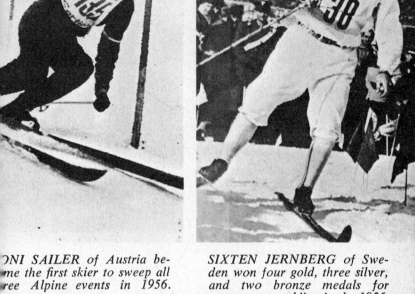

TONI SAILER of Austria became the first skier to sweep all three Alpine events in 1956.

SIXTEN JERNBERG of Sweden won four gold, three silver, and two bronze medals for cross-country skiing in the 1956, 1960, and 1964 Winter Olympic Games.

LYDIA SKOBLIKOVA. The Russian speedskater won a total of six Olympic gold medals in 1960 and 1964.

Jubilant Canadian bob-sledders Doug Anakin, Vic Emery, John Emery and Peter Kirby after causing one of the biggest upsets of the 1964 Winter Olympic Games by winning the 4-man bob-sled event.

PEGGY FLEMING of the United States won the women's figure skating title at Grenoble. 1968.

JEAN CLAUDE KILLY France. Winner of the tv slaloms and the downhill Grenoble. 1968. This was or the second time a skier has w all three Alpine events.

Chapter 18

THE I WINTER OLYMPIAD

Chamonix, 1924

Although figure skating and hockey had been included in the 1908 and 1920 summer Olympics, the first official Winter Olympic Games were held in 1924 at Chamonix in the French Alps. Skiers and speedskaters had finally persuaded the organizers of the summer Olympics in Paris to put on a separate meet for winter sports.

The Norwegians won four gold medals, six silver medals and eight bronze medals; and the Finns four gold, four silver and two bronze.

Norwegian Thorleif Haug won all three skiing events, and Clas Thunberg of Finland got two firsts, a second and a third in the four speedskating races.

Gillis Grafstrom of Sweden retained his men's figure skating title; and Heima Planck-Szabo of Austria beat Beatrix Loughran of the United States in the ladies' competition. Helene Engelmann and Alfred Berger of Austria won the pairs championship from Walter and Ludovika Jakobsson of Finland.

Canada, represented by the Toronto Granites, outscored the opposition 110-3 in the hockey tournament, beating the United States 6-1, Switzerland 33-0, Czechoslovakia 30-0, Sweden 22-0 and Great Britain 19-2.

OFFICIAL I WINTER OLYMPIAD RESULTS

Chamonix, 1924

NORDIC SKIING

18 KM Cross-Country
1. T. Haug, Norway—1:14.31.0
2. J. Grottumsbraaten, Norway—1:15:51.0
3. T. Niku, Finland—1:26:26.0

50 KM Cross-Country
1. T. Haug, Norway—3:44:32.0
2. T. Stromstad, Norway—3:46:23.0
3. J. Grottumsbraaten, Norway—3:47:46.0

Nordic Combined
1. T. Haug, Norway
2. T. Stromstad, Norway
3. J. Grottumsbraaten, Norway

SKI JUMPING
1. J. Thams, Norway
2. N. Bonna, Norway
3. T. Haug, Norway

FIGURE SKATING

Men
1. G. Grafstrom, Sweden
2. W. Bockl, Austria
3. G. Gautschi, Switzerland

Women
1. H. Planck-Szabo, Austria
2. B. Loughran, U.S.
3. E. Muckelt, Great Britain

Pairs
1. H. Engelmann/A. Berger, Austria
2. L. Jakobsson/W. Jakobsson, Finland
3. A. Joly/P. Brunet, France

SPEED SKATING—MEN

500 Metres
1. C. Jewtraw, U.S.—44.0
2. O. Olsen, Norway—44.2
3. R. Larsen, Norway—44.8
   C. Thunberg, Finland—44.8

1,500 Metres
1. C. Thunberg, Finland—2:20.8
2. R. Larsen, Norway—2:22.0
3. S. Moen, Norway—2:25.6

5,000 Metres
1. C. Thunberg, Finland—8:39.0
2. J. Skutnabb, Finland—8:48.4
3. R. Larsen, Norway—8:50.2

10,000 Metres
1. J. Skutnabb, Finland—18:04.8
2. C. Thunberg, Finland—18:04.8
3. R. Larsen, Norway—18:12.2

BOBSLED
4-man Bob
1. Switzerland I—5:45.54
2. Great Britain—5:48.83
3. Belgium—6:02.29

ICE HOCKEY
1. Canada
2. U.S.
3. Great Britain

Chapter 19

THE II WINTER OLYMPIAD

St. Moritz, 1928

When Sonja Henie won her first Oslo figure skating championship at the age of nine, she told her father she wanted to win the world championship. She practised three hours in the mornings and two hours in the afternoons. The following year she became Norwegian champion and at the age of 11 she was the youngest person in history to win the world title. She defended it nine times before turning professional in 1936 and becoming a millionairess. She won the first of her three Olympic championships at St. Moritz in 1928 when she was 15 years old, and the critics likened her performance to a ballet on ice. Sonja said that was because she had seen Pavlova dance in London the year before and she interpreted the same dance, the Dying Swan, on skates.

Also at St. Moritz, Gillis Grafstrom won his third men's figure skating title and Andree Joly and Pierre Brunet of France, who had been third in 1924, won the first of their two Olympic pairs championships.

Canada, represented this time by the University of Toronto Grades, beat Sweden 11-0, Switzerland 11-0 and Great Britain 14-0 to retain the hockey championship. The Canadians were considered so superior to the other teams that the Olympic governing body decided not to bother putting them through the routine of an elimination series to decide the four finalists.

Norway continued to take most of the medals, winning six golds, four silvers and five bronze for a total of 15. The Norwegian skiers did, however, win three of the four skiing events with Johan Grottumsbraaten winning the 18 kilometre cross country and the Nordic combined. The United States won six medals, including both bobsled championships.

OFFICIAL II WINTER OLYMPIAD RESULTS

St. Moritz, 1928

NORDIC SKIING

18 KM Cross-Country
1. J. Grottumsbraaten, Norway—1:37:01.0
2. O. Hegge, Norway—1:39:01.0
3. R. Odegaard, Norway—1:40:11.0

50 KM Cross-Country
1. P. E. Hedlund, Sweden—4:52:03.0
2. G. Jonsson, Sweden—5:05:30.0
3. V. Andersson, Sweden—5:05:46.0

Nordic Combined
1. J. Grottumsbraaten, Norway
2. H. Vinjarengen, Norway
3. J. Snersrud, Norway

SKI JUMPING
1. J. Andersen, Norway
2. S. Ruud, Norway
3. R. Purkert, Czecnoslovakia

FIGURE SKATING

Men
1. G. Grafstrom, Sweden
2. W. Bockl, Austria
3. R. v. Zeebroeck, Belgium

Women
1. S. Henie, Norway
2. F. Burger, Austria
3. B. Laughran, U.S.

Pairs
1. A. Joly/P. Brunet, France
2. L. Scholz/O. Kaiser, Austria
3. M. Brunner/L. Wrede, Austria

SPEED SKATING—MEN

500 Metres
1. { C. Thunberg, Finland—43.4
   { B. Evensen, Norway—43.4
3. { J. O. Farrell, U.S.—43.6
   { R. Larsen, U.S.—43.6
   { J. Friman, Finland—43.6

1,500 Metres
1. C. Thunberg, Finland—2:21.0
2. B. Evensen, Norway—2:21.9
3. I. Ballangrud, Norway—2:22.6

5,000 Metres
1. I. Ballangrud, Norway—8:50.5
2. J. Skutnabb, Finland—8:59.1
3. B. Evensen, Norway—9:01.1

BOBSLED

4-Man Bob
1. U.S. II—3:20.5
2. U.S. I—3:21.0
3. Germany—3:21.9

Skeleton
1. J. Heaton, U.S.—3:01.8
2. J. R. Heaton, U.S.—3:02.8
3. Earl of Northest, Gt. Brit.—3:05.1

ICE HOCKEY
1. Canada
2. Sweden
3. Switzerland

Chapter 20

THE III WINTER OLYMPIAD

Lake Placid, 1932

Norway, which had dominated the first two Winter Olympic Games lost the unofficial championship to the United States in 1932.

American athletes at Lake Placid won six gold medals, four silver medals and two bronze for a total of 12, compared with 10, including three gold medals, for the Norwegians.

After Jack Shea and Irving Jaffee had each won two speedskating races, the Scandinavians complained that this was because they were run under American rules—man-to-man instead of against the clock. On the opening day at Lake Placid, Shea, the 21-year-old son of a local butcher, beat world champion Bernt Evensen of Norway by five yards in the 500 metre race after leading all the way. The following day, in the 1,500 metre race, he finished five yards ahead of Alex Hurd of Canada, the bronze medallist in the 500 metres, Jaffee beat Edward Murphy, also of the U.S., by a few inches in the 5,000 metres.

The 10,000 metre race ended with the first three finishers skidding across the line against a 40-mile-an-hour gale. Jaffee plunged forward and slid across the line three yards ahead of Ivar Ballangrud of Norway and Frank Stack of Canada, both of whom had lost their balance in the last few yards.

The United States' other two gold medals were for bobsledding. J. Hubert Stevens twice piloted his two-man sled to a world record to overtake Reto Capudrutt of Switzerland, and two American teams finished first and second in the four-man bobsled event.

The United States hockey team almost stole the hockey championship from Canada. In the first game, the Americans had a 1-0 lead with less than three minutes to go when Canada tied it up and won 2-1 in overtime. In the second game, three overtime periods failed to break a 2-2 deadlock after Canada had scored the tying goal with 33 seconds left in regulation time.

Sonja Henie was placed first by all seven judges as she defeated Fritzi Burger of Austria once again for the second of her three Olympic figure skating championships.

However, the judges did not have such an easy time picking a winner in the men's figure skating. They studied the score sheets for two hours before awarding the gold medal to world champion Karl Schafer over three-time Olympic champion Gillis Grafstrom of Sweden. Schafer and Grafstrom were such bitter rivals that they refused to speak to each other either before or after the competition.

Defending champions Andree Joly and Pierre Brunet —now Mr. and Mrs. Brunet—retained their pairs title in a close decision over Beatrix Loughran and Sherwin Badger of the United States and Emilia Rotter and Laszlo Szollas of Hungary.

The Scandinavians, as usual, swept the skiing events with the Norwegians getting two gold medals, two silver medals and three bronze medals.

OFFICIAL III WINTER OLYMPIAD RESULTS

Lake Placid, 1932

NORDIC SKIING

18 KM Cross-Country
1. S. Utterstrom, Sweden—1:23:07.0
2. A. Wikstrom, Sweden—1:25:07.0
3. V. Saarinen, Finland—1:25:24.0

50 KM Cross-Country
1. V. Saarinen, Finland—4:28:00.0
2. V. Liikkanen, Finland—4:28:20.0
3. A. Rustadstuen, Norway— 4:31:20.0

Nordic Combined
1. J. Grottumsbraaten, Norway
2. O. Stenen, Norway
3. H. Vinjarengen, Norway

SKI JUMPING
1. R. Ruud, Norway
2. J. H. Beck, Norway
3. K. Wahlberg, Norway

FIGURE SKATING

Men
1. K. Schafer, Austria
2. G. Grafstrom, Sweden
3. M. Wilson, Canada

Women
1. S. Henie, Norway
2. F. Burger, Austria
3. M. Vinson, U.S.

Pairs
1. A. Brunet/P. Brunet, France
2. B. Loughran/S. Badger, U.S.
3. E. Rotter/L. Szollas, Hungary

SPEED SKATING—MEN

500 Metres
1. J. A. Shea, U.S.—43.4
2. B. Evensen, Norway
3. A. Hurd, Canada

5,000 Metres
1. I. Jaffee, U.S.—9:40.8
2. E. S. Murphy, U.S.
3. W. F. Logan, Canada

1,500 Metres
1. J. A. Shea, U.S.—2:57.5
2. A. Hurd, Canada
3. W. F. Logan, Canada

10,000 Metres
1. I. Jaffee, U.S.—19:13.6
2. I. Ballangrud, Norway
3. F. Stack, Canada

BOBSLED

2-Man Sled
1. U.S. I—8:14.74
2. Switzerland I—8:16.28
3. U.S. II—8:29.15

4-Man Bob
1. U.S. I—7:53.68
2. U.S. II—7:55.70
3. Germany I—8;04.00

ICE HOCKEY
1. Canada
2. U.S.
3. Germany

Chapter 21

THE IV WINTER OLYMPIAD

Garmisch-Partenkirchen, 1936

Adolf Hitler's mustache was tainted white from frost and snow when a crowd of 80,000 gathered during a blizzard in the Bavarian Alps to hear him open the fourth Olympic Winter Games.

Canada was represented in the hockey tournament by the Port Arthur Bearcats because the Halifax Wolverines, who had beaten them in the 1935 senior final, could not round up enough of their players. To the astonishment of all, the Bearcats lost the tournament with a 3-2 loss to a British team reinforced by several players trained in Canada.

The Canadians had protested the presence of Canadians on the British team and the Olympic eligibility board originally disqualified them from competition. But when Britain threatened to withdraw its entire team, the Olympic committee reinstated the Canadian players and declared the tournament a non-Olympic championship. However, after some of the games had already been played, the committee again changed its mind and decided to make it official.

Sonja Henie won her third Olympic title and then turned professional. Karl Schafer of Austria successfully defended his men's figure skating title. And Maxi Herber and Ernst Baier of Germany won a close decision in the pairs from Ilse and Erik Pausin of Austria.

Norway won all four speedskating races, with three of them going to Ivar Ballangrud. However he was beaten by compatriot Charles Mathiesen in the fourth event. Ballangrud won four gold medals, two silver and a bronze in three Winter Olympics.

Norway and Sweden divided the skiing honors equally. But in the overall medal total, Norway was far ahead with seven gold medals, five silver medals and three bronze.

OFFICIAL IV WINTER OLYMPIAD RESULTS

Garmisch-Partenkirchen, 1936

NORDIC SKIING—MEN

18 KM Cross-Country
1. E. Larsson, Sweden—1:14:38.0
2. O. Hagen, Norway—1:15:33.0
3. P. Neimi, Finland—1:16:59.0

40 KM Relay Race
1. Finland—2:41:33.0
2. Norway—2:41:39.0
3. Sweden—2:43:03.0

50 KM Cross-Country
1. E. Wiklund, Sweden—3:30:11.0
2. A. Wikstrom, Sweden—3:33:20.0
3. N. Englund— Sweden—3:34:10.0

Nordic Combined
1. O. Hagen, Norway
2. O. Hoffsbakken, Norway
3. S. Brodahl, Norway

Downhill and Slalom—Women
1. C. Cranz, Germany
2. K. Grasegger, Germany
3. L. Schou-Nilsen , Norway

SKI JUMPING

Ski Jumping
1. B. Rudd, Norway
2. S. Ericksson, Sweden
3. R. Andersen, Norway

Nordic Combined
1. O. Hagen, Norway
2. O. Hoffsbakken, Norway
3. S. Brodahl, Norway

FIGURE SKATING

Men
1. K. Schafer, Austria
2. E. Baier, Germany
3. F. Kaspar, Austria

Women
1. S. Henie, Norway
2. C. Colledge, Great Britain
3. V. Hulten, Sweden

Pairs
1. M. Herber/E. Baier, Germany
2. I. Pausin/E. Pausin, Austria
3. E. Rotter/L. Szollas, Hungary

SPEED SKATING—MEN

500 Metres
1. I. Ballangrud, Norway—43.4
2. G. Krog, Norway—43.5
3. L. Freisinger, U.S.—44.0

5,000 Metres
1. I. Ballangrud, Norway—8:19.6
2. B. Wasenius, Finland—8:23.3
3. A. Ojala, Finland—8:30.1

1,500 Metres
1. C. Mathiesen, Norway—2:19.2
2. I. Ballangrud, Norway—2:20.2
3. B. Wasenius, Finland—2:20.9

10,000 Metres
1. I. Ballangrud, Norway—17:24.3
2. B. Wasenius, Finland—17:28.2
3. M. Stiepl, Austria—17:30.0

BOBSLED

2-Man Bob
1. U.S. I—5:29.29
2. Switzerland—5:30.64
3. U.S. II—5:33.96

4-Man Bob
1. Switzerland II—5:19.85
2. Switzerland I—5:22.73
3. Great Britain—5:23.41

ICE HOCKEY
1. Great Britain
2. Canada
3. U.S.

Chapter 22
THE V WINTER OLYMPIAD
St. Moritz, 1948

Nineteen-year-old Barbara Ann Scott became an international sports celebrity by adding the Olympic women's figure skating title to the North American and European championships she had won earlier in the year. The Canadian girl also successfully defended her world championship a week later.

At St. Moritz, Barbara Ann was just about a unanimous choice to win, although the poor ice conditions threatened to cancel the championship after completion of two of the five compulsory figures when she had a lead of 8.4 points over Eva Pawlik of Austria. But after a day off, there was a freeze-up and the ice hardened.

Barbara Ann completed her figures and led Jeanette Altwegg of Great Britain with Miss Pawlik slipping to third.

After the free skating, seven of the nine judges awarded Barbara Ann first place. Almost 40 points behind was Miss Paulik who had overtaken Miss Altwegg on the free skating. Miss Scott was the first non-European to win the Olympic title.

Eighteen-year-old Dick Button of the U.S. won the men's figure skating title, defeating Hans Gerschwiler of Switzerland by 90 points; and the Olympic pairs title went to Pierre Baugniet and Micheline Lannoy of Belgium in a close contest with Ede Kiralt and Andrea Kekassy of Hungary. Wally Siestelmeyer and Suzanne Morrow of Canada were third.

The under-rated Royal Canadian Air Force Flyers beat Switzerland 3-0 to win the hockey championship on a superior goals average, although they had finished in a points tie with Czechoslovakia. The Canadians finished the tournament with seven wins and a 1-1 tie with the Czechs, but they had scored 28 goals to only one against them while the Czechs only scored five goals in the entire tournament.

Not included in the Canadian point total was a 12-1 win over the United States whose games were no counted in the final standings. The U.S. had sent two teams to Switzerland. One was sponsored by he Amateur Athletic Union and the other by the rival Amateur Hockey Association. The International Ice Hockey Association recognized the AHA team and the International Olympic Committee recognized the other one. The IOC then banned both teams and said hockey would not be included in the Olympics. Canada protested and the IOC backed down and allowed the American AHA team to compete, although the results of its games did not count.

Mrs. Gretchen Fraser, a 28-year-old housewife from Vancouver, Wash., won the United States' first skiing gold medal in the women's special slalom. Swedish skiiers won three of the other six events.

The Norwegians swept the four speedskating races, but Sweden won the overall unofficial point total followed by Switzerland and the United States. Thirteen of the 28 competing countries did not score a single point.

OFFICIAL V WINTER OLYMPIAD RESULTS

St. Moritz, 1948

NORDIC SKIING—MEN

18 KM Cross-Country
1. M. Lundstrom, Sweden—1:13:50.0
2. N. Ostensson, Sweden—1:14:22.0
3. G. Eriksson, Sweden—1:16:06.0

40 KM Relay Race
1. Sweden—2:32:08.0
2. Finland—2:42:06.0
3. Norway—2:44:33.0

50 KM Cross-Country
1. N. Karlsson, Sweden—3:47:48.0
2. H. Eriksson, Sweden—3:52:20.0
3. B. Vanninen, Finland—3:57:28.0

Nordic Combined
1. H. Hasu, Finland
2. M. Huhtala, Finland
3. S. Israelsson, Sweden

SKI JUMPING
1. P. Hugsted, Norway
2. B. Ruud, Norway
3. T. Schjelderup, Norway

ALPINE SKIING—MEN

Slalom
1. E. Reinalter, Switzerland—2:10.3
2. J. Couttet, France—2:10.8
3. H. Oreiller, France—2:12.8

Downhill
1. H. Oreiller, France—2:55.0
2. F. Gabl, Austria—2:59.1
3. K. Molitor, Switzerland—3:00.3

ALPINE SKIING—WOMEN

Slalom
1. G. Frazer, U.S.—1:57.2
2. A. Meyer, Switzerland—1:57.7
3. E. Mahringer, Austria—1:58.0

Downhill
1. H. Schlernegger, Switz.—2:28.3
2. T. Beiser, Austria—2:29.1
3. R. Hammerer, Austria—2:30.2

FIGURE SKATING

Men
1. R. Button, U.S.
2. H. Gerschwiler, Switzerland
3. E. Rada, Austria

Women
1. B. A. Scott, Canada
2. E. Pawlik, Austria
3. J. Altwegg, Great Britain

Pairs
1. M. Lannoy/P. Baugniet, Belgium
2. A. Kekessy/E. Kiraly, Hungary
3. S. Morrow/W. Diestelmeyer, Canada

SPEED SKATING—MEN

500 Metres
1. F. Helgesen, Norway—43.1
2. { K. Bartholomew, U.S.—43.2
   T. Byberg, Norway—43.2
   R. Fitzgerald, U.S.—43.2

5,000 Metres
1. R. Liaklev, Norway—8:29.4
2. O. Lundberg, Norway—8:32.7
3. G. Hedlund, Sweden—8:34.8

1,500 Metres
1. S. Farstad, Norway—2:17.6
2. A. Seyffarth, Sweden—2:18.1
3. O. Lundberg, Norway—2:18.9

10,000 Metres
1. A. Seyffarth, Sweden—17:26.3
2. L. Parkkinen, Finland—17:36.0
3. P. Lammio, Finland—17:42.7

BOBSLED

2-Man Bob
1. Switzerland II—5:29.2
2. Switzerland I—5:30.4
3. U.S. II.—5:35.3

4-Man Bob
1. U.S. II—5:20.1
2. Belgium—5:21.3
3. U.S. I—5:21.5

ICE HOCKEY
1. Canada
2. Czechoslovakia
3. Switzerland

Chapter 23

THE VI WINTER OLYMPIAD

Oslo, 1952

The normally jubilant opening day parade for the Olympic Winter Games at Oslo was more like a funeral procession. The parade went on at the same time as the funeral services in London for King George VI. Flags of the Commonwealth nations and Norway were at half mast and the 1,178 athletes from 30 countries proceeded in a slow march past the Royal box and Princess Ragnhild, 21-year-old daughter of Crown Prince Olaf. Her father and grandfather, King Haakon VII, were in London for the funeral.

For several weeks before the Olympics, there had been no snow around Oslo and the ski slopes were almost bare, but a few days before the Games were to open a snowstorm relieved the situation.

Mrs. Andrea Mead Lawrence, 19, of the U.S. won both the giant slalom and the women's special slalom. In the giant slalom she defeated Austrian movie actress Dagmar Rom and collapsed into the arms of her husband, David, also a member of the U.S. ski team. In the women's special slalom, she fell on the first run but recovered on the second to win and become the first skier to win both Olympic slalom events. Mrs. Trude Jochum-Beiser of Austria won the women's downhill, Mrs. Lawrence finishing in seventeenth position. She fell twice on the rugged Norfjell decline.

Stein Eriksen, 22, of Norway, won the men's giant slalom over two Austrians, Christian Pravda and Toni Spiss.

Austrian chemistry student Othman Schneider won the men's special slalom. Eriksen had been the favorite in this event too, and he led on the first two runs; but two mistakes on his final run cost him a second gold medal. Only 33 of the 87 entries qualified for the second run.

The 1950 world champion, Zeno Colo, of Italy, defeated Schneider in the downhill event.

Simon Slattvik of Norway beat defending champion

Heikki Hasu of Finland in the Nordic combined. Hallgeir Brenden of Norway set a world record 49:39.0 in the 15 kilometre portion of the competition but his jumping was so bad that he did not get a medal. Paul Wegeman of the United States suffered a brain concussion when he fell on his third jump.

Husky Veikko Hakulinen, 26, of Finland, won the 50 kilometre cross-country, finishing more than four minutes ahead of fellow countryman Eero Kolehmainen. Norway's Magnar Estenstad, who had been closest to Hakulinen most of the way, tired to finish third. Defending champion Nils Karlsson of Sweden was fifth. The race was run in above freezing temperatures which created watery conditions. Hakulinen admitted that a special wax which enabled his skis to grip the soft snow helped him enormously, while other competitors seemed to slip and fall.

Hallgeir Brenden won the gold medal for the 15 kilometre cross-country, although his time was slower than it had been for the same distance in the Nordic combined.

Speedskater Hjalmar Andersen of Norway then became the first athlete in the Winter Games to win three championships on consecutive days. After winning the 5,000 and 1,500 metres he cut 11.6 seconds off his own 10,000 metre world record. Ken Henry of the United States won the only other speedskating gold medal, for the 500 metres.

Jeanette Altwegg of Great Britain, who had finished third to Barbara Ann Scott in 1948, won the women's figure skating championship, defeating Tenley Albright of the United States.

Defending champion Dick Button easily defeated Helmu Seibt of Austria in the men's figure skating, and Ria and Paul Falk of Austria won the pairs event.

Andreas Ostler of Germany piloted his two-man bobsled to a gold medal with a record breaking run in the first of the four heats. He then steered his four-man bobsled to a second gold medal. The perilous third curve of the bobsled run had to be rebuilt overnight during the competition after two accidents in which two members from both the Belgian and Swiss four-man teams were badly injured.

Canada retained the hockey title with the Edmonton Mercuries winning seven games and tying one. The 1-1 tie with the United States gave the Americans second place over Sweden.

Norway won the unofficial points total over the United States and Finland.

OFFICIAL VI WINTER OLYMPIAD RESULTS

Oslo, 1952

NORDIC SKIING—MEN

15 KM Cross-Country

1. H. Brenden, Norway—1:1:34.0
2. T. Makela, Finland—1:2:09.0
3. P. Lonkila, Finland—1:2:20.0

50 KM Cross-Country

1. V. Kahulinen, Finland—3:33:33.0
2. E. Kolehmainen, Finland— 3:38:11.0
3. M. Estenstad, Norway—3:38:28.0

NORDIC SKIING—WOMEN

10 KM Cross-Country

1. L. Widemen, Finland—41:40.0
2. M. Hietamies, Finland—42:39.0
3. Si. Rantanen, Finland—42:50.0

40 KM Relay Race

1. Finland—2:20:16.0
2. Norway—2:23:13.0
3. Sweden—2:24:13.0

Nordic Combined

1. S. Slattvik, Norway
2. K. Hasu, Finland
3. S. Stenersen, Norway

SKI JUMPING

1. A. Bergmann, Norway
2. T. Flakanger, Norway
3. K. Holmstrom, Sweden

ALPINE SKIING—MEN

Giant Slalom

1. S. Eriksen, Norway—2:25.0
2. C. Pravda, Austria—2:26.9
3. T. Spiss, Austria—2:28.2

Slalom

1. O. Schneider, Austria—2:00.0
2. S. Eriksen, Norway—2:01.2
3. G. Berge, Norway—2:01.7

Downhill

1. Z. Colo, Italy—2:30.8
2. O. Schneider, Austria—2:32.0
3. C. Pravda, Austria—2:32.4

ALPINE SKIING—WOMEN

Giant Slalom

1. A. Lawrence-Mead, U.S.—2:06.8
2. D. Rom, Austria—2:09.0
3. A. Buchner, Germany—2:10.0

Slalom

1. A. Lawrence-Mead—U.S.—2:10.6
2. O. Reichert, Germany—2:11.4
3. A. Buchner, Germany—2:13.3

Downhill

1. T. Jochum-Beiser, Austria—1:47.1
2. A. Buchner, Germany—1:48.0
3. G. Minuzzo, Italy—1:49.0

FIGURE SKATING

Men

. R. Button, U.S.
:. H. Seibt, Austria
. J. Grogan, U.S.

Women

1. J. Altwegg, Great Britain
2. T. Albright, U.S.
3. J. du Bief, France

Pairs

1. R. Falk/P. Falk, Germany
2. K. E. Kennedy/M. Kennedy, U.S.
3. M. Nagy/L. Nagy, Hungary

SPEED SKATING—MEN

500 Metres
1. K. Henry, U.S.—43.2
2. D. McDermott, U.S.—43.9
3. { A. Johansen, Norway—44.0
    { G. Audley, Canada—44.0

1,500 Metres
1. H. Andersen, Norway—2:20.4
2. W. vander Boort, Holland—2:20.4
3. R. Aas, Norway—2:21.6

10,000 Metres
1. H. Andersen, Norway—16:45.8
2. K. Broekman, Neth.—17:10.6
3. C. E. Asplund, Sweden—17:16.6

BOBSLED

2-Man Bob
1. Germany I—5:24.54
2. U.S. I—5:26.89
3. Switzerland I—5:27.71

4-Man Bob
1. Germany—5:07.84
2. U.S. I—5:10.48
3. Switzerland I—5:11.70

ICE HOCKEY
1. Canada
2. U.S.
3. Sweden

Chapter 24

THE VII WINTER OLYMPIAD

Cortina d'Ampezzo, 1956

Russia and an Austrian glamor boy skier dominated the 1956 Winter Olympics at Cortina d'Ampezzo, Italy.

The Russians, competing in the Winter Olympics for the first time, won six of the 24 gold medals and 121 points. Austria, mostly on the unprecedented triple medal performance of Toni Sailer, was second with 78½ points.

The Soviet athletes won three of the four speed-skating events, and then dealt the most stunning blow of all, at least to Canada, by winning the hockey tournament. The Canadians, represented by the Kitchener-Waterloo Dutchmen, were favoured as usual. But they were defeated 4-1 by the United States and then 2-0 by the Russians who displayed far superior passing and stick-handling. The Russian team also beat the U.S. 4-0.

The Russians did their pre-Olympic training at the Grande Hotel de Groce rink, 1,500 feet above Cortina, in comparative isolation. They reasoned that by getting away from the crowds and training at a high altitude they would function better at the lower level. They were right. The Russians were by far the best conditioned team in the tournament.

The Winter Olympics once again was plagued by a dearth of snow. Work crews had to bring it down by the truckload to cover the bare ski slopes. There had been a 23″ fall two weeks before the opening, but most of it had melted. Several skiers were injured in practice runs on the hazardous hills.

Italian speedskating champion Guido Caroli brought in the Olympic torch, but on his way to light the flame he tripped on microphone wires and fell headlong in front of President Giovanni Gronchi's box. With an amazing show of acrobatics he held onto the torch while regaining his feet.

With internationally known skiers tumbling on the icy hills, the lack of snow did not seem to bother Toni Sailer. After winning the giant slalom by almost six seconds, he made two daring descents to win the special slalom by four seconds. Then, in a flawless performance, he won the downhill by 2½ seconds to become the first skier ever to win all three Olympic gold medals.

Norwegian lumberjack Hallgeir Brenden, the defending champion, won the 15 kilometre cross-country race by less than a minute over Sixten Jernberg of Sweden. Jernberg also finished second in the 30 kilometre race won by another lumberjack, Veikko Hakulinen of Finland who had won the 50 kilometre cross-country in 1952. But Jernberg defeated Hakulinen at the 50 kilometre distance this time. Vladimir Kuzin of Russia, who had beaten Hakulinen several times, was the pre-race favorite but finished fifth. However, the Russian skiers picked up valuable points by winning bronze medals in all three races — Pavel Koltschin in the 15 and 30 kilometres and Fyetor Terentyev in the skiing marathon. The Russian skiers also clinched the team championship when Terentyev, Koltschin, Nikolay Anikin and Kuzin won the 40 kilometre relay race. Kuzin, the anchor man, staggered across the finish line six minutes ahead of Hakulinen who had been catching up to him on the last 10 mile leg.

A team of strong Finnish girls won the only Nordic event for women, the 15 kilometre relay. Siiri Rantanen came from behind on the last leg to beat a Russian team by 27 seconds.

Nineteen-year-old Elisabeth Schartz and 21-year-old Kurt Oppelt of Austria won the Olympic figure skating pairs championship in an upset decision over two-time world championships Frances Dafoe and Norris Bowden of Canada. The judges took almost an hour to announce the decision, based on a complicated scoring system. Only a tenth of a point separated the two teams. A minor fault by Miss Dafoe cost the Canadians the championship. The Austrians got four first place votes and five seconds from the nine judges. The Canadians got four firsts, four seconds and a third. Eighteen-year-old Franz Ningel and his 12-year-old partner Marika Kilius of Germany finished fourth behind Mr. and Mrs.

Laszlo Nagy of Hungary. The fans, who thought the young German pair should have been given the bronze medal, threw oranges, bottles and paper on the ice.

Tenley Albright of the United States overcame a severe leg cut, suffered when she fell on soft ice during a warmup, to win the women's championship over 15-year-old Carol Heiss of Ozone Park, N.Y. There was not much doubt in anyone's mind that Tenley was unbeatable after she completed her free skating. Carol, who followed her, knew she was behind and embarked on a daring program of triple jumps and lightning spins to catch up. However, Miss Albright won by 14 points.

Carol Heiss' childhood friend Hayes Alan Jenkins of Colorado Springs won the men's figure skating championship in a close competition with Ronald Robertson of Long Beach, Calif. Jenkins took the lead in the compulsory figures but Robertson was superior in the freeskating. Here again the judges took several minutes before awarding the gold medal to Jenkins, giving him a five point edge. Hayes' brother, David, 19, was third.

Yevgeniy Grischin of Russia set a world record of 40.2 seconds in the 500 metre speedskating and then tied countryman Yuriy Michailov in the 1,500 metres. Both were timed in a world record 2:08.6. Russia got its third speedskating victory in the 5,000 metres with Boris Schilkov beating Sigvard Ericsson of Sweden. Ericsson broke Russia's speedskating monopoly by winning the 10,000 metres. Hjalmar Andersen, the defending Olympic champion and world record holder, was sixth.

Swiss chauffeur Franz Kapus, 45, piloted the winning four-man bobsled and Dalla Costa and Giovanni Conti won Italy's only gold medal in the two-man bobsled.

OFFICIAL VII WINTER OLYMPIAD RESULTS

Cortina d'Ampezzo, 1956

NORDIC SKIING—MEN

15 KM Cross-Country
H. Brenden, Norway—49:38.0
S. Jernberg, Sweden—50:14.0
P. Kolschin, U.S.S.R.—50:17.0

50 KM Cross-Country
1. S. Jernberg, Sweden—2:50:27.0
2. V. Hakulinen, Finland—2:51:45.0
3. F. Terentyev, U.S.S.R.—2:53:32.0

30 KM Cross-Country
V. Hakulinen, Finland—1:44:06.0
S. Jernberg, Sweden—1:44:30.0
P. Koltschin, U.S.S.R.—1:45:45.0

40 KM Relay Race
1. U.S.S.R.—2:15:30.0
2. Finland—2:21:31.0
3. Sweden

Nordic Combined

1. S. Stenersen, Norway
2. B. Eriksson, Sweden
3. F. Gron-Gasienica, Poland

NORDIC SKIING—WOMEN

10 KM Cross-Country

1. L. Kosyryeva, U.S.S.R.—38:11.0
2. R. Yeroschina, U.S.S.R.—38:16.0
3. S. Edstrom, Sweden—38:23.0

15 KM Relay

1. Finland—1:9:01.0
2. U.S.S.R.—1:9:28.0
3. Sweden—1:9:48.0

SKI JUMPING

1. A. Hyvarinen, Finland
2. A. Kallakorpi, Finland
3. H. Glass, Germany

ALPINE SKIING—MEN

Giant Slalom

1. A. Sailer, Austria—3:00.1
3. A. Molterer, Austria—3:06.3
3. W. Schuster, Austria—3:07.2

Slalom

1. A. Sailer, Austria—3:14.7
2. C. Igaya, Japan—3:18.7
3. S. Sollander, Sweden—3:20.2

Downhill

1. A. Sailer, Austria—2:52.2
2. R. Fellay, Switz.—2:55.7
3. A. Molterer, Austria—2:56.2

ALPINE SKIING—WOMEN

Giant Slalom

1. O. Reichert, Germany—1:56.5
2. J. Franal, Austria—1:57.8
3. D. Hochleitner, Austria—1:58.2

Slalom

1. R. Colliard, Switz.—1:52.3
2. R. Schopf, Austria—1:55.4
3. J. Sidorova, U.S.S.R.—1:56.7

Downhill

1. M. Berthod, Switz.—1:40.7
2. F. Danzer, Switzerland—1:45.4
3. L. Wheeler, Canada—1:45.9

FIGURE SKATING

Men

1. H. A. Jenkins, U.S.
2. R. Robertson, U.S.
3. D. Jenkins, U.S.

Women

1. T. Albright, U.S.
2. C. Heiss, U.S.
3. I. Wendl, Austria

Pairs

1. E. Schwara/K. Oppelt, Austria
2. F. Dafoe/N. Bowden, Canada
3. M. Nagy/L. Nagy, Hungary

SPEED SKATING—MEN

500 Metres

1. Y. Grischin, U.S.S.R.—40.2
2. R. Gratsch, U.S.S.R.—40.8
3. A. Gjestvang, Norway—41.0

5,000 Metres

1. B. Schilkov, U.S.S.R.—7:48.7
2. S. Ericsson, Sweden—7:56.7
3. O. Gontscharenko, U.S.S.R.—7:57.5

1,500 Metres

1. { Y. Grischin, U.S.S.R.—2:08.6
   { Y. Michailov, U.S.S.R.—2:08.6
3. T. Salonen, Finland—2:09.4

10,000 Metres

1. S. Ericsson, Sweden—16:35.9
2. K. Johannesen, Norway—16:36
3. O. Gontscharenko, U.S.S.R.—16:42.3

BOBSLED

2-Man Bob

1. Italy I—5:30.14
2. Italy II—5:31.45
3. Switzerland I—5:37.46

4-Man Bob

1. Switzerland I—5:10.44
2. Italy II—5:12.10
3. U.S.—5:12.39

ICE HOCKEY

1. U.S.S.R.
2. U.S.
3. Canada

202

Chapter 25

THE VIII WINTER OLYMPIAD

Squaw Valley, 1960

Mrs. Andrea Mead Lawrence, the 1952 double gold medal winner in the slaloms, got things underway in Squaw Valley by skiing straight down Papoose Peak with the Olympic torch and passing it over to Ken Henry, the 500 metres champion of 1952, who skated once around the rink and lit the flame, but a major snowstorm on the opening day of competition forced the first postponement of an Olympic event since before the war when the men's downhill had to be put off for a day.

French hotel owner Juan Vuarnet, 27, found the newly fallen snow to his liking and beat Hans-Peter Lanig of Germany by half a second in the downhill. Vuarnet was the first Olympic champion to use non-waxed metal skis, now fairly common, and his victory ended a five year domination of downhill and slalom skiing by the Austrians whose best man, Karl Schranz, was seventh.

Roger Staub of Switzerland, who was fourth in the downhill behind another Frenchman, Guy Perillat, beat Josef Steigler of Austria in the giant slalom. The only Austrian gold medal went to Ernst Hinterseer in the special slalom.

The skiers were so inconsistent that Guy Perillat, whose only medal was the bronze in the downhill, was awarded the combined championship by the World Ski Federation. Another Frenchman, Charles Boxon, who only got a bronze medal in the special slalom, was second on the combined points and Hans-Peter Lanig, the silver medallist in the downhill, was third.

Twenty-one-year-old New Englander Penny Pitou won the women's world alpine title on the strength of silver medals in the downhill and giant slalom. Miss Pitou was hampered by a bad cold when she finished the giant slalom just a tenth of a second behind Yvonne Ruegg, a 20-year-old Swiss secretary. There were several spectacular falls and Linda Meyes of the U.S. broke her collarbone.

Heidi Biebl of Germany won the downhill by one second, and twenty-one-year-old Anne Heggtveit of Ottawa, who had finished twelfth in both the giant slalom and the downhill, won Canada's first skiing gold medal in the special slalom which also gave her the world combined slalom championship. She had the fastest time in the first run but lost a tenth of a second at a hairpin turn on the tenth gate. The next fastest time was by Marianne Jahn, the 16-year-old daughter of an Austrian banker, but she fell on the last gate and Miss Heggtveit's combined time was better than three seconds ahead of silver medallist Betsy Snite of the United States. Downhill champion Heidi Biebl was twenty-first, double silver medal winner Penny Pitou fell on her second run and came thirty-third, and the downhill winner Yvonne Ruegg, also fell and was disqualified.

The cross-country relay race on skis, almost unheard of in the United States, turned out to be one of the most exciting events at Squaw Valley. Finnish veteran Veikko Hakulinen caught Haakon Brusveen of Norway on the final leg and held on to his narrow lead until the finish. There was only four fifths of a second between them about three feet, after completing the 24.8 mile course. Hakulinen had started the last leg 20 seconds, or about 150 yards, behind the Norwegian. The Russian team came up from eighth place to finish third on the last leg.

Haakon Brusveen, 32, beat Sixten Jernberg of Norway and Veikko Hakulinen in the 15 kilometre race. But Jernberg, a 31-year-old ski salesman who had finished second to Hakulinen in 1956, led all the way in the 30 kilometre race, beating Rolf Ramgard of Norway by 13 seconds.

In three Olympic appearances, Hakulinen won three gold medals, three silvers and a bronze. Jernberg, whose Olympic career also began in 1952 but who appeared at Cortina in 1964 as well, compiled four gold medals, three silvers and a bronze.

Three-time world champions Barbara Wagner and Bob Paul, of Canada, established themselves at Squaw Valley as perhaps the best pairs skaters in the history of the sport. In their performance they included the overhead axel and the death spin, two of the most difficult and dangerous skating manoeuvres. At the Olympics they were the first couple to receive the unanimous votes of all the judges who gave them a near-perfect score.

David Jenkins, who finished third behind his brother Hayes in 1956, kept the men's Olympic figure skating title in the family with a superb freeskating performance to overcome a 22-point deficit behind Karol Divin of Czechoslovakia after the compulsory figures. One judge gave him a perfect six points for freeskating and the other nine scored 5.9. Donald Jackson of Canada, second to Jenkins in the freeskating, could not overcome Divin's lengthy lead in the compulsory figures and finished third in the combined total.

Carol Heiss, who later married Hayes Alan Jenkins, now a lawyer, got the votes of seven of the nine judges to win the women's figure skating title after finishing second to Tenley Albright in 1956. At Cortina, when she was only 16, she had promised her mother she would win, but she missed by 14 points. Her mother died of cancer a month later. At Squaw Valley, she beat Sjoukje Dijkstra of Holland by 73 points.

The Russians easily won the unofficial team point standings at Squaw Valley coming up with 165½ points, more than double the total points of second placed Sweden. The Soviet athletes brought home 21 medals, compared with the 16 they won in their winter Olympic debut at Cortina.

Six of their seven gold medals were for speedskating and three of these were won by 20-year-old student Lydia Skoblikova. She broke the world record by three tenths of a second in winning the 1,500 metres in 2:25.2 and also won the 1,500 and 3,000 metre races. Another Russian, 22-year-old teacher Klara Guseva, defeated Helga Haase of Germany and world record holder Tamara Rylova of Russia in the 1,000 metres.

The only gold medal the Soviet girls did not get in speedskating was in the 500 metres in which Mrs. Haase defeated Natalie Dontschenko of Russia.

In the men's speedskating, the Russians scored two victories, a tie and one loss when 26-year-old Norwegian carpenter Knut Johannesen defeated Viktor Kositschkin in the 10,000 metres. However, in the 5,000 metres, the 21-year-old Kositschin, regarded as the third stringer on the Russian team, turned the tables on Johannesen.

Yevgeniy Grischin had tied fellow Russian Yuriy Michailov for the gold medal in the 1,500 metres in 1956. In Squaw Valley Grischin was involved in another dead heat for first, but it was a Norwegian, Roald Aas, who crossed the finish line with him this time. However, Grischin did successfully defend his 500 metre title, beating Bill Disney of the United States by a tenth of a second and tying his own Olympic record of 40.2 seconds.

Winning six gold medals out of a possible eight in one sport did not soften the blow of losing the prestigious hockey championship. The Russians only managed a bronze medal with two wins, two losses and a tie. The United States team, which had only been assembled two months before the Olympics, upset Canada 2-1 to take the championship. The Canadians came second.

OFFICIAL VIII WINTER OLYMPIAD RESULTS

Squaw Valley, 1960

NORDIC SKIING—MEN

15 KM Cross-Country

1. H. Brusveen, Norway—51:55.5
2. S. Jernberg, Sweden—51:58.6
3. V. Hakulinen, Finland—52:03.0

30 KM Cross-Country

1. S. Jernberg, Sweden—1:51:03.9
2. R. Ramgard, Sweden—1:51:16.9
3. N. Anikin, U.S.S.R.—1:52:28.2

50 KM Cross-Country

1. K. Hammalainen, Finland—
   2:59:06.3
2. V. Hakulinen, Finland—2:59:26.7
3. R. Ramgard, Sweden—3:02:46.7

40 KM Relay Race

1. Finland—2:18:45.6
2. Norway—2:18:46.4
3. U.S.S.R.—2:21:21.6

Nordic Combined

1. G. Thoma, Germany
2. T. Knutsen, Norway
3. N. Gussakov, U.S.S.R.

BIATHLON

1. K. Lestander, Sweden—1:33:21.6
2. A. Tyrvainen, Finland—1:33:57
3. A. Privalov, U.S.S.R.—1:34:54.2

NORDIC SKIING—WOMEN

10 KM Cross-Country

1. M. Gusakova, U.S.S.R.—39:46.6
2. L. Baranova-Kosyryveva,
   U.S.S.R.—40:04.2
3. R. Yeroschina, U.S.S.R.—40:06.0

15 KM Relay

1. Sweden—1:4:21.4
2. U.S.S.R.—1:5:2.6
3. Finland—1:6:27.5

SKI JUMPING

1. H. Recknagel, Germany
2. N. Halonen, Finland
3. O. Leodolter, Austria

ALPINE SKIING—MEN

Giant Slalom
1. R. Staub, Switzerland—1:48.3
2. J. Stiegler, Austria—1:48.7
3. E. Hinterseer, Austria—1:49.1

Slalom
1. E. Hinterseer, Austria—2:08.9
2. M. Deitner, Austria—2:10.3
3. C. Bozon, France—2:10.4

Downhill
1. J. Vuarnet, France—2:06.0
2. H. Lanig, Germany—2:06.5
3. G. Perillat, France—2:06.9

ALPINE SKIING—WOMEN

Giant Slalom
1. Y. Ruegg, Switzerland—1:39.9
2. P. Piton, U.S.—1:40.0
3. G. Chenal-Minuzzo, Italy—1:40.2

Slalom
1. A. Heggtveit, Canada—1:49.6
2. B. Snite, U.S.—1:52.9
3. B. Henneberger, Germ.—1:56.6

Downhill
1. H. Biebl, Germany—1:37.6
2. P. Piton, U.S.—1:38.6
3. T. Hecher, Austria—1:38.9

FIGURE SKATING

Men
1. D. Jenkins, U.S.
2. K. Divin, Czechoslovakia
3. D. Jackson, Canada

Women
1. C. Heiss, U.S.
1. S. Dijkstra, Holland
3. B. Roles, U.S.

Pairs
1. B. Wagner/R. Paul, Canada
2. M. Kilius/H. Baumler, Germany
3. N. Ludington/R. Ludington, U.S.

SPEED SKATING—MEN

500 Metres
1. Y. Grischin, U.S.S.R.—40.2
2. W. Disney, U.S.—40.3
3. R. Gratsch, U.S.S.R.—40.4

5,000 Metres
1. V. Kositschkin, U.S.S.R.—7:51.3
2. K. Johannesen, Norway—8:00.8
3. J. Pesman, Neth.—8:05.1

1,500 Metres
1. {R. Aas, Norway—2:10.4
{Y. Grischin, U.S.S.R.—2:10.4
3. B. Stenin, U.S.S.R.—2:11.5

10,000 Metres
1. K. Johannesen, Norway—15:46.6
2. V. Kositschkin, U.S.S.R.—15:49.2
3. K. Backman, Sweden—16:14.2

SPEED SKATING—WOMEN

500 Metres
1. H. Hause, Germany—45.9
2. N. Dontschenko, U.S.S.R.—46.0
3. J. Ashworth, U.S.—46.1

1,500 Metres
1. L. Skoblikova, U.S.S.R.—2:25.2
2. E. Seroczynska, Poland—2:25.7
3. H. Pilejeyk, Poland—2:27.1

1,000 Metres
1. K. Guseva, U.S.S.R.—1:34.1
2. H. Haase, Germany—1:34.3
3. T. Rylova, U.S.S.R.—1:34.8

3,000 Metres
1. L. Skoblikova, U.S.S.R.—5:4.3
2. V. Stenina, U.S.S.R.—5:16.9
3. E. Huttunen, Finland—5:21.0

ICE HOCKEY
1. U.S.
2. Canada
3. U.S.S.R.

Chapter 26

THE IX WINTER OLYMPIAD

Innsbruck, 1964

Once again, the Winter Olympics suffered from barren slopes. Austrian soldiers brought down tons of snow, but it was not enough to prevent a rash of accidents and two fatalities. A 50-year-old British tobogganer, Kazimierz Kay-Skyszpeski was killed during a practice run on Mount Patscherkofel. Three days later, a 19-year-old Australian, Ross Milne, was fatally injured in a fall on the men's downhill ski run when he crashed into a tree.

On the opening day, Russia won the first of 11 gold medals when Ludmilla Belousiva, 28, and her husband, Oleg Protopopov, 31, won the figure skating pairs championship by less than one point from the favored Marika Kilius and Hansjurgen Baumler of West Germany, who had also finished second to Canada's Bob Paul and Barbara Wagner in 1960. A Canadian judge, Dr. Suzanne Morrow, burst into tears when she was booed off the ice by German sportswriters and fans who thought she had not given enough marks to the German pair. Dr. Morrow, a former North American pairs champion who won a bronze medal in 1948, had placed Miss Kilius and Baumler behind Canadians Debbie Wilks, 17, and Guy Revell, 22, who finished third.

From then on, the Russians stayed ahead in medals won and also points, finishing with 195½ to 98 for Norway and 91 for Austria.

Four of these 11 gold medals were won by a husky, 24-year-old Siberian school teacher, Lydia Sloblikova, who won all the women's speedskating events. First, she led a Russian sweep of the 500 metres, clipping almost a full second off the 1960 Olympic record of Germany's Helga Haase who finished eighth this time. Then she broke her own Olympic record by 2.4 seconds in the 1,500 metres and took nine tenths of a second off the Olympic record for the 1,000 metres. Only slushy ice stopped her from a fourth record when she had to splash through puddles to win the 3,000 metres.

Sjoukje Dijkstra, 22, of The Netherlands, compiled such a commanding lead in the compulsory figures of the women's figure skating that the rest had no chance of catching her. Petra Burka of Canada won the freeskating competition, but still finished third behind silver medallist Regine Heitzer of Austria.

Twenty-year-old Manfred Schnelldorfer of Munich completed a European sweep of the figure skating titles by turning in a near-perfect freeskating performance to defeat European champion Alain Calmat, 23, of France who lost valuable marks in a fall. Fourteen-year-old Scott Allen of the U.S., finished third to become the youngest skater ever to win an Olympic medal.

The Goitschel sisters from France, Marielle, 18, and Christine, 19, dominated the women's alpine skiing. Marielle was supposed to be the better of the two, but Christine beat her in the women's special slalom. The order was reversed in the giant slalom. It was the only time that sisters had placed one-two in an Olympic event. Jean Saubert of the United States was third in both slaloms, but had to argue her way past an officious guard to receive one of her bronze medals. Miss Saubert had lost her pass. The rigid security also irked Marielle Goitschel. She punched a policeman after a slalom race when he tried to prevent her coach from reaching her.

Neither of the Goitschels nor Miss Saubert got a medal in the downhill, won by Chrisl Haas of Germany over Edith Zimmerman of Austria. Bronze medallist Traudl Hecher of Austria, who had sprained her ankle in the special slalom, had been told by her doctor that she was finished for the rest of the Games. But her skimaker persuaded her to see another doctor who froze the ankle, enabling her to compete in the downhill.

French skier Francois Bonlieu was disowned by his own countrymen when it was discovered that he had been using skis made in the United States during preOlympic trials. French manufacturers persuaded him to use their skis during the Olympics, but he was still in disgrace until he vindicated himself, and the French skimakers, by winning the men's giant slalom on a slushy course.

The favored Egon Zimmerman almost fell near the finish in the downhill but recovered his balance and won. Another Austrian, Josef Stiegler, took the men's special slalom.

Finnish ski patrol border guard Eero Maentyranta won the 15 and 30 kilometre cross-country races. He also won a silver medal as a member of the 40 kilometre relay team which finished second to a Swedish team led by 35-year-old ski salesman Sixten Jernberg who picked up his third gold medal in three Olympics. Jernberg won the 30 kilometre race in 1960 and the 50 kilometre race at Innsbruck. He also won three silver medals in his Olympic career, finishing second in the 15 kilometre in 1956 and 1960 and second in the 30 kilometre race also in 1960.

Klaudia Boyarskikh won all the women's Nordic skiing events, winning the five kilometre cross-country and then beating two other Russion girls at 10 kilometres and leading the Russian relay team to victory.

The hockey tournament was the closest one in Olympic history. Russia won it by beating Canada 3-2 in the final game. But if the Canadian team had won by just one goal, it would have got the gold medal. The loss, however, put Canada fourth in the standings and the Canadians missed a medal for the first time in Olympic hockey. Sweden was second and Czechoslovakia third.

During the Canada-Sweden game Karl Oberg of Sweden was suspended for one game for hitting Canadian coach Father David Bauer over the head with his hockey stick. The referee in turn was suspended for two games because he did not give Oberg a 10-minute misconduct penalty. Father Bauer showed remarkable restraint over the incident and prevented a possible fight by ordering his players back on the bench and forcibly preventing them from retaliating . His conduct was rewarded by a special gold medal from president Bunny Ahearne of the International Ice Hockey Federation, but the Canadian team boycotted the ceremony. The Swedes had already gone home.

While Canadians, listening to the Canada-Russia game by radio, were muttering about not winning a hockey medal, their loss was somewhat offset by an unexpected gold medal in the four-man bobsled race.

Brothers Vic and John Emery, Peter Kirby and Doug Anakin broke the existing record and beat the favored Austrian team by nearly a full second. Not having a bobsled of their own, they had practiced at Lake Placid, N.Y., the only run in North America, and had only four 4-man training runs on the Innsbruck course before the Olympic competition started. Tony Nash and Robin Dixon won the two-man bobsled event for Great Britain.

OFFICIAL IX WINTER OLYMPIAD RESULTS

Innsbruck, 1964

NORDIC SKIING—MEN

15 KM Cross-Country
1. E. Maentyranta, Finland—50:54.1
2. H. Gronningen, Norway—51:34.8
3. S. Jernberg, Sweden—51:42.2

30 KM Cross-Country
1. E. Maentyranta, Finland— 1:30:50.7
2. H. Gronningen, Norway— 1:32:02.3
3. I. Voronchikin, U.S.S.R.— 1:32:15.8

50 KM Cross-Country
1. S. Jernberg, Sweden—2:43:52.6
2. A. Roennlund, Sweden—2:44:58.2
3. A. Tiainen, Finland—2:45:30.4

400 KM Relay Race
1. Sweden—2:18:34.6
2. Finland—2:18:42.4
3. U.S.S.R.—2:18:46.9

Nordic Combined
1. T. Knutsen, Norway
2. N. Kiselev, U.S.S.R.
3. G. Thoma, Germany

15 KM Relay
1. U.S.S.R.—59:20.2
2. Sweden—1:1:27.0
3. Finland—1:2:45.1

NORDIC SKIING—WOMEN

5 KM Cross-Country
1. K. Boyerskikh, U.S.S.R.—17:50.5
2. M. Lehtonen, Finland—17:52.9
3. A. Kolchina, U.S.S.R.—18:08.4

10 KM Cross-Country
1. K. Boyerskikh, U.S.S.R.—40:24.3
2. E. Mekshil, U.S.S.R.—40:26.6
3. M. Gusakova, U.S.S.R.—40:46.6

SKI JUMPING

90 Metres
1. T. Engan, Norway
2. V. Kankkonen, Finland
3. T. Bvandtzaeg, Norway

70 Metres
1. V. Kankkonen, Finland
2. T. Engan, Norway
3. T. Bvandtzaeg, Norway

ALPINE SKIING—MEN

Giant Slalom
1. F. Bonlieu, France—1:46.71
2. K. Schranz, Austria—1:47.09
3. J. Stiegler, Austria—1:48.05

Slalom
1. J. Stiegler, Austria—2:21.13
2. W. Kidd, U.S.—2:21.27
3. J. Heuga, U.S.—2:21.52

Downhill
1. E. Zimmermann, Austria—2:18.16
2. L. Lacroix, France—2:18.90
3. W. Bartels ,Germany—2:19.48

ALPINE SKIING—WOMEN

Giant Slalom
1. M. Goitschel, France—1:52.24
2. C. Goitschel, France—1:53.11
3. J. Saubert, U.S.—1:53.11

Slalom
1. C. Goitschel, France—1:29.86
2. M. Goitschel, France—1:30.77
3. J. Saubert, U.S.—1:31.36

Downhill
1. C. Haas, Austria—1:55.39
2. E. Zimmerman, Austria—1:56.42
3. T. Hecher, Austria—1:56.66

BIATHLON

1. V. Melyanin, U.S.S.R.—1:20:26.8
2. A. Prevalov, U.S.S.R.—1:23:42.5
3. O. Jordet, Norway—1:24:38.8

FIGURE SKATING

Men

1. M. Schnelldorfer, Germany
2. A. Calmat, France
3. S. Allen, U.S.

Women

1. S. Dijkstra, Holland
2. R. Heitzer, Austria
3. P. Burka, Canada

Pairs

1. L. Belousova/O. Protopopov, U.S.S.R.
2. M. Kilius/H. Baumler, Germany
3. D. Wilkes/G. Revell, Canada

SPEED SKATING—MEN

500 Metres

1. R. McDermott, U.S.—40.1
2. Y. Grischin, U.S.S.R.—40.6
   A. Gjestvang, Norway—40.6
   A. Orlov, U.S.S.R.—40.6

5,000 Metres

1. K. Johannesen, Norway—7:38.4
2. P. Moe, Norway—7:38.6
3. F. Maier, Norway—7:42.0

1,500 Metres

1. A. Antson, U.S.S.R.—2:10.3
2. C. Verkerk, Neth.—2:10.6
3. V. Haugen, Norway—2:11.25

10,000 Metres

1. J. Nilsson, Sweden—15:50.1
2. F. Maier, Norway—16:06.0
3. K. Johannesen, Norway—16:06.3

SPEED SKATING—WOMEN

500 Metres

1. L. Skoblikova, U.S.S.R.—45.0
2. I. Yegorova, U.S.S.R.—45.4
3. S. Idorova, U.S.S.R.—45.5

1,500 Metres

1. L. Skoblikova, U.S.S.R.—2:22.6
2. K. Mustonen, Finland—2:25.5
3. P. Han. North Korea—2:27.1

1,000 Metres

1. L. Skoblikova, U.S.S.R.—1:33.2
2. I. Yegorova, U.S.S.R.—1:34.3
3. K. Mustonen, Finland—1:34.8

3,000 Metres

1. L. Skoblikova, U.S.S.R.—5:14.9
2. V. Stenina, U.S.S.R.—5:18.5
   P. Han, North Korea—5:18.5

BOBSLED

2-Man Bob

1. Great Britain—4:21.90
2. Italy II—4:22.02
3. Italy I—4:22.63

4-Man Bob

1. Canada I—4:14.46
2. Austria I—4:15.48
3. Italy II—4:15.60

TOBOGGANING

Single-Seater—Men

1. T. Koehler, Germany—3:26.77
2. K. Bonsack, Germany—3:27.04
3. H. Plenk, Germany—3:30.15

Two-Seater—Men

1. J. Feistmantl/M. Stengl, Austria—1:41.62
2. R. Senn/H. Thaler, Austria—1:41.91
3. W. Aussendorfer/S. Mair, Italy—1-42.87

Single-Seater—Women

1. O. Enderlein, Germany—3:24.67
2. I. Geisler, Germany—3:27.42
3. H. Thurner, Austria—3:29.06

ICE HOCKEY

1. U.S.S.R.
2. Sweden
3. Czechoslovakia

Chapter 27

THE X WINTER OLYMPIAD

Grenoble, 1968

Russia finished a poor second to Norway in the un-official point standings in the 1968 Winter Olympics at Grenoble.

The only major championship the Russians won was hockey when they came back from a 5-4 beating to defeat Czechoslovakia for the gold medal, beating third place Canada 5-0 in the final game. The Canadians, who had been upset by Finland 5-0, in turn upset the Czech's chances for a gold medal by beating them 3-2. After winning the championship for the second time in a row, Russian coach Anatoli Tarasov, a colonel in the Soviet Army, boasted: "Bring on the National Hockey League, like Montreal Canadiens or Chicago Black-Hawks, and you'll see we'll cream them too."

Secretary manager Gordon Juckes of the Canadian Amateur Hockey Association partially agreed with him. He was so impressed with the Russian team that he admitted they would not look out of place in the NHL.

The Winter Olympics in the French Alps opened amid the usual controversy. This time, some female competitors objected to taking a sex test to make sure they were all female. It was the first time the girls had to prove their femininity in Olympic competition and they did not like it.

Also, Avery Brundage, President of the International Olympic Committee, threatened to cancel all skiing events if the skiers persisted in exhibiting the manu-facturers' labels on their skis. The outcry was so strong that he backed down but still insisted that skiers should not be photographed with their equipment.

Another major flareup occurred while the Games were in progress. The East German women's luge team was caught with hot runners. Someone had heated the steel to make the toboggans go faster. The Germans were disqualified but later reinstated when International Luge Federation president Bert Isatitch of Austria said there was no proof that officials or members of the East German team had actually used blow torches.

Skiers John Claude Killy of France and Nancy Greene of Canada stole the spotlight at Grenoble. Killy became the second skier to win three gold medals, winning both slaloms and the downhill as Toni Sailer of Austria had done in 1956.

After winning the downhill and the giant slalom, he was favored in the special slalom, but the 24-year-old Killy was lucky to do it. Both Haakon Mjoen of Norway, and 29-year-old Karl Schranz of Austria beat him but were disqualified for missing gates.

24-year-old Nancy Greene recovered from a disappointing tenth place finish in the downhill, won by Austrian gasoline station operator Olga Pall, to get a silver medal in the special slalom and a gold in the giant slalom. It was the best Olympic performance by a Canadian athlete since Percy Williams won the 100 and 200 metre sprints in the Amsterdam summer games of 1928. In the special slalom, she lost by only 29 one-hundredths of a second to Marielle Goitschell of France.

In Nordic skiing, a 27-year-old Italian, Franco Nones, ended Scandinavia's unbroken record of Olympic victories in the 30 kilometre cross-country. Nones stayed in front over the last 20 kilometres to beat Odd Martinsen of Norway and the defending champion, Eero Maentyranta of Finland.

Maentyranta, 30, who had also won the 15 kilometre race in 1964, was defeated this time by a 33-year-old Norwegian lumberjack, Harold Groenningen.

Twenty-nine-year-old Norwegian pop singer Olle Ellefsaeter defeated Vyacheslav Vedenine of Russia by almost a minute in the 50 kilometre race.

In the women's 10 kilometre cross-country won by 30-year-old Swedish housewife Toini Gustafsson, the first five finishers were Scandinavians.

Vladimir Beloussov won Russia's first ski jumping medal, defeating Czechoslovakian locksmith Jiri Raska on the 90-metre jump. Raska had already won the 70-metre jump. World champion Bjoern Wirkola of Norway was a major disappointment, finishing fourth at 70-metres and twenty-fourth in the longer jump.

Norwegian policeman Magnar Solberg, 31, won the biathlon. He was second in the 20 kilometre race and one of only two of the 60 competitors to score hits on all 20 rifle shots from standing and prone positions.

Russian engineer Oleg Protopopov, 36, and his 33-year-old wife, Ludmila Belousova, successfully defended their Olympic pairs figure skating championship. Several judges said afterwards that they would have been given the full six points in the compulsory skating except for a minor slip towards the end which spoiled a perfect performance.

Nineteen-year-old Peggy Fleming of Colorado Springs compiled a commanding lead of 77.2 points in the compulsory figures and then coasted through the free-skating for an easy win over Gabriele Seyfert of East Germany. However, the biggest ovation during the women's figure skating competition went to 11-year-old Beatrice Hustiu of East Germany, the youngest athlete at Grenoble. Beatrice, who had only been skating for two years, finished second to last among the 32 figure skaters.

The oldest athlete, incidentally, was 57-year-old Matias Stinnes, a German-born luge fanatic who was the one-man Argentine team. He did not do any better than Miss Hustiu.

The men's figure skating gold medal went to Wolfgang Schwarz of Austria. Five of the nine judges gave him first place in the freeskating which was just enough points to beat Tim Wood of the United States.

Speedskaters set three world records. Kees Verkerk of Holland broke his own world mark to win the 1,500 metre race in 2:03.4 with Art Schenk of Holland and Ivar Eriksen of Norway tied for second. Verkerk also set a world records for 5,000 metres, but it only lasted for 20 minutes when Fred Anton Maier of Norway cut it by 3.3 seconds to win in 7:22.4. Verkerk had to settle for a silver medal.

Defending champion Terry McDermott, 27, of the United States would probably have set a world record for the 500 metres, but he skated in the last heat when the soft ice was choppy. He was beaten by one fiftieth of a second by Erhard Keller of West Germany.

A 23-year-old Dutch leather factory clerk, Johanna Schut, knocked a tenth of a second off two-time world champion Christina Kaiser's world record in skating the 3,000 metres in 4:56.2. Kaija Mustonen, 26, of Finland, who had won the 1,500 metres gold medal, was second in 5:01.3. In the 1,500 metre race, Miss Mustonen defeated two Dutch girls, world champion Stien Kaiser and Carolina Geijssen. The Finnish typist had finished second to Russia's great Lidia Skoblikova in 1964.

In the women's 500 metres, there was an unprecedented triple tie between three Americans, Jenny Fish, Dianne Holum and Mary Meyers, who all finished a fifth of a second behind world champion Ludmila Titova of Russia. No bronze medal was awarded.

Carolina Geijssen, 22, broke an Olympic record set only minutes before to take the 1,000 metre championship away from Miss Titova. 16-year-old Dianne Holum was third.

Forty-year-old Eugenio Monti of Italy had won nine world titles in bobsledding after he took up the sport when a knee injury knocked him out of skiing competition. He had never been able to win an Olympic title, getting silver medals for both events in 1956 and bronze medals in 1964. In Grenoble his luck finally turned. Monti made no mistakes and won two gold medals by piloting both the two-man and four-man sleds to victory. The third and fourth runs of both events were cancelled because of bad weather.

The fourth and final runs of the luge competitions were also cancelled, giving Manfred Schmid of Austria a gold medal in the single seater and a silver in the double in which he teamed with Ewald Walch to finish second behind Klaus Bonsack and Thomas Koehler of East Germany. Koehler, the singles champion at Innsbruck, finished second to Schmid at Grenoble.

OFFICIAL X WINTER OLYMPIAD RESULTS

Grenoble, 1968

NORDIC SKIING—MEN

15 KM Cross-Country
1. H. Groenningen, Norway—47:54.2
2. E. Maentyranta, Finland—47:56.1
3. G. Larsson, Sweden—48:33.7

30 KM Cross-Country
1. F. Nones, Italy—1:35:39.2
2. O. Martinsen, Norway—1:36:28.9
3. E. Maentyranta, Finland—
1:36:55.3

50 KM Cross-Country
1. O. Ellefsaeter, Norway—2:28:45.8
2. V. Vedenine, U.S.S.R.—2:29:02.5
3. J. Haas, Switzerland—2:29:14.8

40 KM Relay Race
1. Norway—2:08:33.5
2. Sweden—2:10:13.2
3. Finland—2:10:56.7

Nordic Combined
1. F. Keller, Germany
2. A. Kaelin, Switzerland
3. A. Kunz, East Germany

NORDIC SKIING—WOMEN

5 KM Cross-Country
1. T. Gustafsson, Sweden—16:45.2
2. G. Koulakova, U.S.S.R.—16:48.4
3. A. Koltchina, U.S.S.R.—16:51.6

10 KM Cross-Country
1. T. Gustafsson, Sweden—36:45.6
2. B. Moerdre, Norway—37:56.4
3. I. Aufles, Norway—37:59.6

15 KM Relay Race
1. Norway—57:30.0
2. Sweden—57:51.0
3. U.S.S.R.—58:30.6

SKI JUMPING

90 Metres
1. V. Beloussov, U.S.S.R.
2. J. Raska, Czechoslovakia
3. L. Griny, Norway

70 Metres
1. J. Raska, Czechoslovakia
2. R. Bachler, Austria
3. B. Preiml, Austria

Combined
1. F. Keller, Germany
2. H. Hagaki, Japan
3. E. Fiedor, Poland

BIATHLON

Relay
1. U.S.S.R.—2:13:02.4
2. Norway—2:14:50.2
3. Sweden—2:17:26.4

Individual
1. M. Solberg, Norway—1:13:45.9
2. A. Tikhonov, U.S.S.R.—1:14:40.4
3. V. Goudartsev, U.S.S.R.—
1:18:27.4

ALPINE SKIING—MEN

Giant Slalom
1. J. C. Killy, France—3:29.28
2. W. Favre, Switz.—3:31.50
3. H. Messner, Austria—3:31.83

Slalom
1. J. C. Killy, France—1:99.73
2. H. Huber, Austria—1:39.82
3. A. Matt, Austria—1:40.09

Downhill
1. J. C. Killy, France—1:59.85
2. D. Perrillat, France—1:59.93
3. D. Daetwyler, Switz.—2:00.32

ALPINE SKIING—WOMEN

Giant Slalom
1. N. Greene, Canada—1:51.97
2. A. Famose, France—1:54.61
3. F. Boschatay, Switz.—1:54.74

Slalom
1. M. Goitschel, France—1:25.86
2. N. Green, Canada—1:26.15
3. A. Famose, France—1:27.89

Downhill
1. O. Pall, Austria—1:40.87
2. I. Mir, France—1:41.33
3. C. Haas, Austria—1:41.41

FIGURE SKATING

Men

1. W. Schwarz, Austria
2. T. Wood, U.S.
3. P. Pera, France

Women

1. P. Fleming, U.S.
2. G. Seafert, East Germany
3. H. Maskova, Czechoslovakia

Pairs

1. L. Belousova/O. Protopopov, U.S.S.R.
2. T. Joukchesternava/A. Gorelik, U.S.S.R.
3. M. Glockshubert/W. Danne, Germany

SPEED SKATING—MEN

500 Metres

1. E. Keller, Germany—40.3
2. { R. McDermott, U.S.—40.5
   { M. Thomassen, Norway

5,000 Metres

1. F. Maier, Norway—7:22.4
2. C. Verkerk, Netherlands—7:23.2
3. P. Nottet, Netherlands—7:25.5

1,500 Metres

1. C. Verkerk, Netherlands—2:03.4
2. { A. Schenk, Netherlands—2:05.5
   { I. Eriksen, Norway

10,000 Metres

1. J. Hoeglin, Sweden—15:23.6
2. F. Maier, Norway—15:23.9
3. D. Sandler, Sweden—15:31.8

SPEED SKATING—WOMEN

500 Metres

1. L. Titova, U.S.S.R.—46.1
2. { M. Meyers, U.S.—46.3
   { D. Holum, U.S.
   { J. Fish, U.S.

1,500 Metres

1. K. Mustonen, Finland—2:22.4
2. C. Geijssen, Netherlands—2:22.7
3. C. Kaiser, Netherlands

1,000 Metres

1. C. Geijssen, Netherlands—1:32.6
2. L. Titova, U.S.S.R.—1:32.9
3. D. Holum, U.S.—1:33.4

3,000 Metres

1. J. Schut, Netherlands—4:56.2
2. K. Mustonen, Finland—5:01.1
3. C. Kaiser, Netherlands—5:01.3

BOBSLED

2-Man Bob

1. Italy—4:41.54
2. Germany—4:41.54
3. Roumania—4:44.6

4-Man Bob

1. Italy—2:17.39
2. Austria—2:17.48
3. Switzerland—2:18.04

TOBOGGANING

Single-Seater—Men

1. M. Schmid, Austria—2:52.48
2. T. Koehler, E. Germ.—2:52.66
3. K. Bonsack, E. Germ.—2:53.33

Single-Seater—Women

1. E. Lechner, Italy—2:28.66
2. C. Schmuck, Germany—2:29.37
3. A. Duenhaupt, Germany—2:29.56

Two-Seater—Men

1. T. Koehler/K. Bonsack, East Germany—1:35.85
2. M. Schmid/E. Walch, Austria—1:36.34
3. W. Winkler/F. Nachmann, Germany—1:37.29

ICE HOCKEY

1. U.S.S.R.
2. Czechoslovakia
3. Canada

OLYMPIC

GAMES

RECORDS

OLYMPIC GAMES RECORDS

1. TRACK AND FIELD—MEN

100 Metres	Jim Hines (U.S.)	9.9	1968
200 Metres	Tommie Smith (U.S.)	19.8	1968
400 Metres	Lee Evans (U.S.)	43.8	1968
800 Metres	Ralph Doubell (Australia)	1:44.3	1968
1,500 Metres	Kipchoge Keino (Kenya)	3:34.9	1968
5,000 Metres	Vladimir Kuts (Russia)	13:39.6	1956
10,000 Metres	Billy Mills (U.S.)	28:24.4	1964
Marathon	Abebe Bikila (Ethiopia)	2:12:11.2	1964
110 Metres Hurdles	Willie Davenport (U.S.)	13.3	1968
400 Metres Hurdles	David Hemery (Great Britain)	48.1	1968
3,000 Metres Steeplechase	Gaston Roelants (Belgium)	8:30.8	1964
400 Metres Relay	Charles Greene Mel Pender (U.S.) Tommie Smith Jim Hines	38.2	1968
1,600 Metres Relay	Vince Matthews Ron Freeman (U.S.) Larry James Lee Evans	2:56.1	1968

Event	Athlete	Record	Year
20,000 Metres Walk	Kenneth Matthews (Great Britain)	1:29:34.0	1964
50,000 Metres Walk	Abdon Pamich (Italy)	4:11:12.4	1964
High Jump	Dick Fosbury (U.S.)	7'4¼"	1968
Broad Jump	Bob Beamon (U.S.)	29'2½"	1968
Triple Jump	Viktor Saneyev (Russia)	57'0¾"	1968
Pole Vault	Bob Seagren (U.S.)	17'8½"	1968
Shot Put	Randy Matson (U.S.)	67'10¼"	1968
Discus	Al Oerter (U.S.)	212'6½"	1968
Hammer Throw	Gyula Zsivotzky (Hungary)	240'8"	1968
Javelin	Janis Lusis (Russia)	295'7¼"	1968

2. TRACK AND FIELD—WOMEN

Event	Athlete	Record	Year
100 Metres	Wyomia Tyus (U.S.)	11.0	1968
200 Metres	Irene Szewinska (Poland)	22.5	1968
400 Metres	Betty Cuthbert (Australia)	52.0	1964
800 Metres	Madeline Manning (U.S.)	2:00.9	1968
80 Metres Hurdles	Maureen Caird (Australia)	10.3	1968
400 Metres Relay	Barbara Ann Ferrell	42.8	1968
	Mildrette Netter (U.S.)		
	Margaret Bailes		
	Wyomia Tyus		
High Jump	Iolanda Balas (Roumania)	6'2¾"	1964
Long Jump	Viorica Viscopoleanu (Roumania)	22'4½"	1968
Javelin	Michaela Penes (Roumania)	198'7½"	1964

Event	Record Holder	Record	Year
Shot Put	Margitta Gummel (East Germany)	64'4"	1968
Discus	Lia Manoliu (Roumania)	191'2½"	1968
Pentathlon	Irini Press (Russia)	5,246 pts.	1964

3. SWIMMING—MEN

Event	Record Holder	Record	Year
100 Metres Free-Style	Michael Wenden (Australia)	52.2	1968
200 Metres Free-Style	Michael Wenden (Australia)	1:55.2	1968
400 Metres Free-Style	Michael Burton (U.S.)	4:09.0	1968
1,500 Metres Free-Style	Michael Burton (U.S.)	16:38.9	1968
100 Metres Backstroke	Roland Mattes (East Germany)	58.7	1968
200 Metres Backstroke	Roland Mattes (East Germany)	2:09.6	1968
100 Metres Breast Stroke	Donald McKenzie (U.S.)	1:07.7	1968
200 Metres Breast Stroke	Ian O'Brien (Australia)	2:27.8	1964
100 Metres Butterfly	Douglas Russell (U.S.)	55.9	1968
200 Metres Butterfly	Kevin Berry (Australia)	2:06.6	1964

200 Metres Individual Medley	Charles Hickcox (U.S.)	2:12.0	1968
400 Metres Individual Medley	Richard Roth (U.S.)	4:45.4	1964
400 Metres Free-Style Relay	Zachary Zorn Stephen Rerych (U.S.) Mark Spitz Kenneth Walsh	3:31.7	1968
800 Metres Free-Style Relay	Stephen Clark Roy Saari (U.S.) Gary Inman Don Schollander	7:52.1	1964
400 Metres Medley Relay	Charles Hickcox Donald McKenzie (U.S.) Douglas Russell Kenneth Walsh	3:54.9	1968

4. SWIMMING—WOMEN

100 Metres Free-Style	Dawn Fraser (Australia)	59.05	1964
200 Metres Free-Style	Debbie Meyer (U.S.)	2:10.5	1968
400 Metres Free-Style	Debbie Meyer (U.S.)	4:31.8	1968

Event	Name	Time	Year
800 Metres Free-Style	Debbie Meyer (U.S.)	9:24.0	1968
100 Metres Backstroke	Kaye Hall (U.S.)	1:06.2	1968
200 Metres Backstroke	Pokey Watson (U.S.)	2:24.8	1968
100 Metres Breast Stroke	Djurdjica Bejdov	1:15.8	1968
200 Metres Breast Stroke	Sharon Wichman (U.S.)	2:44.4	1968
100 Metres Butterfly	Sharon Stouder (U.S.)	1:04.7	1964
200 Metres Butterfly	Aagje Kok (The Netherlands)	2:24.7	1968
200 Metres Individual Medley	Claudia Kolb (U.S.)	2:24.7	1968
400 Metres Individual Medley	Claudia Kolb (U.S.)	5:08.5	1968
400 Metres Relay Free-Style	Jane Barkman Linda Gustavson (U.S.) Susan Pedersen Jan Henne	4:02.5	1968
400 Metres Relay Medley	Kaye Hall Ellie Daniel (U.S.) Catie Ball Susan Petersen	4:28.3	1968

6. WEIGHT-LIFTING

Bantamweight	Mohannad Nassiri (Iran)	809¾ lb.	1968
Featherweight	Yoshinobu Mikaye (Japan)	876 lb.	1964
Lightweight	Waldemar Baszanowski (Poland)	964½ lb.	1968
Middleweight	Victor Kurentsov (Russia)	1,047 lb.	1968
Light-Heavyweight	Boris Selitsky (Russia)	1,068¾ lb.	1968
Middle-Heavyweight	Kaaorlo Kangasniemi (Finland)	1,140½ lb.	1968
Heavyweight	Leonid Zhabotinsky (Russia)	1,262 lb.	1964

7. SPEED SKATING—MEN

500 Metres	Richard McDermott (U.S.)	40.0	1964
1,500 Metres	Kees Verkerk (The Netherlands)	2:03.4	1968
5,000 Metres	Fred Anton Maier (Norway)	7:22.4	1968
10,000 Metres	Johnny Hoeglin (Sweden)	15:26.6	1968

8. SPEED SKATING—WOMEN

500 Metres	Lydia Skoblikova (Russia)	45.0	1964
1,000 Metres	Carolina Geijssen (The Netherlands)	1:32.6	1968
1,500 Metres	Kaija Mustonen (Finland)	2:22.4	1968
3,000 Metres	Johanna Schut (The Netherlands)	4:56.2	1968

May they display cheerfulness and concord so that the Olympic torch may be carried on with ever greater eagerness, courage and honour for the good of humanity throughout the ages.

> Included in the remarks of the President of the Olympic Committee at the Closing Ceremonies of the Games.